"To Chef Jeff"
a special friend,
and a special meal!
Thanks Loads
Love
Amy + Jim

124

Georges Perrier

Le Bec-Fin Recipes

with Aliza Green

Photographs by David Fields

RUNNING PRESS

PHILADELPHIA · LONDON

9   8   7   6   5   4   3

Digit on the right indicates the number of this printing

Library of Congress Cataloging-in-Publication Number 96-72572

ISBN 0-7624-0170-2

Designed by Ken Newbaker

Edited by Mary McGuire Ruggiero

Typography by Deborah Lugar: Weiss with Palace Script

This book may be ordered by mail from the publisher.
Please include $2.50 for postage and handling. *But try your bookstore first!*

Running Press Book Publishers
125 South Twenty-second Street
Philadelphia, Pennsylvania 19103-4399

Dedication

I dedicate this book to my mother, Yvonne.
She told me she would never see it, but it's finally done.
And to my daughter, Geneviève, for all the days I was not home.

Acknowledgements

Peter Gilmore, for his loyalty and hard work;
without him this book would not be possible.

Robert Bennett, for his friendship and his
beautiful talent as Pastry Chef at Le Bec-Fin.

Gregory Moore, for all the years and his
incredible talent to discover wine.

Clare Pelino, "My PR," who has kept me
organized and made this project possible.

Foreword

GEORGES PERRIER DEVELOPED his skills at some of the most prestigious restaurants in France and became part of a generation of young French entrepreneurs who wanted to try their luck in the United States. Thirty years spent in America have brought him much satisfaction and many awards—the just crowning for a chef who has been able to bring Americans to the discovery and appreciation of all that makes French cooking successful.

In over twenty-five years of operation in Philadelphia, Georges Perrier's Le Bec-Fin has succeeded in developing a faithful and exclusive clientele. There are clear reasons why: Georges is a perfectionist who has managed to share with his staff his taste for a job well done. He has created a pleasing establishment, and his warm welcome makes his patrons wish to return. He provides a range of offerings that are well-balanced and most creative. In turn, his patrons respect the taste of ingredients from which Georges extracts a full symphony of flavors, such as in his famous Lobster Bisque and his Roast Pigeon with Mushroom Cannelloni and Confit of Cabbage; the impressive cheese selection served with fruit and walnut bread; as well as the extravaganza of spectacular desserts. A wine list full of promises and a cart with a judicious assortment of liquors complete the feast.

Great establishment. Great chef. America can be true to its word: it has given Georges, thanks to the quality of his work, the success that his talents deserve. He remains, in my eyes, one of the best ambassadors of French cuisine, and I congratulate him.

—Paul Bocuse

. . .

EACH CITY HAS its superlative and unique restaurant. In Philadelphia this restaurant is, without contest, Le Bec-Fin. And Le Bec-Fin is Georges Perrier. A flamboyant persona in the tradition of the classically trained French chef, Georges's impeccable credentials, talent, and drive work together to create the superb food and elegant atmosphere that his restaurant is so noted for.

Georges Perrier • Le Bec-Fin Recipes reflects Georges's eclectic and protean artistry at interpreting classic dishes in modern and inventive ways, as evidenced in his Fricassee of Wild Morel Mushrooms with Asparagus Tips and his Baked Penne Pasta with Lobster. These recipes coexist with more traditional renditions of old favorites like Veal Rib Chop with Natural Juices and Fresh Baby Peas and his Sweetbreads in Brioche Crumb Crust.

This extensive, very personal cookbook perfectly exemplifies contemporary French cuisine, which is grounded in the past but intelligently adapted to encompass the culinary innovations of the last decade of the twentieth century.

—Jacques Pépin

*I*T IS ALMOST impossible for a Philadelphian to imagine Le Bec-Fin anywhere but in Philadelphia. Yet in our hearts, we know that Georges Perrier's ongoing gift to our city would be an award-winning, long-playing hit almost anywhere in the world.

That we are so proudly, even loudly, possessive of both the restaurant and its perfectionist owner/chef is uncharacteristic of a population known for minimizing, occasionally even booing, its own. As a community, we have bonded with Le Bec-Fin to the extent that even those Philadelphians of modest means who feel that they can't afford the restaurant, never stop dreaming of dining there one day.

In a sense, this book is for them in that its pages contain the recipes that—even made in a home kitchen by a cook less gifted or dedicated than Perrier and his crew—promise to recreate a bit of the magic of a Le Bec-Fin meal.

But the book is also a keeper of memories for the faithful who have followed Perrier from his arrival in Philadelphia as a talented but insecure young chef to today when he and the restaurant are ranked with the world's best. We who were in place in 1967, the year Perrier arrived here, will enjoy being reminded of the instant excitement generated by those first meals prepared by him at La Panetiere, the tiny Spruce Street restaurant where he first began his career in America.

As the *Philadelphia Inquirer*'s restaurant critic—I was then—as I am today on the receiving end of vast amounts of reader feedback on local dining establishments. While I've reviewed Le Bec-Fin periodically over the years, I can remember only one unhappy reaction to a review.

The caller, a woman, wanted me to know that she had read my most recent assessment of Le Bec-Fin a few weeks earlier, and had, as a consequence, gone there with her husband to celebrate their anniversary. The food and setting, even the service, were everything I had said, she admitted. Yet she and her spouse had been "disappointed."

Genuinely puzzled, I asked why.

"Your review didn't tell us they didn't have any music," she said. The lack of an opportunity to waltz between courses had spoiled the evening for the couple. I apologized and promised to remember her words when writing about the restaurant in the future.

I'm honoring that promise here with the information that this book—though crammed with Le Bec-Fin recipes and insights—contains not a single fox-trot number or show tune.

Somehow, I don't think you will mind.

—Elaine Tait

Contents

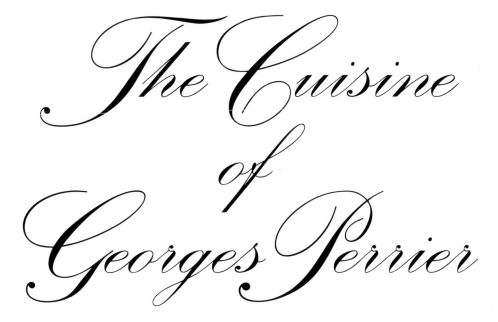

The Cuisine of Georges Perrier

INTRODUCTION

WRITING MY BOOK

*F*OR MANY YEARS, I've wanted to share my passion for *la cuisine* with readers. Since opening Le Bec-Fin twenty-seven years ago, I've served thousands of fine meals. While I consider myself to be a classic chef, I keep adding new dishes to my repertoire. Both long-time favorites and newer dishes are included in this collection. Because I've cooked these dishes so many times, I know they work. I'm not one to run after the latest trend. Instead, I keep refining my technique and ingredients until I get just what I've created in my imagination.

I emphasize here my *specialités maison* (house specialties): fish and seafood cookery, my light but flavorful sauces, and desserts from my famous cart. Because I don't want to eat sophisticated food every day, I have also included a separate section of simpler bistro recipes, including salads, soups, main dishes, and desserts. The last chapter is devoted to *Les Fonds de Cuisine*, the basics, including the stocks that are the foundation of French cuisine.

For those who enjoy a challenge, I share the recipes for some of my more complex dishes, but I balance these with simpler, equally delicious recipes. I've indicated when any special equipment is needed. It's not my nature to hide my secrets. I like to share so other people can enjoy my recipes. I would never hold anything back. I think the young should learn from more experienced chefs, and I'm happy to give back what I've learned over the years.

ACKNOWLEDGING MY ROOTS

*W*HEN YOU COOK, inspiration comes from your roots—your background. Who inspired me? I was lucky enough to grow up in a home where cooking was tremendously important. Every Sunday afternoon dinner was a holy occasion. The entire family sat down together to an impeccably appointed table. With great precision, my father chose all of the appropriate wines. The food was marvelous; inspirational to me. I am grateful to both of my parents for giving me a strong feeling for food at such an early age.

My best recollections of childhood are the ones with my wonderful mother. She had a great sense of *accueil*, a gift for making friends always feel welcome—every day of the week, at any hour. The love and attention to detail my mother gave to meals gave our large family of five children the chance to

A photograph of Georges Perrier's parents, Yvonne and Eugène.

get together and to grow up close. My mother cooked with so much love.

We lived in a lovely home in the beautiful French countryside near the culinary mecca of Lyon. On grand occasions such as holidays or family celebrations, my mother always bought the best ingredients at the market. She also kept a beautiful garden where she grew strawberries, raspberries, peas, and salad greens. We would go out to the garden before dinner to pick our salad greens and pencil-thin *haricots verts* (young green beans). I remember this marvelous *Civet de Lièvre*, a slow-cooked game stew she would make with a wild hare. In the winter, she served *Choucroute*, a dish of braised meats and sauerkraut—cooked in beer—because she was from Alsace. Her *Choucroute* was an enchantment.

My mother has been extremely important in my *carrière*.

She worked as a doctor, but her two passions have always been for antiques and cooking, both of which she transferred to me. Living and working in France forty to fifty years ago, she had a great deal to prove as a woman doctor. She is a great, passionate cook with an extraordinary palate. I've included some of my favorites of her recipes in this book. I could write a whole book just with my mom's recipes. I learned so much about cooking and about life from her.

I developed my palate by cooking for my mother's dinner parties, because she entertained often. I learned about being critical of myself from my dad, who was extremely difficult to please. He would say, "It's good, but . . ." or "I like it, but . . ." Maybe it would have been easier if he had liked everything, but it forced me to stretch my abilities, to become aware of nuances and subtleties.

My two grandmothers were also a great influence on me. Mamienette, from Alsace, was a terrific, wonderful cook; Mamie d'Aix, from the Lyon area, was beautiful in pastry. Though I was only twelve years old at the time, I can still remember the incredible taste and texture of Mamienette's *Ris de Veau à la Crème* (Sweetbreads in Cream) and Mamie d'Aix's sublime chocolate truffles.

THE IMPORTANCE OF MY APPRENTICESHIP

MY DAD WAS A JEWELER and wanted me to continue in his business. My mom wanted me to become a doctor. I shocked them when I told them I wanted to do a culinary apprenticeship, but then they supported me. My mom pushed me very hard to succeed as a chef. I've had my good and bad moments. I've had some very difficult times, though I try to leave behind any sadness when I come to work.

In the traditional French way, I began my apprenticeship at fifteen years of age. For three years I worked at a casino hotel near Lyon. It was extremely difficult for me to adjust to that life, coming as I did from a bourgeois background. I had to learn how to survive in a totally different environment. I needed much *esprit*. Sometimes it took tremendous willpower to see it through. At that time, there were some pretty nasty people in kitchens. This was in the late 1950's. We worked long hours every day. I began at 5 AM and worked until 2 PM. Then I took a two-hour break and came back to work from 4 PM to midnight. The pay was little, but I did receive room and board.

When I came home with my first recipes, I was so proud. I had learned how to make *Pommes de Terre à la Crème*, a dish of potatoes cooked in cream that was so rich I know I couldn't eat it today. I saw the look on my parents' faces. They told me, "I don't think it should be done this way; I think it needs this, I think it needs that." What I learned is that criticism is the best way to learn.

Another high point in those days was when the casino's chef, Michel Lorrain, gave me a position as *chef de partie*. I was responsible for the soups and all the vegetables. I cooked my first chicken stock and my first consommé. I cooked the *haricots verts*, I *tournéd* (cut into barrel shapes) the artichokes, and I did all the other garnishes for the main courses. Thinking the days would never end, I always started my work about three hours before everybody else came in and finished two hours later than the rest.

INFLUENCES IN MY EARLY CAREER

I WAS LUCKY ENOUGH to be hired by the late Raymond Thuillier at his famous three-star restaurant, l'Oustau de Baumanière at Les Baux de Provence. As a chef, Thuillier was extremely demanding and difficult because he was a perfectionist. Though I have met many passionate people in my life, the owner of Baumanière was one that still stands out. When you meet people like this, they give you the strength to be as dedicated as they are.

Working there was one of the highlights of my *carrière*. I learned so much. Thuillier made a marvelous *Sauce Baumanière*, made with Provençal wine and finished with anchovy butter, that he served with fillet of beef. I still can't replicate this sauce to my satisfaction.

After two years at Baumanière, I tried to get a job at Fernand Point's great restaurant, La Pyramide, near Lyon. I had always wanted to work at this legendary restaurant, so I went to see Madame Point, his widow. With no positions available, she advised me to work at a ski resort to gain more experience. So I found a job in the Alps, promising that I would work through the season. One day, I received a call from La Pyramide inviting me to work there. I had to tell them that I couldn't leave my job because I had given my word. To my relief, a few days later, they called back and asked me to start when the skiing season ended. I became the *chef poissonier* at La Pyramide at age twenty-two.

Point's restaurant was the precursor to nouvelle cuisine. We were already cooking *la cuisine moderne* when I started there. We made reductions for our sauces, something that had never been done before. He introduced so many of the cooking techniques we use today. Many of the most famous French chefs of our day trained under this culinary genius. Fernand Point had already died by the time I started, but Madame Point, who became the proprietor, continued to strengthen his ideas and style in a beautifully run restaurant.

One day, Madame Point called me into her office. I was shy and didn't know what to say or how to act because I was standing in the office with Madame Point who was one of the most famous restaurateurs in the world. *What had I done wrong?* I wondered. To my surprise, she sat me down and told me that I would accomplish great things because I was very talented. She could not promote me to a chef or *sous*-chef position because she had no openings but she wished to encourage me in my chosen *métier* (craft). It was a great moment in my life. La Pyramide was such a fabulous and influential restaurant. I'm so lucky to have had the chance to work there.

COMING TO AMERICA

W HEN I WORKED at l'Oustau de Baumanière, there was an American working in the kitchen, Peter Von Starck. Peter had the honor of being the first American ever to be hired by a three-star restaurant in France. Though we both worked there at the same time, we really didn't get to know each other then. I think it was destined that Peter and I meet again.

A year later, I was driving down Avenue La Pyramide, coming home from work very late one night. I saw Peter walking down the street near the restaurant, so I invited him to join me for a drink at the station brasserie. We drank so much Scotch. We were up until 4 or 5 AM. (I've never touched Scotch since that night. The very thought of it could make me ill.)

Peter was getting ready to open a restaurant in Philadelphia. He invited me to come to the United States and become his chef. Most chefs in France come from restaurateur families, some of them for generations. Eventually they take over their family businesses. Though I didn't come from such a family, my parents had offered to buy me a

restaurant in my home town of Aix les Bains, near Lyon.

In 1966, I made my decision to move to Philadelphia to help open La Panetière and work with Peter. People just didn't understand him here. In my opinion, he was the greatest restaurateur the city of Philadelphia has ever known. He had great talent, great vision, and great taste. I learned so much from him.

I worked for Peter for three years at La Panetière before leaving to open my restaurant. I thank Peter very much for what he taught me over the years. Memory is the source of my culinary inspiration. I think that, when you are a chef, there is always great feeling and great memory. Peter was a great influence on me as a chef.

OPENING THE FIRST LE BEC-FIN

W ITH PETER'S BLESSING, I opened my own restaurant at 1312 Spruce Street—the site of the original La Panetière, which had moved to larger, more sumptuous quarters. From 1970 until 1983, Le Bec-Fin was a tiny, thirty-five-seat restaurant with just nine tables. At the beginning, I had to prove myself. I was competing against a beautiful, well-established restaurant, La Panetière, much the same as Le Bec-Fin is today.

My restaurant was so small that there was no waiting room for the guests. They would line up on the street, patiently waiting for the first seating to finish. Sometimes we were running late, so I figured out a great solution. We would invite the guests back into the kitchen and give them a glass of wine. They loved it! I made them touch the food, taste the food. Not many other restaurants would do this. Many years later, I still hear from people who remember their visits to my tiny kitchen.

The restaurant and the contact with the customers, some of whom have become my dear friends, are the pleasures of my life and bring me much happiness. We chefs are a different breed. We do pay a personal price in our lives because of the long hours and the extreme pressures of our work. Though I have always been dedicated to my restaurant, I still feel guilty when I remember the night of the birth of my one and only child, my daughter Geneviève.

I had newly opened my restaurant the night I brought her mother to the hospital. Telling her that I was terribly sorry, I left to return to the restaurant and cook. I had just started preparing my *mise en place* for the evening's service when they called me from the hospital to tell me I had a baby girl. I rushed back to the hospital, saw my beautiful baby girl for ten minutes, and then had to rush back to the restaurant.

When I first came to the United States in 1967, and later, when I opened my restaurant in 1970, people in France told me, "You can't cook in the United States. You won't have the fresh herbs, you won't have good meat or poultry." At the beginning it was difficult, but I always found the best products. When I couldn't find it, I found people to grow what I didn't have. There is always a way to do things the right way, if you want. There is always a way to find the best ingredients.

One day, this beautiful lady named Julia Street came to see me. She brought me many fragrant herbs from her garden: French tarragon, tender chives, and chervil sprigs. I was so happy to get

Georges Perrier in the kitchen of the original Le Bec-Fin, c. 1983.

these fresh herbs, so I asked Julia to grow them for me. Three months later, she was in business growing herbs for all of the finer restaurants in Philadelphia.

In those days, I could only find frozen pigeon. A woman named Sally Miller learned that I was looking for game birds. So next thing I know, she shows up with pheasants, partridge, quail, and pigeon from her farm near Lancaster, Pennsylvania. Later, I helped her customize the feed for each bird, giving each bird a distinctive flavor.

I was famous in the early days for my *Quenelles de Brochet* (Pike Dumplings). When I worked at La Pyramide, I kept trying to learn the recipe for *quenelles* from the chef. He always hid when he made them. I kept trying to figure out how to make them because he would always omit something from his recipe. Finally I succeeded in recreating his feather-light pike

dumplings. (I include a precise recipe in this book.) Later the *quenelles* brought me my first national recognition in the press, from Craig Claiborne of the *New York Times*.

I learned so much from my customers, especially in the early days. They would comment and criticize and I would try to improve. They would make suggestions and I would listen. I was still only twenty-seven years old. I had so much to learn from their experience. One of my favorite customers was a man named Carl Baird, who was such a wonderful gourmet that I created a special dish, Vermicelle de Caviare, and named it for him. He loved food and he loved life. When he came in to eat, he always inspired me with his *joie de vivre* and his charm. It's a great memory for a restaurateur.

I've done some unbelievable things, especially as a young chef. Once, when I was first open and still struggling in 1971, I read an article about wine in the Sunday *Philadelphia Inquirer*. I quite agreed with the writer's point that, as the customer, you should never be intimidated into accepting a wine that you feel isn't right. If the wine isn't good, send it back. Even though we had a wine cellar and kept the wine at proper temperature and humidity, sometimes wine is quirky.

The next day, Monday, a party of four came into my restaurant and ordered my finest wines, including a Château Lafite Rothschild, 1955, a great year. At the time it cost about $300, which was a fortune to a struggling restaurateur. When my sommelier came into the kitchen to tell me what they'd ordered, I decided to go out myself to serve it to them.

I uncorked the wine and decanted it carefully. I poured out a little to taste it myself and check that it was in prime condition. I swirled it around in the glass, then sipped. I put the glass down and said to them in my beautiful French accent, "This wine isn't right. Let me replace it for you!" When the sommelier brought the second bottle, I tasted again and said, "Oh, this is perfect."

The customers were astounded; my manager almost had a heart attack. I wanted people to know that, at Le Bec-Fin, we were not afraid to change a bottle of wine if it wasn't right, no matter what the cost. This was just one day after the article and I wanted to make a big statement. That's the personality of Georges Perrier. I've always felt you have to be a great giver to receive.

I'm reminded of the late Jack Kelly who was one of my friends in those early years. I kept asking him when he was going to bring his sister, Princess Grace, to my restaurant. He always promised that, when she came to Philadelphia for a visit, he would bring her. I wanted to create a special dish for her when she came. At that time, she wore her blonde hair in *tresses* (braids) wrapped around her head, which inspired me to make a *Tresse de Saumon et de Sole* (Braid of Salmon and Sole)

served on a rosy pink sauce. This dish became one of my signatures and I served it for many years. You'll find both a recipe and a photo in this book.

MOVING LE BEC-FIN TO WALNUT STREET

*I*N 1983, I took a big risk and moved my restaurant to its present location on Walnut Street. Here I've been able to follow my dream. I designed the entire restaurant in Louis XVI style, with magnificent chandeliers, lovely wall coverings, and beautiful but comfortable chairs and tables. My appointments have always been a source of pride for me. I make sure to serve my food on the best porcelain with substantial silverware. My wine list consists of over four hundred carefully chosen and properly aged offerings. I always give these wines what they deserve, including room to breathe in sparkling crystal glasses.

When guests enter my restaurant, they immediately feel the *chaleur*, the warmth of the ambiance. The colors are

The jewel-box entrance to Le Bec-Fin, Walnut Street, Philadelphia

flattering, the light is intimate, and the waiters are friendly. As a restaurateur, I never want any guest to feel intimidated or uncomfortable in my establishment. They should feel welcome and relaxed in this luxurious setting.

After being seated, guests are handed a magnificent menu and equally impressive wine list from which to choose their selections for their *prix-fixe* dinner. I change the menu seasonally, which is especially important because so many of my customers are regulars. To start, accompanying perhaps a glass of Champagne, I may send out a few *amuse-bouche*, tiny tastes to "tickle the throat."

Guests start with an *Entrée*, a first course that includes everything from *Terrine de Foie Gras au Truffes* (Terrine of Foie Gras with Fresh Black Truffles) to *Fricassée de Morilles aux Asperges* (Wild Morel Mushrooms with Asparagus Tips). Many guests request my signature *Galette de Crabe* (Crab Cake with Light Mustard Sauce).

The next course is *Les Fruits de Mer*, "fruits of the sea." I take special pride in my fish and seafood cookery. My menu always includes fresh Dover sole, no matter what the price. My suppliers search out the best seasonal fish and seafood for me, including hand-harvested sea scallops, Maine lobster full of flavorful roe, and imported Rouget Barbet, the famed European Red Mullet.

Next comes the *Plat de Résistance*, the main course, which will most often be a fully flavored meat that deserves a fine, aged wine, perfectly decanted if appropriate. Depending on the season, customers may choose from *Filet d'Agneau en Eventail au Curry et Chutney de Courgettes* (Fanned Fillet of Lamb in a Light Curry Sauce with Zucchini Chutney) to the simpler *Tournedos de Boeuf, Sauce Médoc* (Fillet of Beef in Bordeaux Wine Sauce).

I especially love pigeon, so I nearly always include a dish like my *Pigeon Rôti au Cannelloni de Champignons au Jus et Choux Confits* (Roast Pigeon with Mushroom Cannelloni and Confit of Cabbage). Accompanying the main dish will be a small plate of seasonal vegetables, perhaps including my *Mousse de Carottes* (Carrot Mousse) or my all-time favorite *Gratin Dauphinois* (Potatoes Baked in Cream). All of this is served flawlessly by my waitstaff who orchestrate each course magically. Each plate arrives at the table covered by a silver cloche, an elegant and dramatic way of keeping the food hot and at its best.

As a palate refresher between courses, the guest may choose either a light green mesclun salad (baby mixed greens

from a local, organic farm) or a selection of marvelous French cheeses accompanied by our famous *Pain aux Fruits et Noix*, a homemade fruit and nut bread.

Guests at Le Bec-Fin know to leave room for what is, to many, the best part of the meal: desserts from our celebrated multi-tiered cart. This is a sumptuous offering of more than forty classic desserts made daily in our pastry shop, including homemade sorbets, ice creams, and of course, the best fruits of the season. Many people order a *dégustation*, a tasting array of the desserts that most appeal to them. This way they don't have to make any painful decisions about which to choose. With a service of fresh-pressed *café filtre*, a plate of our own *mignardises* (tiny cookies and sweetmeats) and perhaps a final glass of cognac or Armagnac, the meal is complete.

EXPLAINING MY CULINARY PHILOSOPHY

*M*Y COOKING and my philosophy have always been simple: It can't be great cooking without a classical base. I received my training in some of the finest restaurants of France. The regional cooking of France is my heritage, the strength behind French cuisine. It's tremendously important to maintain these culinary traditions. Men like Antonin Carême, a founder of La Grande Cuisine Française and head of Talleyrand's kitchen, and Auguste Escoffier, the brilliant master chef at the turn of the century, were the visionaries of cooking. As a chef, you must always acknowledge your debt to others.

While classical cooking has been my foundation and my inspiration, my culinary style has changed tremendously through the years. When I think of the *Beurre Blanc* I made twenty-five years ago, I know I couldn't eat it today. It was a wonderfully lavish reduction of large amounts of butter and cream.

Of course, I want to be thin, not fat, and so do my customers. They are very conscious of the lightness and of the flavor. Nowadays, everyone still wants wonderful taste, but they want it lighter. That is difficult to do. We find better combinations of ingredients and better techniques. We even beat air into our sauces to make them lighter. Cooking must evolve to stay fresh. As a chef, I look to the source of my cooking, the great regional cuisine of France. However, I also dine at the fine restaurants of my contemporaries in this country to experience their styles.

The object of cooking is to maintain and highlight the intrinsic flavor. Why make it more complicated? Freshness is number one! The simpler the food, the more important the ingredients. In a great dish, you can see, eat, taste, and smell everything. No one thing is overpowering. These days, my obsession is to extract as much flavor as possible to make a sauce that is as light as possible. When I cook, I don't like to confuse the palate with too much going on. My goal is to perfectly balance three different flavors in a dish. If I achieve this, I know I've created an apotheosis, a quintessence, of all three flavors—a dish that is much more than the sum of its parts.

As a chef, you must come to an understanding to use restraint, not to overdo anything. This is the way of success in the long run. I aim for simplicity with elegance while always using what's fresh and at its best.

I believe the French proverb "One can become a chef; one must be *born* a *rôtisseur*," to be correct. I have the good fortune to be a great *saucier*, that is my magic power. By now, I know many things just by feel. When I make a salad, I *feel* just how much oil to drizzle on top, how much salt to sprinkle in, how many drops of vinegar it will take for perfection. It takes years of experience to develop and refine your palate. I stress to my cooks that they must continue to taste to get it right.

In the early years, I had just myself and a few others to worry about. In this restaurant, I now have eighty-seven employees for whom I'm responsible. Now I must taste and correct all of their work. That's what I'm here for. It's vital to work with people who have talent. It's so exciting to see young people develop and so rewarding to see them succeed. Some of my employees, including my trusted chef de cuisine, Peter Gilmore, and my erudite sommelier, Gregory Moore, have been with me for twenty years. There's a saying among the staff at Le Bec-Fin: "You either stay one day or ten years. It depends on your character."

New employees quickly learn that when we plate a dish, I can't stand for it to sit more than three seconds before a waiter serves it to the customer. We cook our food *à la minute*, to order. I refuse to watch it deteriorate while I wait for it to be served. Years ago, if a waiter didn't pick up immediately, I might just push the plate full of food off the front of the line so it would break on the floor in front of him. Then he would know that I will never tolerate less-than-perfect food being served in my restaurant. I'm much calmer than I was when I was younger, but I'm still just as critical.

Understanding the Character of a Chef

*P*ASSION FOR COOKING is the force behind me. You need a great deal of motivation to become a chef. As a young man, I would always try to finish my assigned work quickly so that I could learn new things. I try to inculcate this philosophy in the young chefs who come to work for me. I push them hard to learn the habit and the spirit of working with efficiency and concentration.

As a chef, I know I'm demanding and tough. I suffered so much in my own youth as an apprentice. But, I believe this is how you develop character. I believe you should be most critical of yourself in order to develop fully. You've got to keep questioning yourself to stay ahead. Nothing is guaranteed, because you're only as good as the last meal you cooked.

A chef must have character, willpower, and above all, discipline to stay on top, to continue day after day. While a chef might be born with a unique talent, I believe you have to work at it, or it will just stagnate.

I truly admire the courage of anyone who marries a chef. Their mates are never home for special occasions. One truly must sacrifice to become a great chef. It's not just a *carrière*, it's a way of life. Over the years in this very demanding business, you have to constantly reinvent yourself to stay on top.

My advice to young chefs: Believe in yourself. Do what you think is right. *Garde manger* (pantry or salad station) is where it all starts. First you have to learn how to taste. I want to tell young people not to get discouraged. Sometimes it's frustrating to spend days making a dish to know that in a few minutes it will no longer exist. Keep your curiosity but remember, success is in continuity, doing things right over and over again.

Being a Conductor in the Kitchen

*C*OOKING HAS so much to do with feeling and emotion. Because the pressure in the kitchen is very dramatic, it accentuates any problems. The restaurant is like a theater show. I am the conductor of my restaurant, my cooks and staff are the artists. As the conductor, I must conduct in a harmonious way to accomplish the perfect meal, not only in the kitchen, but in the dining room as well.

I am influenced by my surroundings tremendously. I can walk into the restaurant and feel the energy right away. If there's a problem with a cook I call him right into my office to talk. Whether it's a financial problem or a personal problem, I try to solve it right away. I want my cooks particularly to feel free when they work. They need to concentrate fully without worrying about outside matters.

To direct a business is to orchestrate it. To create and maintain a successful restaurant, you have to have a great staff that works with you through the years. In my opinion, the staff makes the restaurant. You must grow with your employees. They have to make it along with you. The employees are the force, the strength behind you. It's just unrealistic to think you can do it alone.

SOURCES OF CULINARY INSPIRATION AND ART

SOMETIMES INSPIRATION comes from adapting other chef's recipes. Back as a young chef, I kept trying to figure out the special taste in a dish of escargot made by my chef, Monsieur Cleuvenot. It finally came to me that it was green Chartreuse liqueur. I still make my escargot using this *digestif* liqueur made with all kinds of mountain herbs. I've included a recipe my for *Escargots au Champagne* (Snails in Champagne), a signature dish from early in my *carrière*. Another fabulous dish I learned in the early years came from Monsieur Beck, one of the first chefs I worked under. His *Grenouilles à la Meunière* (Sautéed Frog's Legs) were superb. I still adore his *Rognon au Whisky* (Veal Kidney with Scotch Whisky).

I'll never forget visiting my great friend Paul Bocuse in his kitchen. I looked in the walk-in refrigerator and it was practically empty. Paul told me that they only buy what they need for the day—the fish, the produce, the meats—everything! That way the ingredients are always at their best. There was no ice on the fish he explained (something we do commonly at Le Bec-Fin), because the ice might bruise the delicate flesh. Because they always cook and serve the fish the same day, they didn't need to preserve it with ice.

I found this to be a great way of working, but something that's much more possible in France. Many of the great restaurants have their own gardens. The *baricots verts*, the lettuce, the fresh, tender herbs are all picked that day from the garden. Paul really inspired me that day. He gave me a goal that I'm still trying to reach: To cook only with ingredients that are at their peak.

Though I do find creativity when I need it, I can't create a new dish every day. For myself, inspiration has always been difficult. To be creative, you have to feel good about yourself. Sometimes, it takes weeks for me to put myself in the special mood that permits me to be creative. For new dishes, the inspiration I need might come from eating a dish in a small restaurant, or from a conversation about food ideas with my chefs. I must be in the right *état d'âme* (condition of the soul), fully relaxed and with concentration. Finally it comes. It gives me joy to accomplish and to create and to make our customers happy. It's always a treat for me when a customer gets such a thrill out of a new dish I've created.

LIVING THE LIFE OF A CHEF

I NEVER FORCED the issue. I never said I wanted to be the top chef. I just wanted to have a successful restaurant. How can any one chef be number one? It's not about thinking you're better than this one or that one. There's always going to be someone else coming along that might surpass you. The important thing is to have focus and concentration. A top chef must be able to turn out superb food day after day, not just when he or she is in the mood. I'm still always learning, always trying to stretch my boundaries.

In the early years I would experiment over and over till I got the food to taste the way I wanted. Many times it didn't work and I'd have to throw the whole thing out. I remember many pots of *quenelles* that I discarded in frustration. Now it's a whole lot different, because I've refined my style through the years. I have so much experience, I'm more able to control my destiny, my results.

It helped me to be in the right place at the right time. As a young chef, I worked with some great teachers. From the beginning, I was committed to *mon métier*. I could never do anything else in life. I love the contact with people. I love to talk to my customers. I am so pleased when people respond to my cooking.

I don't know any other job where people will thank you so profusely. It still amazes me that a customer can feel such gratitude to the one who created their meal. Cooking is so rewarding. I have so much passion for it. Though some days are difficult and some days you fall short, you try your best every day. Some days are just magical.

Les Vins

NOTES ON WINE

by Le Bec-Fin Sommelier, GREGORY MOORE

WINE WITH FOOD

$\mathcal{M}$OST OF US AGREE that in the role of a beverage to accompany fine food, wine has no equal. In my experience, many otherwise confident and adventurous friends of fine cuisine, like Chef Perrier's, find the selection of a wine to complement a dish unnecessarily difficult. Too bad that a natural wish to experiment is frequently inhibited by too much concern over what may or may not be "correct" or "appropriate." The worst is that the most memorable marriages of food and wine (which can be the most unexpected) are missed because of slavish adherence to rigid wine snob protocol. Far too many rely on mass market wines designed for expense account dining.

Classified Bordeaux and famous Burgundies, well-oaked Chardonnays and Cabernets from Napa and Sonoma certainly have their place. The problem is that aside from being expensive, these wines address only a narrow range of aesthetic values. The craft of the sommelier would be boring indeed without the tremendous variety of wines available.

Basic guidelines for matching food and wine are really not very difficult to understand. Truly horrible combinations are so rarely encountered that they should in no way discourage experimentation. Generally, simple wines successfully accompany complicated preparations; complex wines show their best when paired with simple, elegant dishes.

Chef Perrier refines regional French cuisine in much the same way that a fine tweed jacket refines an English farmer. As sommelier at Le Bec-Fin, I have been privileged to taste some of the greatest wines produced in our time, alongside the most exquisite cooking imaginable. Nevertheless, many of the happiest *"marriages entre mets et vin"* (marriages between food and wine) at which I have officiated, have been between regional dishes refined by Georges' elegant touch and country wines polished (only to a degree) by modern winemaking. I hope it won't be surprising or disappointing that the wines suggested in this book are mostly French, and mainly French country wines. In my opinion, there is no higher quality and wider range of versatile wines at fairly reasonable cost available from any other country.

NOTES ON THE SERVICE OF WINES WITH CHEESE

$\mathcal{I}$ WELL REMEMBER an occasion when, quite by accident, I stumbled onto what must be one of the most miserable combinations of wine and food imaginable. An important client had come to dinner on the occasion of his wife's birthday, bringing with him two bottles of Château Lafite; the 1945 and the 1953, both very great years. The wines were opened and tasted, and the '53 selected for the dinner. That left the open bottle of '45, which our distinguished client generously left for me.

Alone as usual, closing the restaurant at one or two o'clock in the morning. I put the key in the front door, and fairly trembling with anticipation, poured a glass of one of the greatest wines I had ever seen. To accompany the Lafite, I chose a thick slice of pungent, raw-milk Reblochon, one of the world's greatest cheeses. The wine was sublime; the cheese was perfect. Together, they were atrocious and proof that conventional wisdom should always be taken with a grain of salt.

It is simply untrue that the cheese course demands the finest red wine served at the dinner. The most exquisitely complex and subtle wine should be served alongside the most elegant but simple food.

Remember that wine and cheese are country foods that evolved together in a wide range of styles. Pair a cheese with a wine that comes from the same place. Try Sancerre with

Crottin de Chavignol or other upper-Loire goat's milk cheese. See if a nervy Maconnaise Chardonnay like Pouilly Fuissé or St. Veran doesn't better accompany a runny Epoisses than a red Bordeaux. Rich Pinot-dominated Champagne is wonderful with a fine ripe Brie. The list could go on and on. Think of Alsatian Gewurztztraminer with Muenster, or Arbois blanc with Morbier. Notice how many of these wines are white.

Consider wines which complement the characteristics of the cheese. One of the great classic combinations is Sauternes with Roquefort, where the saltiness of the cheese is offset by the sweetness of the wine. Ditto for port and Stilton. If you do drink fine red wine with your cheese course, be sure that the cheeses don't overwhelm the wine. The finer the wine, the milder and more subtle the cheese. The stronger, more pungent the cheese, the simpler and more direct the wine.

WINE WITH DESSERT

AS MANY TIMES as I try to enjoy a glass of Barsac or Beerenauselese with sweets, I find more conflict than harmony in the marriage. The perfect balance of sweetness between the dessert and the wine is so critical, but so difficult to achieve, that I have found few combinations that work.

If the wine is less sweet than the dessert, it tastes tinny to me. Maybe that's why I hate dry Champagne with wedding cake. It must be that various degrees of sweetness are not complementary the way that contrasts between saltiness and sweetness can be. For me, sweet wine is to drink alone or with cheese. Dessert should be eaten without wine, and dessert wine drunk afterwards.

Dessert wine is a wider category that many believe. Besides Sauternes, France alone supplies a wide range of sweet wines, ranging from Vouvray *moelleux* through late-harvested Riesling, Gewurztztraminer, and Pinot Gris from Alsace. Provence and Rousillon provide examples of fortified,

sweet Muscat; and the Southwest has Monbazzaillac and Pacherenc de Vic Bilh. Even Champagne is sometimes made in a sweet style called *demi-sec* or *doux*, which can be delicious after dinner with petits fours.

That I prefer no wine with dessert should in no way be interpreted as disapproval of sweet wine. Some of the most memorable bottles that have come my way have been sweet. The claim that only dry wine has aesthetic merit, or that it is more sophisticated to prefer dry wine, is simply false.

WINE WITH BISTRO FOOD

BISTRO CUISINE IS infrequently served in formal courses, so normally only one wine is needed for the meal. Because of the variety of flavors in the food, the wines should be as versatile as possible. Sometimes remarkable marriages can be arranged, but the best usually are accidental. "Bistro Wine" includes the whole range of southern French reds: Côte du Rhône, Languedoc, Roussilon, and Provence.

Any of the direct, low-acid reds, which come from every part of France qualifies. Middle Loire reds like Chinon, Bourgueil, and Saumur-Champigny are tremendously popular in Parisian *bistrots*. Beaujolais and Bourgogne Passetoutgrains are enjoyed everywhere. Especially useful are the wines of the Southwest, like Cahors and Madiran, which are so delicious with grilled foods.

The white wines include, of course, Vouvray, the most underappreciated of all the great wines of France. The lesser wines of all the great regions are frequently the best with the cuisine. So, rather than the fine Riesling of Alsace, choose instead the less delicate Pine Blanc or Chasselas. Instead of Côte de Beaune wines like Meursault and Puligny-Montrachet, look for one of the wines of the Côte Chalonnaise like Rully or Aligoté de Bouzeron. Chablis Grand Cru is great wine, but sometimes a little Sauvignon de St. Bris is more fun.

Les Entrées

FIRST COURSE

Bisque de Homard

Lobster Bisque with Scotch Whisky

n my Lobster Bisque, I substitute Scotch whisky for the traditional cognac. The whiskey adds a slightly smoky nuance to my justly famous bisque. In the classic method for bisque, chefs use rice as a thickener. I mix beurre manié with lobster roe to both lightly thicken and flavor the bisque.

.... SERVICE FOR 8 ....

THE LOBSTERS

Two 1½-pound lobsters

2 tablespoons olive oil

1½ cups mirepoix (see page 217)

1 ripe tomato, quartered

4 cloves garlic, halved

2 sprigs fresh thyme

1 sprig fresh tarragon

1 sprig fresh Italian parsley

1 bay leaf

Preparing the Lobsters

Split the lobsters lengthwise from head to tail. Separate the halves. Remove the "sand sac" (the small bag), from inside each side of the head and discard. Remove any dark green roe sacs and set aside for the Sauce Américaine. Cut off both claws. Break the claw shells by hitting with a meat mallet.

In a large sauté pan, heat the oil over high heat until it just begins to smoke. Sear the lobster pieces until they turn bright red. Remove the claws from the pan and set aside for garnish. Add the mirepoix, tomatoes, garlic, thyme, tarragon, parsley, and bay leaf. Cook for 5 minutes.

Making the Sauce Américaine

Transfer the cooked lobster mix to a 1-gallon stockpot. Add the cognac, port, and Madeira and *flambé* (ignite with a long match). When the flames subside, add the tomato paste and white wine along with Fond Blanc de Volaille, Demi-Glace, and wine and bring to a boil. Simmer, stirring occasionally so nothing sticks to the bottom and burns, for 1 hour.

Strain through a sieve, reserving both the solids and the broth. Put solids through a meat grinder (or coarsely chop, then place in a food processor and finely grind). Return the reserved broth to the stockpot. Stir together the beurre manié and the reserved lobster roe. Whisk into the broth to thicken, and bring to a boil. Simmer, stirring occasionally, for 1 hour.

Strain the mixture through a fine sieve. (If you're preparing this ahead of time, chill the sauce at this point by placing the pot in a sink filled with ice water. Stir occasionally until the liquid cools, replacing the ice if necessary.) Refrigerate for up to 3 days, until you're ready to finish the bisque.

Finishing the Bisque

Remove the meat from the reserved claws and discard the shells. Cut the claw meat into ⅛-inch dice and set aside. Soak the saffron threads in Scotch until the liquid becomes bright yellow, about 10 minutes. Stir into the broth and return to a boil. Skim off any foamy impurities with a ladle and discard. Stir in the heavy cream, return to a boil and season with salt, white pepper, and cayenne. (The bisque should be creamy and just lightly coat the back of a wooden spoon.) Ladle the bisque into hot soup plates and sprinkle with the reserved diced lobster meat. Serve immediately, while piping hot.

❧ *Chef's Truc* ☙

BUYING LOBSTERS: Buy female lobsters, if possible. Look at the first set of feelers below the thorax; they are soft on a female, hard on a male. Female lobsters also have shorter, wider tails than males. The females contain the dark green roe or "coral" that turns bright red when cooked and adds an intense flavor to this bisque. Sometimes fish stores sell "culls" (lobsters missing a claw). These culls are less expensive and fine for this bisque because the whole lobster isn't served here.

THE SAUCE AMÉRICAINE

¼ cup cognac

¼ cup port

¼ cup Madeira

1 tablespoon tomato paste

½ cup dry white wine

4 cups Fond Blanc de Volaille
    (see page 214)

2 cups Demi-Glace
    (see page 212)

2 tablespoons Beurre Manié
    (see page 216)

Reserved lobster roe

THE LOBSTER BISQUE

Pinch of saffron threads

2 tablespoons Scotch whisky

4 cups Sauce Américaine

2 cups heavy cream

Salt and white pepper

Pinch of cayenne pepper (optional)

Dodine de Poulet aux Ris de Veau, Foie Gras et Champignons Sauvages

Mold of Chicken with Sweetbreads, Foie Gras, and Wild Mushrooms

*M*y dodine is a complex dish, a chef's tour de force, but well worth the effort. For perfect results, you will need to buy a special U-shaped dodine mold (see Sources page 219). I also make a summer version of this dodine, using salmon instead of chicken and adding a julienne of snow peas and carrots. Allow three days to complete the dodine in stages.

.... SERVICE FOR 12 TO 16 ....

THE SWEETBREAD

1 calf sweetbread (about ½ pound)

2 tablespoons olive oil

2 tablespoons butter

¾ cup mirepoix (see page 217)

¼ cup Madeira

2 tablespoons cognac

1 cup Fond Blanc de Volaille
(see page 214)

¼ cup Demi-Glace (see page 212)

THE CHICKEN AND FOIE GRAS

6 large boneless, skinless chicken breasts
(about 2½ pounds)

8 ounces Mousse de Foie Gras
(store-bought)

Nonstick spray or oil (for mold)

THE BINDING SAUCE

½ cup cold water

1½ tablespoons powdered gelatin

3 cups Jus de Poulet (see page 214)

1½ cups dry white wine

1½ cups heavy cream

2 shallots, finely chopped

1-inch length gingerroot, peeled

Salt and white pepper

Preparing the Sweetbread

Soak the sweetbread in cold water for 2 to 3 hours, then drain and discard the water. Place the sweetbread in a sauté pan, cover with cold water and bring to a boil. Simmer for 5 minutes, then drain and cool. Pull off and discard the outer skin and any hard connective tissue. Wrap the sweetbread in plastic and place in a flat dish. To compress and firm the sweetbread, cover with a heavy weight such as a can of tomatoes. Refrigerate overnight.

The next day, in a medium sauté pan, brown the sweetbread on all sides in the olive oil and butter. Add the mirepoix and brown together lightly. Then add the Madeira and cognac and bring to a boil over high heat. Stir in the Fond Blanc de Volaille and Demi-Glace, bring back to a boil and braise, cooking either on top of the stove or in a 350°F oven, for about 20 minutes. Allow the sweetbread to cool in its cooking liquid, then remove it and chill. (Discard the cooking liquid or set aside for a braised veal or beef stew.) The sweetbread can be prepared up to 2 days ahead. Cut the chilled sweetbread lengthwise into ¼-inch thick slices and set aside.

Preparing the Chicken and the Foie Gras

Bring a large pot of water to a boil. Meanwhile, trim the chicken breasts, reserving the tenders for another use. Cut off and discard any fat and connective tissue. Place each chicken breast between two sheets of plastic wrap. Using a meat mallet, evenly pound until ¼-inch thick. Sprinkle with salt and pepper. Arrange on a wire rack over boiling water. Cover with foil, and steam about 2 minutes. Set aside.

Remove the Mousse de Foie Gras from its package and freeze for 1 hour. Using a hot knife, slice the mousse lengthwise into ¼-inch-thick strips. Refrigerate until ready to use.

Preparing the Binding Sauce

Pour the water into a small pan. Sprinkle in the gelatin and let it soak for 15 minutes. Cook over low heat until the liquid is clear. Set aside. Meanwhile bring the Jus de Poulet, wine, heavy cream, shallots, and ginger to a boil in a small pan. Cook until reduced by half. Strain out and discard the shallots and ginger. Return to the

THE GARNISHES

½ pound medium-sized shiitake
mushrooms, stems removed

1 tablespoon olive oil

1 tablespoon butter

2 tablespoons finely chopped truffles

THE SALAD

1½ tablespoons balsamic vinegar

3 tablespoons walnut oil

Salt and white pepper

¾ pound mesclun greens

With this dish I recommend a direct white wine like a Pinot Blanc of Alsace made by **Barmès Buecher**, **Albert Mann**, or **Léon Beyer**.

heat and cook until reduced to 1½ cups of liquid. Stir in the gelatin and season generously with salt and white pepper. Let cool until syrupy.

Preparing the Garnishes and Assembling the Dodine

In a sauté pan, brown shiitake mushroom caps in the olive oil and butter. Drain on paper towels to absorb any excess liquid and set aside.

Lightly oil the dodine mold (or a long narrow bread pan that holds about 6 cups of liquid). Lay the chilled chicken breast paillards side by side on a cutting board. Cut the breasts lengthwise into 3-inch-wide strips.

Lay the strips next to each other crosswise in the terrine mold without overlapping. Trim off any overlapping tips and set aside for the last layer of the mold. Ladle in about ½ cup of the sauce and spread evenly over the chicken. Lay the shiitakes, cap-side down, in a line down the center of the terrine. Cover with ¼ cup of the sauce, then lay the sweetbread slices down the center of the mold. Cover with ¼ cup of the sauce. Sprinkle the truffles in a line down the center of the terrine and cover with another ¼ cup of the sauce.

For the last layer, place the sliced Mousse de Foie Gras over the truffles. Ladle in ¼ cup of the sauce, then cover with the remaining chicken strips and any reserved trimmings. Top with the remaining ¼ cup of sauce. Chill for 3 to 4 hours, or until firmly set.

Serving the Dodine

Using an electric or very sharp knife cut the dodine into 12 to 16 slices. Clean off and heat the knife under hot water between each slice. Lay the slices out on a baking pan lined with parchment (or wax) paper. Whisk together the vinegar and oil, and season to taste with salt and pepper. Toss the mesclun lightly with the dressing and arrange on individual plates. Lay a slice of the dodine alongside. *Voilà!*

FRICASSÉE DE MORILLES AUX ASPERGES

FRICASSEE OF WILD MOREL MUSHROOMS WITH ASPARAGUS TIPS

I do love morels, especially when fresh ones are in season. Both morels and asparagus spring up from the soil, ready to be plucked and enjoyed together in this lovely spring dish. I can't imagine a more perfect combination. Morels with dark-colored caps have the best flavor. Many kinds of mushrooms are now cultivated including morels, but the cultivated varieties tend to be rather bland. We get them from foragers who search out the woodland hiding places of these delicacies. Honeycomb-shaped morels are often full of dirt. Wash them gently but thoroughly before using.

.... SERVICE FOR 6 ....

Preparing the Morels

Pour the water into a bowl. Add the morels and let soak for 10 minutes to wash out any sand. Remove the morels from the water, reserving the washing water. Trim off the stems and cut the caps into halves or quarters, depending on their size. Strain the washing water through a fine sieve lined with a damp paper towel. Into a small saucepan, bring the strained washing water and the morel stem trimmings to a boil. Cook until the liquid is reduced to ½ cup. Push through a sieve and discard the solids.

Sauté the shallots in butter until translucent, then add the morels and sauté for 2 to 3 minutes until lightly browned. Add the vermouth and the wine. Reduce the heat and cook, covered, for 5 to 10 minutes. Remove the cover and add the reduced morel liquid and the heavy cream. Cook until the sauce lightly coats the back of a wooden spoon. Keep the sauce warm.

Preparing the Asparagus

Meanwhile, cut off the top 2 to 3 inches of the asparagus tips. (Save the stalks for another use.) Bring a pan of salted water to a boil. Cook the asparagus tips just until they turn brilliant green. Remove the tips, reserving the cooking liquid, and refresh under ice water to set the color.

Whisk in 2 to 3 tablespoons of the asparagus cooking water into the mayonnaise. Add the herbs, lemon juice, salt, and pepper. Slowly heat the sauce, then add the asparagus tips and heat until warmed through.

Assembling the Dish

Arrange the morels in their sauce in the center of each serving plate. Arrange the asparagus tips in a spoke pattern around the morels. Drizzle the herb sauce over the asparagus tips and serve immediately.

THE MORELS

4 cups cold water

¾ pound fresh morels

2 tablespoons unsalted butter

2 shallots, finely chopped

½ cup dry white vermouth

½ cup dry white wine

1 cup heavy cream

Salt and white pepper

THE ASPARAGUS

1 pound fresh asparagus

½ cup Sauce Mayonnaise (see page 216)

1 tablespoon chopped fresh chervil

1 tablespoon chopped fresh Italian parsley

1 tablespoon freshly squeezed lemon juice

Salt and white pepper

A versatile white wine like **Vouvray** will make a good marriage between the morels and the asparagus in this dish. **Gaston Huet** and **Prince Poniatowski** make the best wines.

ESCARGOTS AU CHAMPAGNE

SNAILS IN CHAMPAGNE WITH HAZELNUT-CHARTREUSE BUTTER

I've had many, many requests for my Escargots au Champagne, a longtime favorite of my customers. What makes it so good? First I gently poach the snails in a flavorful broth, enriched with demi-glace and gelatin. It's important to cook the snails in their broth for a long time to reduce the liquid properly. To maintain all the delicate flavor of the Champagne, I stir it in at the very end of cooking. Because of the bubbles, the Champagne also gives a "moussy," or frothy, quality to the sauce. At the last minute, I combine the sauce and the escargot butter, boiling rapidly to make a creamy emulsion. We serve these escargots in their own individual cassolette or small silver pot. Try this recipe for a party, because it makes enough for twelve.

.... SERVICE FOR 12 ....

THE ESCARGOTS

2½ cups water

1 can 96-count Helix snails,
    drained and rinsed well

2 tablespoons unflavored gelatin

1½ cups Fond Blanc de Volaille
    (see page 214)

¾ cup dry white wine

¼ cup Demi-Glace (see page 212)

¾ cup Champagne

BEURRE D'ESCARGOT

1 pound unsalted butter, cut into bits

8 to 10 cloves garlic, peeled

2 teaspoons salt

¼ teaspoon ground white pepper

1 tablespoon green Chartreuse

2 sprigs fresh Italian parsley, stems removed

½ cup whole blanched hazelnuts

1 shallot, peeled

With this dish serve a large-scaled **Champagne** based on **Pinot Noir** grapes such as the **Carte Jaune Brut** from **Veuve Clicquot**, my favorite.

Cooking the Escargot

You may cook the snails up to 2 or 3 days ahead of time, but they must be prepared at least a day ahead of time. In a small bowl, pour ½ cup of the water. Sprinkle in the gelatin and let soak for 10 minutes to soften. Meanwhile, in a medium saucepan, bring the Fond Blanc de Volaille, wine, and the remaining water to a boil. Add the gelatin, snails, and the Demi-Glace and cook at a simmer for 1 hour or until the liquid has reduced to ½ cup. Add the Champagne, return to a boil, and remove the pan from the heat. Cool to room temperature, then chill overnight in the refrigerator. The juices surrounding the snails should be jellied when cold.

Preparing the Beurre d'Escargot

Place the butter, garlic, salt, white pepper, and Chartreuse into the bowl of a food processor. Process until creamy, then transfer to a bowl. Finely chop together the parsley, nuts, and shallot and mix with the butter until well blended. Chill the butter until ready to finish the dish.

Finishing the Escargot

To serve the escargot in individual cassolettes, place 8 snails, 1 tablespoon of the jellied liquid from the snails, and approximately 2 tablespoons of Beurre d'Escargot into each cassolette. Or place the snails, jellied liquid, and Beurre d'Escargot in a shallow pan.

Set the cassolettes or the pan over medium-high heat and cook, stirring often to prevent burning, until piping hot. The sauce should be "moussy" and creamy, never oily looking. Stir in a sprinkle of water if the sauce separates. Serve very hot.

❧ *Chef's Trucs* ❧

BUYING HELIX SNAILS: At Le Bec-Fin, I use only the European Helix variety of snails, that I buy in a can of ninety-six. In France, these snails are called *Petit Gris*. While a different variety of less expensive snails from Southeast Asia is available, I don't care for their flavor or texture. Ask before you buy; be sure you're paying for the Helix variety.

CRÈME D'ASPERGES AU CRABE
CREAM OF ASPARAGUS SOUP WITH CRAB

Early in the spring, asparagus spears are tender and green from stem to tip. Later in the year, the stalks are much tougher and only a small portion of the spear is good for this soup. Asparagus and East Coast blue crab are both at their best at the same time of year. Make this soup as a starter for a memorable spring dinner.

SERVICE FOR 8

THE SOUP

4 pounds asparagus (small to medium)

2 medium onions, peeled and chopped

2 ribs celery, sliced

2 cloves garlic, peeled

4 tablespoons unsalted butter

1 quart (4 cups) Fond Blanc de Volaille
   (see page 214)

1 cup heavy cream

Salt and white pepper

THE GARNISH

1 bunch Italian parsley, stems removed

½ pound jumbo lump crabmeat,
   picked clean

Reserved asparagus tips

Preparing the Soup

Cut off the tips (the top 1 inch) of the asparagus stalks and set aside for garnish. Trim off and discard the asparagus bottoms—anything that's not green will be tough. Cut the remaining part of the stalks into 1-inch lengths and set aside. In a medium stockpot, lightly sauté the onions, celery, and garlic in butter, cooking until translucent. Add the cut up asparagus stalks and the Fond Blanc de Volaille and bring to a boil. Simmer for 30 minutes, then puree in a blender and strain through a food mill or fine sieve. (Be sure to force all the liquid through or the asparagus flavor will be lost.) Stir in the cream, season with salt and pepper to taste, and return to a boil.

Preparing the Garnish

Prepare the garnish while the stock is simmering. Bring a small saucepan of water to a boil. Add the reserved asparagus tips and return to a boil. Cook just until the asparagus tips turn brilliant green. Remove the asparagus tips with a skimmer and set aside the cooking liquid. Refresh the tips under cold running water to set the color. Add the parsley to the cooking liquid and return to a boil. Simmer for 5 minutes. Drain the water and refresh the parsley under cold water to set the color.

Puree the parsley leaves, adding just enough cold water to blend, then add to the soup. (This green chlorophyll brightens the color of the soup.) Place 1 ladleful of soup in a small pan and bring to a boil. Add the crabmeat and the asparagus tips and heat together for 1 minute. Ladle the remaining soup into hot soup plates, then divide the crab-meat-asparagus mixture evenly among the portions. Serve immediately.

GALETTE DE CRABE "LE BEC-FIN"

LE BEC-FIN CRAB CAKE WITH LIGHT MUSTARD SAUCE

This Galette de Crabe is a signature dish at my restaurant. I'm extremely particular about the crabmeat I buy. I use only the best jumbo lump crabmeat with plenty of the orange roe that gives the crab its flavor. I've made this recipe over and over so I know you'll have perfect results. Serve the galette with my light mustard sauce or accompanied by a simple wedge of lemon and a small green salad. At Le Bec-Fin we often garnish the galette with lightly blanched haricots verts arranged in a spoke pattern.

SERVICE FOR 8 TO 10

THE GALETTES

14 ounces large shrimp, peeled and deveined

1 bunch scallions, sliced into thin rings

3 tablespoons butter

2 whole eggs, cold

2 cups heavy cream, icy cold

2 tablespoons Dijon mustard

1 tablespoon Worcestershire

1 tablespoon Tabasco

1 pound jumbo lump crabmeat, picked clean

2 tablespoons olive oil

THE SAUCE

1 egg yolk

1 tablespoon sherry vinegar

2 tablespoons Dijon mustard

½ cup Fond Blanc de Volaille

   (see page 214)

1½ cups olive oil

2 tablespoons whole-grain mustard

Salt and white pepper

Preparing the Galettes

Chill the shrimp along with the bowl and blade of a food processor in the freezer for about 30 minutes. Sauté the scallions in 1 tablespoon butter until just wilted. Set aside to cool.

Place the shrimp in the processor and puree on high speed for 1 minute or until smooth and shiny. Using a rubber spatula, scrape down the sides of the bowl, then add the eggs. Process again until the mixture is smooth and shiny, about 2 minutes. Scrape the bowl again. With the machine running, slowly pour in the heavy cream. Scrape the bowl and process again to make sure the cream is completely incorporated. Remove the mixture and place in a bowl. Stir in the mustard, Worcestershire, and Tabasco, then gently fold in the cooled scallions and the crabmeat.

Place four or five 3-inch oiled ring molds into a lightly oiled nonstick pan. Fill each mold with the mixture, smoothing off the tops with a spoon. Over medium heat, cook the crab cakes until golden brown, about 2 minutes on each side. Once the cakes have browned, push down on the ring molds to cut off any excess crab mixture and remove the rings from around the cakes. Remove the crab cakes from the pan. Repeat the procedure until all of the crab mixture has been cooked. (The cakes may be made up to 1 day ahead, up to this point, and refrigerated.)

Preparing the Sauce

Place the egg yolk, vinegar, Dijon mustard, and Fond Blanc de Volaille into a blender. Blend until smooth, about 30 seconds. Drizzle in the olive oil until the sauce is emulsified (creamy looking). Add the whole-grain mustard and season with salt and pepper to taste.

Preparing the Endive

In a small sauté pan, heat the butter and the lemon juice. Add the cut endive and the sugar and toss together. Cook over medium heat until the endive is wilted but not soft and the pan juices have been absorbed. Season to taste and set aside.

Assembling the Dish

Preheat the oven to 400°F. Place the crab cakes on a buttered nonstick baking pan.

THE ENDIVE AND HARICOT VERTS

1 tablespoon butter

2 teaspoons lemon juice

3 heads Belgian endive, cored and cut into
1-inch lengths

1 teaspoon sugar

Salt and ground white pepper

1 pound haricot verts,
trimmed and blanched (optional)

Bake for 5 minutes or until the cakes are springy to the touch.

In a small pot, slowly heat the sauce over low heat without letting it boil. Place a small mound of the endive in the center of each serving plate. Top with 1 or 2 crab cakes then ladle the sauce over the crab cakes and serve immediately.

❧ *Chef's Truc* ❧

USING FLAN RINGS: At Le Bec-Fin, we use special metal "flan" rings to shape the crab cakes (see Sources page 219). For the smaller crab cakes you can improvise with round biscuit cutters. For the large cakes substitute a cleaned empty tuna can with both ends removed. Lightly oil the rings before filling with the crab mix.

With this dish I would serve a clean, full-bodied white wine like a **Chardonnay** from the **Maconnais** by **André Bonhomme** or **Gilles Corsin**. Especially good is **Corsin's St. Véran "Tirage Precoce" 1995**. An **Hermitage Blanc**, with its hint of toasted hazelnut, would work as well.

Saumon Fumé Maison

House Smoked Salmon

If you have access to a cold smoker, try our house recipe for smoked salmon. It's a perfect hors d'oeuvre, stimulating to the palate but not too filling. We serve it at Le Bec-Fin in the traditional way: paper-thin slices are garnished with mounds of chopped tiny capers, cooked egg whites and yolks, and red onion. With a wedge of lemon and a couple of twists from the pepper mill, it is a classic that can't be improved upon. Don't forget to serve it with crispy toast triangles. Many days I enjoy this smoked salmon for a light lunch.

·· SERVICE FOR 20 TO 25 ··

Smoking the Salmon

Make 5 or 6 shallow slits in the skin along the length of the side of salmon fillet. Spread a layer of salt in a stainless steel or enamel pan. Lay the salmon, skin-side down, on the salt. Spread another layer of salt over the fillet, covering completely. Cover loosely with plastic wrap and refrigerate for 24 hours.

Remove the salmon from the salt and rinse in cold water. Fill a large container or sink with cold water and soak the salmon for 2 hours, changing the water every 30 minutes to remove the salty taste. Remove from the water and drain. Place the side of salmon, skin-side down, on a strong wire baker's cooling rack set over a pan to catch the drips. Air-dry the salmon in the refrigerator for 24 hours.

Following the manufacturer's instructions, cold-smoke the salmon over hickory with apple wood chips for 4 hours. Transfer the salmon to a deep container. Cover with the oil and refrigerate, covered, for 24 hours. Remove the salmon from the oil, wipe dry with a towel, and wrap tightly with plastic wrap to store. The salmon will keep for 1 to 2 weeks. To slice, use an electric or very sharp knife, cutting the salmon on the bias into paper-thin slices.

THE SALMON

1 fillet Atlantic salmon
    (about 2½ pounds),
    pin bones removed
1½ pounds kosher salt
2 quarts (8 cups) vegetable oil
Hickory chips
Apple wood chips

MILLE-FEUILLE DE SAUMON FUMÉ AVEC SA SALADE DE CONCOMBRES

LAYERED TERRINE OF HOUSE SMOKED SALMON WITH CUCUMBER SALAD

In this beautiful dish, I stack thin layers of our own cold-smoked salmon between layers of creamy chervil mousse. Make my Mille-Feuille de Saumon if you enjoy a challenge. What a magnificent impression it will make for your next gathering. Because the mille-feuille keeps perfectly for two to three days, make it ahead of time, slicing into portions the day of your event.

SERVICE FOR 12 (MAKES ONE 12 x 2 x 2-INCH LOAF)

THE SMOKED SALMON

1½ pounds fillet of smoked salmon

THE MOUSSE

1 tablespoon unflavored gelatin

Juice of 1 lemon

8 ounces smoked salmon trimmings

8 ounces cream cheese

8 tablespoons (1 stick) unsalted butter,
    cut into bits

2 drops of Tabasco

¼ cup olive oil

½ cup Fond Blanc de Volaille
    (see page 214)

Ground white pepper (no salt)

1 bunch fresh chervil, stems removed

Preparing the Smoked Salmon

Using an electric or very sharp knife, slice the smoked salmon into thin, even slices, laying out on plastic wrap as you cut. Line three 10- x 15-inch jelly-roll pans with parchment paper. Cover the paper completely with the smoked salmon, slightly overlapping the slices. Cover with a second sheet of parchment paper, pressing so it adheres to the salmon. Repeat with the remaining two trays. Place the three trays in the freezer until firm, about 20 minutes.

Making the Mousse

Pour the lemon juice in a small pan. Sprinkle in the gelatin and let soak for 10 minutes to soften. Gently heat until the liquid is clear. Let cool to room temperature.

Process the smoked salmon trimmings in the food processor until smooth. While the machine is running, gradually add the cream cheese and the butter. Add the Tabasco, oil, Fond Blanc de Volaille, pepper, and gelatin and process again until smooth. Add the chervil, and process just to combine. Transfer the mousse to a bowl. Set aside.

Assembling the Mille-Feuille

Remove the trays of salmon from the freezer. Discard the top pieces of parchment paper. Spread one-quarter of the mousse over the first tray and invert the second tray of smoked salmon on top of the mousse. Remove the paper and spread with one-quarter of the mousse. Invert the third tray on top and remove and discard the remaining sheet of parchment paper. Spread with one-quarter of the mousse. Cover the top layer with a sheet of parchment paper and press down gently but firmly so the layers of salmon and mousse adhere. Refrigerate until firm, about 1 hour.

Remove the terrine from the refrigerator and discard the parchment paper. Transfer the terrine from the tray onto a work surface. Using an electric or very sharp knife and the edge of a metal ruler, cut lengthwise, slicing the layers into 4 equal 2½-inch-wide strips. Stack the layered strips, spreading the remaining one-quarter of the mousse evenly between each one. Press firmly so that each stack adheres to the next. (You should end up with one 2½-inch wide by 4-inch high by 15-inch long terrine.) Wrap the terrine tightly with plastic wrap and place in the

THE CUCUMBER SALAD

2 *English cucumbers*

½ *cup heavy cream*

2 *tablespoons sherry wine vinegar*

1 *tablespoon finely snipped fresh chives*

1 *tablespoon finely snipped fresh chervil*

Salt and white pepper

Fresh chervil sprigs (for garnish)

With this dish I suggest a rich, vinous **Champagne**, like **Egly-Orlet Rosé**, or a white wine with just a little sweetness like **Poniatowski's Clos Baudoin 1993**.

freezer until firm, about 1 hour. Using an electric or very sharp knife, trim the edges to make a neat rectangle. Refrigerate until ready to serve.

Preparing the Cucumber Salad

Peel the cucumbers in alternating thin and wide strips. Cut off the tip and ends of the cucumbers and discard. Slice the cucumbers in half lengthwise. Using a spoon, scoop out and discard the seeds. Slice the cucumbers into thin half-moons and set aside in a bowl.

Just before serving, lightly whip the cream until soft peaks form. Gently fold the vinegar and herbs into the cream and season to taste with salt and pepper. Toss the dressing with the cucumbers.

Serving the Terrine

To serve, slice the cold terrine crosswise in ⅜-inch-thick slices. Serve on cold plates accompanied by a small portion of the cucumber salad. Decorate with sprigs of fresh chervil.

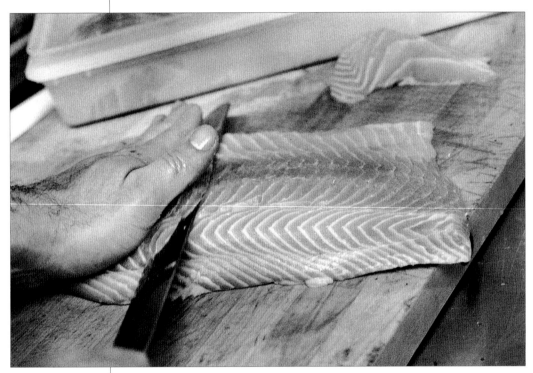

PARFAIT DE FOIES DE VOLAILLES ET SA SALADE

LIGHT MOUSSE OF CHICKEN LIVERS WITH COGNAC AND A SALAD

Because this mousse has such a creamy melt-in-your mouth texture, it's called a parfait, which usually refers to a smooth, airy dessert. Take the trouble to search out the pale-pink livers of free-range or grain-fed chickens to make this inexpensive yet luxurious mousse. Here the parfait is served in slices as a first course with its salad, but you can also serve it whole accompanied by toast triangles as part of a buffet dinner.

.... THE MOUSSE SERVES 12 TO 15; THE SALAD SERVES 4 TO 6 ....

Preparing the Parfait

Soak the chicken livers for 1 hour in the milk, then drain and discard milk. Dry the livers on a towel. Using a sharp paring knife, remove any veins.

Sauté the livers and shallots in the olive oil over high heat for about 3 minutes, or until the livers are lightly browned, but still pink inside. Drain off the olive oil and cooking juices from pan into a container and set aside.

Add the cognac to the pan and *flambé* (ignite with a long match). Remove the pan from heat and let the livers cool for 30 minutes.

Place the livers and the butter in a food processor and process just until smooth. (Don't process too long or the mixture will become white.) Pour in the reserved cooking juices, salt, and pepper and process 30 seconds longer. Using the back of a rubber spatula, press the parfait mixture through a fine mesh sieve. Spray a 1-quart decorative mold with nonstick spray and fill with the mousse mixture. Refrigerate until firm, about 8 hours.

To unmold, choose a shallow pot with a diameter larger than the mold, fill it halfway with water and bring to a boil. Briefly dip the mold up to the rim in the boiling water and then invert it onto a cutting board or serving platter. Remove the mold. Loosely cover the parfait with plastic wrap and refrigerate until ready to serve.

Preparing the Salad

Place the oil and vinegar in a small glass jar with a lid and shake well, until the dressing looks creamy. Season to taste with salt and pepper. Place the mesclun greens in a large bowl and add the dressing to coat. Toss gently but thoroughly.

Serving the Parfait

Cut the parfait into ⅜-inch-thick slices. Place 1 slice on each chilled plate. Using a pair of salad tongs, gently arrange the dressed salad alongside.

❧ *Chef's Truc* ❧

SLICING THE PARFAIT: To slice the parfait, have ready a long, thin sharp slicing knife. Run the knife under hot water, shake dry, then slice. Rinse the knife under the hot water after each slice to get clean, even slices.

THE PARFAIT

1 pound chicken livers, preferably from free-range, grain-fed chickens

1 cup milk

2 tablespoons olive oil

2 shallots, finely chopped

3 tablespoons cognac

1 pound (4 sticks) unsalted butter, softened

Salt and white pepper

THE SALAD

½ cup walnut oil

¼ cup cider vinegar

Salt and ground white pepper

½ pound mesclun greens, gently washed and towel-dried

With this dish I recommend an aristocratic dry white **Alsace Riesling** like a 1990 **Cuvée Frederick Emile of Trimbach.**

LES OEUFS SURPRISE AU CAVIAR

EGG SHELLS FILLED WITH OSETRA CAVIAR

A dramatic dish, perfect for an elegant hors d'oeuvre. I especially like to serve these eggs for a New Year's Eve dinner. If you can, use brown eggs for their warm color. I use a special egg cutter made for soft-boiled eggs to clip off their tops. Top the eggs with the very best caviar you can afford. I like to use osetra caviar for this dish. Osetra is a small-grain caviar, more even in size than the richer, milder beluga. Osetra is nutty flavored and its color varies from golden yellow to light brown. Present the eggs in individual ceramic egg cups, if you have them. If not, make a mound of coarse salt on each plate with a depression in the middle to hold the egg, placed larger end down.

.... SERVICE FOR 8 ....

THE EGGS

12 extra-large eggs (reserve the carton)

THE FILLING

½ cup heavy cream

2 teaspoons vodka

2 teaspoons lemon juice

Salt and ground white pepper

8 teaspoons osetra caviar, chilled

Rather than wine, serve icy, icy cold **vodka** with this dish. My favorite is **Stolichnaya Cristal**.

Preparing the Egg Shells

Using kitchen shears, poke a hole into the side of the eggs, about ½ inch below the pointy end. Carefully snip around the circumference of the eggs and remove and discard the top. Drain off and discard the contents of the eggs. Repeat until you have 8 perfect egg shells, reserving the remaining 4 eggs for the filling. Carefully rinse out the inside of each shell using hot water, then drain on paper towels. Set aside the shells in the reserved egg carton.

Preparing the Filling

Hard cook the remaining 4 eggs until the yolks are just set (see *Chef's Truc* below). Refresh the cooked eggs under cold water to prevent them from overcooking. Shell the eggs, then separate the yolks and whites and chop each separately.

Whip the cream until soft peaks form. Fold in the egg yolks and egg whites, vodka, and lemon juice. Season with salt and pepper to taste. Spoon the filling into a pastry bag fitted with a medium-sized plain round tip then pipe into the reserved shells, filling them all the way to the top. Top each egg with 1 teaspoon of caviar and serve.

~ Chef's Truc ~

COOKING EGGS: To cook perfect eggs, never boil them! Rubbery, overcooked eggs are unpleasant and can ruin this marvelous dish. Place the eggs in a small, heavy saucepan. Cover with cold water and bring to a boil. When the water reaches a boil, turn off the heat and cover. Allow the eggs to set in the water, about 8 minutes. Test by running cold water over one egg. Gently crack the shell. The egg should feel soft but not liquidy. Cut open an egg if you're not sure. The yolks should be set but not grainy and hard.

Ravioli de Champignons, Sauce Ivoire

Mushroom Ravioli with Ivory Sauce

I serve my ravioli day after day and my customers keep ordering more. Try this recipe and you'll see why they love it so much. It makes a light but satisfying main course for lunch or brunch. Hedgehog, chanterelle, shiitake, or any strong-flavored exotic or wild mushroom is delicious for this ravioli filling. True wild mushrooms, rather than exotic cultivated mushrooms, still have the most intense flavor. Try using morels, chanterelles, or cèpes if they are in season. I use an inexpensive plastic ravioli mold (available at most kitchen supply stores) to shape my ravioli.

SERVICE FOR 8 (MAKES 32 RAVIOLI)

THE CHICKEN MOUSSE

½ pound boneless, skinless chicken breast

1 egg

2 cups heavy cream, chilled

THE RAVIOLI

1 pound assorted wild mushrooms,
    cleaned and dried

2 tablespoons butter

3 shallots, peeled and finely chopped

Salt and ground white pepper

1 egg

2 tablespoons milk

½ pound fresh Pâte aux Oeufs
    (see page 215)

With this dish I recommend a light-bodied red with some rustic character like the **Vin de Pays de Vaucluse 1995** from **Christian Vache** or a **Marcillac** from **Philippe Teuilier's Domaine du Cros.**

Preparing the Chicken Mousse

Trim the chicken breast of all fat and connective tissue. Cut into large cubes. Place in the freezer along with a food processor bowl and blade and chill for 45 minutes. Process the chicken and the egg together until smooth and shiny. Leave the mixture in the processor bowl and chill again for 20 minutes. Remove bowl from the freezer and with the motor running, slowly pour in the heavy cream, stopping once or twice to scrape down the sides of the bowl. Scrape the mixture into a bowl, cover, and refrigerate until well chilled, about 1 hour.

Preparing the Ravioli Filling

Trim off any tough mushroom stems and set aside for the Sauce Ivoire. Finely chop the mushrooms. In a small sauté pan, cook the shallots in the butter until translucent, then add the mushrooms. Sauté, stirring often, until the mixture is extremely dry. Cool slightly, then combine with the chicken mousse using a plastic spatula. Season with salt and pepper. In a small sauté pan, cook a spoonful of the mixture, then taste for seasoning. (Don't taste the uncooked mixture; it contains raw chicken.) Season again if necessary. Place the mixture in a pastry bag fitted with a large round tip and set aside in the refrigerator.

Assembling the Ravioli

Lightly beat together the egg and milk. Using a roller-type pasta machine, roll out 2 sheets of pasta dough for each batch. Drape 1 sheet over the ravioli mold. Pipe about 1 tablespoon of the mushroom mixture into each ravioli form. Brush the edges of the pasta with the egg wash. Lay the second sheet of pasta on top. Using your fingers, press together the 2 layers to seal. Then, using a rolling pin, roll over top of pasta to cut out the individual ravioli. Repeat until you have 32 ravioli. If serving within 24 hours, refrigerate until needed. (If you wish to freeze the ravioli at this point, cover a jelly-roll pan with parchment paper and arrange the ravioli on the paper without touching. Freeze until firm, then transfer to a heavy plastic freezer bag, seal and keep frozen.)

Preparing the Sauce Ivoire

Cook the mushroom stems in 1 tablespoon of the butter until softened and translucent. Deglaze the pan with Madeira and vermouth. Add the Fond Blanc de Volaille and cook until the mixture is reduced by half. Off the heat, whisk in the ½ pound butter a little at a time into the sauce. Season with salt and white pepper. Puree the sauce in a blender, then strain through a fine sieve. Keep the sauce warm while cooking the ravioli.

Preparing the Mushroom Garnish

Heat the butter and olive oil in a sauté pan. Cook the mushrooms on a low heat until soft, then sauté at high heat to brown. Season with salt and pepper to taste and cook until the liquid has evaporated. Set aside.

Finishing the Ravioli

Bring a large pot of water with 1 tablespoon of salt to boiling. Cook 4 ravioli for each portion as an appetizer or 7 to 8 ravioli for a main course. Add the ravioli, one at a time, into the center of the boiling water. Be careful not to let them touch as you add more ravioli. Bring the water back to a boil and cook until tender, 2 minutes if fresh, 4 minutes if frozen.

Scoop the ravioli out of the water and gently lay on a clean towel to drain. Transfer to heated plates. Ladle the sauce over each serving. Place small spoonfuls of the mushroom garnish in the center of the plate and in between each ravioli. Serve immediately.

THE SAUCE IVOIRE

2 cups chopped assorted mushroom stems
    (plus extra mushrooms if needed)
½ pound (2 sticks) plus 1 tablespoon
    unsalted butter, softened
2 tablespoons Madeira wine
2 tablespoons dry white vermouth
2 cups Fond Blanc de Volaille
    (see page 214)
Salt and ground white pepper

THE MUSHROOM GARNISH

1 tablespoon butter
1 tablespoon olive oil
½ pound assorted mushrooms,
    cleaned and dried, sliced or quartered
    (depending on their size)
Salt and white pepper

SALADE DE CREVETTES, SALSA DE MANGUES ET COULIS DE TOMATES

SALAD OF GRILLED SHRIMP WITH CRAB, MANGO SALSA, AND TOMATO COULIS

*T*his light but flavorful summer dish makes a striking presentation with its curved streaks of brilliant sauces. I love this dish because the many flavors and textures blend so well. The dish calls for six different sauces, making it an ambitious dish for the home cook. It may be simplified if desired by choosing just one or two of the sauces with delicious, though not quite so spectacular, results.

SERVICE FOR 8

THE MANGO SALSA

2 ripe but firm mangoes, peeled
   (see Chef's Truc page 48)

½ red bell pepper, roasted, peeled, and seeded

1 tablespoon Japanese sesame oil

1 tablespoon rice wine vinegar

Salt and white pepper

1½ cups Tomates Concassées
   (see page 217)

THE TOMATO COULIS

¼ cup chopped garlic

½ cup chopped shallots

½ cup extra-virgin olive oil

4 cups halved ripe plum tomatoes

Salt and white pepper

THE SWEET AND SOUR SAUCE

¾ cup sugar

½ cup red wine vinegar

½ cup rice wine vinegar

1 cup Demi-Glace (see page 212)

½ cup Fond Blanc de Volaille
   (see page 214)

1 tablespoon tomato paste

1 cup Tomates Concassées (see page 217)

Making the Mango Salsa

Cut the mango into ¼-inch cubes and set aside.

Cut the bell pepper into ⅛-inch dice and set aside. Combine the diced mango with the bell pepper, sesame oil, vinegar, and Tomates Concassées. Season to taste with salt and pepper.

Making the Tomato Coulis

In a large saucepot, heat the garlic and shallots in the oil, cooking until lightly browned. Add the tomatoes and simmer until tender, stirring occasionally. Puree in a blender then strain through a fine sieve. Season to taste and set aside.

Making the Sweet and Sour Sauce

In a 2-quart heavy-bottomed saucepan, gently heat the sugar until it melts. Then raise the temperature and caramelize, cooking the sugar until it's golden brown. Add both vinegars and bring the mixture to a boil, melting the now-hardened sugar to a syrup. Add the Demi-Glace, Fond Blanc de Volaille, and tomato paste and simmer 10 minutes. Strain through a sieve and stir in the Tomates Concassées. Use the remaining sauce for grilled fish or seafood.

Making the Mango Coulis

In a small saucepan, bring the mango, ginger, vinegar, sugar, salt, and water to a boil. Simmer for about 15 minutes or until the ginger is tender. Puree in a blender, then strain through a sieve. Refrigerate until needed.

Making the Tomato Garlic Oil

Heat the garlic in the oil until the garlic just begins to brown. Strain the oil, reserving the oil and discarding the garlic. Add the Tomates Concassées and bring to a boil. Simmer 5 minutes, then season to taste with salt and pepper.

Making the Crabmeat

Gently toss the crabmeat, oil, vinegar, and chives, season with salt and pepper, and refrigerate until needed. Peel the cucumber, leaving alternating strips of skin and flesh. Slice thinly and set aside.

THE MANGO COULIS

2 ripe but firm mangoes, peeled
(see Chef's Truc below)
and coarsely chopped

One 2-inch piece ginger root,
peeled and sliced

1 tablespoon red wine vinegar

⅛ teaspoon sugar

⅛ teaspoon salt

1 cup water

THE TOMATO GARLIC OIL

2 tablespoons chopped garlic

½ cup extra-virgin olive oil

½ cup Tomates Concassées (see page 217)

Salt and white pepper

THE CRABMEAT

1 pound jumbo lump crabmeat, picked clean

½ cup hazelnut oil

¼ cup raspberry vinegar

1 tablespoon finely snipped chives

Salt and white pepper

½ European seedless cucumber

THE SHRIMP

2 tablespoons extra-virgin olive oil

Salt and white pepper

12 jumbo shrimp (1½ under-12-count
shrimp per person), peeled and deveined

THE GARNISH

½ cup Jus de Persil (see page 88)

Grilling the Shrimp

Combine the oil, salt, and pepper with the shrimp and marinate 10 minutes. Preheat a grill to red-hot, then grill the shrimp until just opaque. Remove from grill and let cool slightly. Slice each shrimp in half lengthwise and keep warm.

Assembling the Salad

Have ready 8 large dinner plates and three plastic squeeze bottles, one filled with Tomato Coulis, one filled with Jus de Persil, one filled with Mango Coulis. Mentally divide the plate into three sections. Spiraling out from the center of each plate, make one swirl each of the three different sauces in each section. (You should have a total of nine swirls on each plate.)

Divide the Mango Salsa into 8 portions. Using a small open ring mold, shape the salsa into an even round, filling the mold about three-quarters full. Arrange cucumber slices on top and crown with a spoonful of the crabmeat salad. Place a ring of Mango Salsa in the center of each plate then remove the mold. Dot 1 teaspoon of the Tomato-Garlic Oil in three places around each mold. For each portion, place 3 shrimp halves on top of the oil, leaning them against the salsa. Dot the Sweet and Sour Sauce in between the swirls of sauce and serve.

❧ Chef's Trucs ❧

PEELING A MANGO: Slice ½ inch off the top and bottom. Using a small, sharp knife, pare off the skin in strips. Slice away the flesh from the flat, tongue-shaped pit and cut as directed.

· · ·

THINNING THE JUS DE PERSIL: If the Jus de Persil is too thick, blend it with a little of its cooking liquid and a few ice cubes so the color stays bright.

With this dish I would serve an excellent **Chardonnay** from California's South Central Coast. Two of my favorites are the **Babcock Grand Cuvée** and **Au Bon Climat's Talley Vineyard Reserve**.

LENTILLES AUX TRUFFES ET PETITS OIGNONS CARAMELISÉS

LE PUY LENTILS WITH WINTER TRUFFLES AND CARAMELIZED PEARL ONIONS

We think of lentils as earthy, even plebeian, but not in this dish. I use the French Le Puy lentils that are speckled deep green, tiny, and firm. Truffles are certainly earthy, but they are hardly plebeian. The truffles may be enjoyed to their fullest in this dish. I especially like my garnish of sweet caramelized tiny pearl onions cooked in duck fat. You can buy duck fat or make your own as in my Chef's Truc below. Don't be tempted to leave it out. Cooking with duck fat is one of the secrets of French cuisine, especially in the romantic country of Southwest France—Three-Musketeer country.

.... SERVICE FOR 6 ....

Cooking the Lentils

Soak the lentils overnight in a bowl of cold water. Drain off and discard the water and rinse the lentils under fresh water. Place the lentils and the Fond Blanc de Volaille in a heavy-bottomed pot and bring to a boil. Reduce heat to very low and simmer about 30 minutes, until cooked through but still firm—the skins shouldn't split open. (You can also cook the lentils in a 300°F oven, covered, until they're tender but still firm.) Drain off and set aside any cooking juices and keep the lentils warm in the pot.

Preparing the Garnish

Preheat the oven to 300°F. In a small pot, combine the reserved lentil cooking juices and the truffle juice. Cook until reduced to ¼ cup. Whisk the butter into this reduction, then mix it back with the lentils and set aside.

In an ovenproof sauté pan, heat the duck fat until sizzling. Add the pearl onions and cook until they begin to brown. Add the sugar, salt, and pepper and cover with aluminum foil. Place the onions in the oven and roast until tender, about 15 minutes. Drain off and discard the duck fat, reserving the onions.

Serving the Lentils

Have ready 6 shallow soup plates. Reheat the lentils, then divide into 6 portions. Cover each with the reserved truffle sauce and the reserved truffle dice. Divide the caramelized pearl onions and arrange among the soup plates.

❧ *Chef's Truc* ❧

RENDERING DUCK FAT: If you roast your own duck, save the fat you pull out of the carcass along with any drippings. Pour into a small container. Chill overnight or until the fat congeals. Remove the layer of white fat from the jellied juices. Simmer the fat at very low heat, skimming often until it's clear. Strain into a container and chill. The clarified fat will keep for several months if refrigerated.

THE LENTILS

1 cup green Le Puy lentils

1 quart (4 cups) Fond Blanc de Volaille
  (see page 214)

1 canned black winter truffle,
  cut into ⅛-inch dice

2 tablespoons truffle juice
  (from the canned truffles)

2 tablespoons unsalted butter

1 pint pearl onions, peeled

1 tablespoon sugar

Salt and white pepper

½ cup rendered duck fat
  (see Chef's Truc below)

With this dish from the Southwest of **France** I would serve a wine from the same place of origin, like a **Côte du Frontonnais** of **Chateau Bellevue la Forêt** or a **Gaillac** from the **Domaine des Terrisses**.

SALADE DE CAILLES

SALAD OF QUAILS WITH MÂCHE IN RASPBERRY HAZELNUT VINAIGRETTE

Quail is a tasty, delicate bird that can be a bit intimidating to Americans. At Le Bec-Fin, we cook quail on the bone to keep them juicy but we serve them off the bone to make them easier to eat. The trimmings and bones of the quail add another dimension of flavor to the sauce. Like all my sauces, this one is built layer by layer—the result is balanced perfection.

.... SERVICE FOR 4 ....

THE QUAIL

1 tablespoon unsalted butter

1 tablespoon olive oil

4 whole quail

Salt and white pepper

½ cup Madeira

1 cup Jus de Poulet (see page 214)

¼ cup Vinaigrette Maison (see page 216)

THE SALAD

½ cup sliced almonds

1 ripe tomato, insides scooped out

2 tablespoons olive oil

4 quail eggs

4 cups mâche (lamb's leaf lettuce), gently washed and dried

½ cup hazelnut oil

¼ cup raspberry vinegar

Salt and white pepper

With this dish I would serve a low-acid red wine from the **Côte du Rhône**, like **Oratoire St. Martin's 1995**, served cool.

Cooking the Quail and Preparing the Vinaigrette Sauce

Heat the butter and oil in a large sauté pan until sizzling hot. Meanwhile, season the quail with salt and pepper. Brown the whole quail on all sides, cooking only until rare inside. (The juices should still be pink.) Remove the quail and juices and cool, setting the pan aside. Turn the quail so its back faces you. Cut down on either side of the backbone. Remove and set aside the backbone. Flatten the quail and split it down the breastbone. Cut off the wings and set aside. Using your fingers, remove the ribcage and set aside. You should now have 2 boneless breast halves and 2 leg-thigh sections on the bones.

Return the reserved bones to the pan and brown well on all sides. Pour in the Madeira and bring the liquid to a boil, scraping up the browned bits with a wooden spoon. Add the Jus de Poulet to the pan and simmer, reducing the liquid by half, about 20 minutes. Strain the liquid through a sieve, whisk together with Vinaigrette Maison and set aside.

Preparing the Salad

Preheat the oven to 350°F. Place the almonds on a baking sheet and roast 6 to 8 minutes or until lightly but evenly browned. Shake the pan once or twice while roasting. Remove from the oven and set aside. Cut twelve ¾-inch diamond shapes from the scooped out tomato shell and set aside.

Assembling the Salad

Heat a nonstick sauté pan with 1 tablespoon olive oil, then add the quail pieces and brown until medium-rare or until the juices run slightly pink. Remove the quail from pan, and add the remaining tablespoon of olive oil. Carefully break the quail eggs into the pan, cooking sunny-side up for about 1 minute, or until the egg whites have set. Turn off the heat and set aside the eggs in the pan.

Toss the mâche with hazelnut oil, vinegar, salt, and pepper. Divide among 4 large salad plates. Place 3 tomato diamonds on each plate surrounding the mâche. Top the salad with roasted almonds. Arrange quail sections in a cross shape over the mâche, with 2 breast halves opposite each other and 2 leg-thigh pieces in between. Place a sunny-side up egg in center of each salad. Dot the salad plate with the reserved Vinaigrette Sauce.

Terrine de Foie Gras au Poivre Szechuan

Terrine of Duck Foie Gras Scented with Szechuan Peppercorns

A delicacy for thousands of years, the technique of producing foie gras (fattened liver) goes back as far as the Egyptians. The Moullard ducks used for foie gras, a sterile cross of two breeds, tend naturally to fatten themselves in preparation for their long migratory flights. Fresh foie gras, raised in New York state, is sold by grade. I use "A" grade, the highest, which is large, pale in color, and blemish free. I use two special seasonings for my terrine, Szechuan peppercorns and a Moroccan spice mix dominated by cinnamon, coriander seed, ginger root, and paprika.

.... SERVICE FOR 12 TO 16 ....

THE FOIE GRAS

1 whole "A" grade foie gras, about
    2 pounds (see Sources page 219)

2 teaspoons Moroccan spice mix
    (see Sources page 219)

1 teaspoon sel rose (see Chef's Truc below)

1 teaspoon Szechuan peppercorns

1 teaspoon sea salt

1 cup Sauternes

½ cup port

White pepper

1 whole black winter truffle
    (fresh or canned), thinly sliced

With this dish I would serve a **Sauternes** like **Chateau Guiraud**, the property next to **Chateau d'Yquem**, or a late harvest **Riesling** like the **Vendange Tardive Clos Hauserer of Zind-Humbrecht**.

Preparing the Foie Gras

Soak the foie gras in warm water for 30 minutes or until the liver softens. After removing it from the water, place the liver smooth-side down on a flat work surface. Using your fingers and a pair of tweezers or surgical forceps, open up the liver in the center to find the main vein. Gently pull out the vein and any smaller veins. Keep opening up the liver as you pull, until all the veins have been removed. (The veins would give a bitter taste and unpleasant rubbery quality to the terrine).

Combine the Moroccan spice, sel rose, Szechuan peppercorns, sea salt, wines, and pepper. Place the foie gras, smooth-side down, in a roasting pan just large enough to hold it. Rub with spice-wine mixture. Marinate for 1 hour in the refrigerator.

Cooking the Terrine

Preheat oven to 300°F. Place the foie gras in the oven and cook for 10 minutes only. Pour off and set aside any cooking juices. Meanwhile, line a terrine mold with plastic wrap, leaving several inches overlapping on the sides. Divide the foie gras in half. Place half, smooth-side down, in the terrine and cover with a line of truffle slices down the middle. Place the second half over the truffle layer, smooth-side up.

Cut a piece of cardboard to fit the terrine. Fold the overhanging plastic over the top of the foie gras and cover with the cardboard. Apply weight evenly (with cans) and refrigerate for 1 hour.

Pour the reserved cooking juices into a small pot and simmer, skimming off all impurities. When the remaining fat is clear, let it cool slightly. Remove the weights and plastic wrap from the terrine. Pour the cooled fat over top, then cover again with plastic wrap and chill for 1 hour. Using a hot knife, cut thin slices of the terrine. Serve with a small green salad and crisp toast.

❧ *Chef's Truc* ❧

USING SEL ROSE: Pink salt is a special curing salt that contains saltpeter, used in small amounts in preserved meats. In sausages, prosciutto, and in this terrine, the sel rose helps preserve the meat and gives it a lovely rose-pink color.

Velouté de Cocos Blancs aux Truffes

Velvety Soup of White Coco Beans and Grated Truffle

This soup was inspired by an unforgettable meal I had at Joël Robuchon's eponymous now-closed restaurant in Paris. After experiencing it, I was inspired to recreate the dish for my own menu. The perfume of the freshly grated truffles and slightly smoky, creamy French white coco beans both have a goût du terroir, a taste of the earth, that I find irresistible. If I'm lucky enough to have fresh truffles, I don't cook them. Instead I grate them over the hot soup at the last minute in order to release their powerful, evanescent aroma.

.... SERVICE FOR 6 ....

Preparing the Soup

Soak the white beans in cold water for 6 hours, then drain, rinse, and set aside. Soak the leeks in a large bowl of cold water, swishing around several times to release any sand. Remove the leeks from the water, leaving behind any sand. Drain the leeks. Sauté the bacon in a large pot until browned. Add the leeks, onion, celery, and garlic and cook over medium heat until translucent, about 10 minutes.

Add the ham hocks, the drained white beans, the Fond Blanc de Volaille, and the herbs then let simmer 1 hour. Remove the meat from the ham hocks and discard

bones. Return the meat to the soup then puree in small batches in a blender. Strain the soup through a fine sieve. Stir in the heavy cream. Bring soup to a simmer and season with salt and pepper to taste.

Serving the Soup

Soak the truffle in cold water for 10 minutes then scrub well to remove any dirt. Dry it on a towel. Carefully peel the truffle, using a sharp paring knife. Ladle the soup into 6 heated soup plates. At the table, grate a generous portion of truffles over each soup plate.

THE SOUP

1 cup dried white beans
    (cocos blancs, navy beans,
    or cannellini)
¼ pound (4 ounces) bacon, diced
3 leeks (white part only),
    cut into 1-inch rings
1 onion, peeled and chopped
3 celery ribs, chopped
3 whole cloves garlic, peeled
2 ham hocks
4 quarts Fond Blanc de Volaille
    (see page 214)
4 bay leaves
4 sprigs fresh thyme
2 cups heavy cream
1 fresh black truffle, or more to taste
Salt and white pepper

❧ Chef's Truc ❧

BUYING BLACK TRUFFLES: The best black truffles come from the Perigord region in France. Pungent, aromatic winter truffles have a mottled dark-brown to black color. They should be firm, never spongy. Summer truffles cost less but don't have nearly the flavor of the genuine article.

Vichyssoise d'Huîtres Caspienne
à la Crème de Ciboulette

WARM VICHYSSOISE SOUP WITH OYSTERS, CHIVE CREAM, AND CAVIAR

The Caspian Sea is the source of nearly all the world's supply of sturgeon caviar. Here, a lowly leek and potato soup is transformed into an elegant warm Vichyssoise Caspienne. Poached oysters float on a cloud of chive cream. The dish becomes sublime when you top the oysters with jet black caviar beads. Place the garnish on the soup at the last second before serving so both the caviar and the cream stay cold.

SERVICE FOR 6

THE SOUP

3 leeks (white part only), cut into
   1-inch wide rings
2 tablespoons unsalted butter
2 Idaho potatoes, peeled and diced
1 quart (4 cups) Fond Blanc de Volaille
   (see page 214)
1½ cups heavy cream
Salt and white pepper

THE GARNISH

18 freshly shucked oysters (3 per person)
½ cup heavy cream, lightly whipped
3 tablespoons thinly snipped chives
1 tablespoon vodka
2 tablespoons beluga caviar

Preparing the Soup

Soak the leeks in a large bowl of cold water, swishing around several times to release any sand. Skim from water, leaving any sand at the bottom of the bowl. Melt butter in a large pot and cook the leeks until transparent. Add the potatoes and cook 5 minutes longer. Add the Fond Blanc de Volaille and simmer for 45 minutes. Puree the soup and force through a fine mesh sieve. Stir in heavy cream and season with salt and pepper to taste.

Preparing the Garnish and Serving the Soup

In a small saucepan, poach the oysters in their own juices, cooking just until their edges curl. Drain the oysters on paper towels, discarding the cooking liquid. Fold the chives and vodka into the whipped cream. Ladle the soup into individual heated soup plates. Arrange 3 poached oysters at the ten, two, and six o'clock positions in the center of each soup plate. Top each serving with an egg-shaped spoonful of chive whipped cream (see *Chef's Truc* below) and 1 teaspoon of caviar. Serve immediately.

∂ Chef's Trucs ∂

SNIPPING HERBS: One of the most useful kitchen tools is a pair of sharp scissors—especially for snipping chives into thin rings. If you chop instead, the chives will bruise and darken. Scissors are also good for snipping off the sharp, tough ends of artichoke leaves and for clipping fresh herb sprigs.

• • •

MAKING WHIPPED CREAM "EGGS": To form whipped cream into egg shapes, use 2 large tablespoons. Dip one spoon into hot water, then scoop up a mound of cream. Dip the second spoon into the hot water and use it to smooth the top of the whipped cream "egg." Carefully float the cream on top of the soup.

Les Fruits de Mer

FISH COURSE

Homard Rôti aux Légumes Caramélisés

Roast Lobster with Caramelized Vegetables

What a striking presentation: shiny vermilion-red lobster atop diced fava bean and garden vegetables. The fresh fèves or fava beans I use here are just about the most delicious vegetable of all. Before making the sauce, you will first need to make a lobster stock. The balance of the sauce is most important here. Judge for yourself when you've added enough lobster roe butter. You're aiming for a sweet sauce that is not overly buttery nor too strong from the concentrated flavor of the roe.

.... SERVICE FOR 4 ....

THE LOBSTERS

4 gallons water

¼ cup salt

¼ cup white vinegar

Four 1½ pound whole live lobsters,
*   preferably female (see*
*   Chef's Truc page 25)*

THE VEGETABLES

2 tablespoons unsalted butter

1 cup diced turnips

1 cup diced carrots

1 tablespoon sherry vinegar

1 cup thinly sliced scallions
*   (white part only)*

1 cup fava beans, blanched, shelled,
*   and peeled (see Chef's Truc page 60)*

Salt and white pepper

THE SAUCE

½ pound (2 sticks) unsalted butter

1 quart (4 cups) Fond de Homard
*   (see page 213)*

Salt and white pepper

2 tablespoons olive oil

Blanching the Lobsters

In a large stockpot, combine the water, salt, and vinegar and bring to a boil. Plunge the lobsters into the water and cook for 4 minutes. Using a pair of tongs, remove the lobsters from the water and place on a large tray to cool. Discard the cooking water.

When cool enough to handle, twist off the tail where it meets the body of the lobsters. Remove and set aside the dark green roe sacs at the center of the tails. Split the tail lengthwise then remove and discard the intestine that runs down the center. Loosen—but don't remove—the tail meat from its shell. Twist off the claws where they meet the body of the lobster. Using a mallet or hammer, crack the claw shells, without breaking them up too much. Remove the claw meat from their shells, trying to leave them as intact as possible. Repeat with the remaining lobsters.

Caramelizing the Vegetables

In a large heavy sauté pan, heat the butter until sizzling. Add the turnips and carrots. Cook until well browned and evenly caramelized. Add the vinegar and scrape the pan. Cook until the vegetables are coated with the pan juices, then add the scallions and the fava beans. Cook 2 to 3 minutes until warmed through, season to taste, and remove from the heat.

Finishing the Sauce

In a food processor, combine the butter and the reserved lobster roe, processing until smooth. Remove from processor and set aside. In a saucepan over medium heat, reduce the Fond de Homard to 1 cup, then whisk in the butter-roe mixture. (For best results, use a hand-held blender to incorporate the butter. You'll get a lighter, smoother sauce.) Season the sauce with salt and pepper to taste and keep warm.

Assembling the Dish

Preheat the oven and a roasting pan to 400°F. Rub the lobster tails and claws with the olive oil, then lay them shell-side down in the pan. Roast 5 to 6 minutes or until the tails curl and the meat turns opaque. Reheat the caramelized vegetables and the claw meat in a pan on top of the stove. Divide the vegetables among 4 large, heated dinner plates. Arrange 2 lobster tail halves and 1 each of the 2 different types of

claws on each plate. (Each lobster has one large, rounded crusher claw and a smaller, sharp pincher claw.) Drizzle the sauce over the top and serve immediately.

❧ *Chef's Truc* ❧

COOKING FRESH FAVA BEANS: Shell fava pods just as you would peas. Bring a small pot of water to a boil. Blanch the shelled fava beans for 2 minutes, then refresh in cold water. Using your fingertips, pull off the thick outer skin, exposing the beautiful green beans inside. If your fava beans are young and bright green, they will only need reheating. The shelled fava beans in their skins are also available frozen where Mediterranean foods are sold.

With this dish I would serve a great white **Burgundy** from the **Côte de Beaune** like **Robert Ampeau's Meursault Perrières 1986** or a **Puligny Montrachet** from **Domaine Sauzet**.

COQUILLES D'AUTOMNE

SEA SCALLOPS FOR AUTUMN

I created this dish as an ensemble of three favorite ingredients: potatoes, wild mushrooms, and scallops. I use only firm, dry diver scallops. These scallops are hand-harvested eight or ten at a time by deep-sea divers, ensuring that each is whole with an unbroken shell. Most common scallops are fished by dredging the ocean floor, which often breaks and tears them apart. This simple dish is light and flavorful, using just a few ingredients. It makes an ideal starter because it's not too filling.

.... SERVICE FOR 4 ....

Preparing the Scallops

In a large nonstick pan, sauté the potato in 2 tablespoons butter until browned. Pour in 1 tablespoon of the red wine vinegar and scrape the pan. Season to taste with salt and white pepper, stir in the chives and set aside.

Sauté the mushrooms in the remaining 2 tablespoons butter, then season and set aside.

Wipe out the sauté pan, then heat 1 tablespoon olive oil until almost smoking. Sprinkle the scallops with salt and white pepper. Sauté half the scallops in the oil until browned, remove from the pan and set aside. Sauté the remaining half in 1 tablespoon olive oil. Pour in the remaining 1 tablespoon vinegar. Pour over the scallops and set aside.

Assembling the Dish

Have ready 4 large ring molds (see *Chef's Truc*, page 36), set on 4 serving plates. Place one-quarter of the scallops on the bottom of each ring, cover with one-quarter of the mushroom mix, then top with one-quarter of the potatoes. Press down gently and evenly to set, then remove the rings. Sprinkle with the chervil sprigs. Serve immediately.

THE SCALLOPS

1 large Idaho potato,
     peeled and cut into ⅛-inch dice

4 tablespoons unsalted butter

2 tablespoons red wine vinegar

Salt and white pepper

1 tablespoon thinly snipped chives

½ pound shiitake mushrooms, stems
     removed, cut into ⅛-inch dice

½ pound chanterelles, cleaned, trimmed,
     cut into ⅛-inch dice

2 tablespoons olive oil

1 pound large diver sea scallops,
     muscle removed, cut into ⅛-inch dice

THE GARNISH

1 tablespoon tiny, whole chervil sprigs

With this dish, serve a white **Burgundy** from the **Côte Chalonnaise** like **Aubert de Villaine's** marvelous **Rully "Les St. Georges"** 1994, or a **Montagny Les Coeres** from **Jean Vachet.**

HUÎTRES CHAUDES EN FEUILLES VERTES

POACHED OYSTERS WRAPPED IN GREEN LEAVES

Here the earthy-sweet flavor of celery root is a special complement to the iodine-tinged oysters. Cold water oysters from northern waters are firmer and have a stronger iodine flavor. In France, we especially appreciate this pronounced flavor in oysters like our Belons and the green-tinted oysters of the Marennes. In the United States, I prefer Malpeques from the cold waters of the St. Lawrence seaway in Quebec. I do dislike milky, soft overly-large oysters. An oyster should have all the briny freshness of the sea. Use small, firm, freshly shucked oysters here for this palate-teasing appetizer.

.... SERVICE FOR 3 ....

THE OYSTERS

12 freshly shucked cold-water oysters,
* juices and shells reserved*
¼ cup dry white wine
2 shallots, peeled and finely chopped

THE VEGETABLES

1 celery root, tough outer skin removed
1 carrot, peeled
1 tablespoon unsalted butter

THE SAUCE

1 teaspoon Madras curry powder
¼ cup heavy cream
4 tablespoons unsalted butter, cut into bits
Salt and white pepper

12 large outer leaves from
* 2 heads Boston lettuce*
Salt and white pepper

For this dish, my choice would be a stony and unadorned **Chablis**, such as one from **François Raveneau** and **René Dauvissat**.

Poaching the Oysters

Combine ¼ cup of the oyster juice with wine and shallots. Bring liquid to a simmer and poach oysters, cooking them just until their edges curl. Set aside the poaching liquid for the sauce. Set aside the bottom oyster shells for presentation.

Preparing the Vegetables

If the celery root is large cut it in half. Julienne the celery root and carrot using a mandoline or a Benriner cutter. Cook the vegetables in the butter until al dente.

Making the Sauce

Add the curry powder to the poaching liquid and reduce the liquid by half. Stir in the heavy cream and reduce by half again. Whisk in the butter, season with salt and pepper, strain and keep warm.

Finishing the Dish

Bring a medium pot of salted water to a boil. Add the lettuce leaves and blanch for 10 seconds, or just until they wilt. Refresh under ice water. Arrange each leaf rib-side down and spread open. Place a small amount of the vegetables in the center of each leaf, seasoning to taste with salt and pepper. Set a poached oyster on the vegetables and wrap the lettuce leaf around the filling. Place the packets in the reserved shells. Place the filled oyster shells in a sauté pan with ½-inch of water in the pan. Cover and reheat for 2 minutes. Serve with heated sauce.

❧ *Chef's Truc* ❧

SHUCKING OYSTERS: You will need a special oyster knife and most importantly, a heavy glove to protect your hand. Scrub the oysters well in cold water. Holding each oyster, bowl shape down, in your gloved hand, insert the knife into the place where the two points meet and twist until you pop the oyster open. (It may take a few tries until you get the feel of it.) Never rinse the oyster because its natural juice contains the essence of the oyster flavor.

ESCALOPES DE SAUMON AU BEURRE DE CIBOULETTE

SCALLOPS OF SALMON IN CHIVE BUTTER SAUCE

*O*ne of my trademarks is to use mussel juice in my fish sauces. To me it adds a sweet but pronounced taste of the sea. Here I cut the salmon on the bias into "scallops" for a beautiful and quick way to prepare and cook this fish. I use the freshest farm-raised Atlantic salmon from Maine. Because salmon is an oily fish, it deteriorates quickly. Only buy the freshest fish. If you make this sauce ahead of time, whisk in the chive butter just before serving or the sauce will lose its bright green color. (This recipe will yield extra butter sauce that you can freeze for later.) At Le Bec-Fin, we serve this dish accompanied by Basmati Rice Pilaf with Truffles (page 131).

.... SERVICE FOR 4 ....

THE BEURRE DE CIBOULETTE SAUCE

½ pound (2 sticks) unsalted butter

1 cup snipped fresh chives

¾ cup Jus de Moules (see page 213)

½ cup Fumet de Poisson (see page 213)

1 shallot, peeled and chopped

1 mushroom, cleaned and sliced

1 tablespoon dry white vermouth

2 tablespoons dry white wine

½ cup heavy cream

Salt and white pepper

THE SALMON

1½ pounds boneless and skinless
    salmon fillet

Salt and white pepper

1 tablespoon olive oil (to coat the salmon)

With this dish I would serve a **Sauvignon Blanc** from the **Loire Valley** like the **Sancerre** of **Dominique Roger** or a **Quincy** of **Domaine Mardon**. My favorite is **Roger's** Sancerre "La Jouline."

Making the Beurre de Ciboulette Sauce

Puree butter and chives in food processor until bright green in color. Set aside. In a medium, heavy-bottomed pot, place the Jus de Moules, Fumet de Poisson, shallot, mushroom, vermouth, and wine. Bring to a boil and cook on medium-high heat until reduced by half. Add the heavy cream and reduce again until the sauce lightly coats a spoon. Just before serving, whisk in the chive butter. Season with salt and pepper and strain through a fine mesh sieve.

Cooking the Salmon

Using a sharp boning knife, cut the salmon on the bias into eight ½-inch-thick scallops. Lightly oil the salmon scallops and season on both sides with salt and pepper. Heat a large nonstick sauté pan without adding any oil to the pan. Sauté the salmon scallops for 1 minute on each side, then drain on paper towels. Serve immediately with Beurre de Ciboulette sauce ladled over top.

FILET DE ST. PIERRE AUX COEURS D'ARTICHAUTS

FILLET OF JOHN DORY WITH ARTICHOKES

John Dory is a large, firm-fleshed gelatinous fish that, unfortunately, doesn't have much meat for its size. The same species of fish comes into this country from two different parts of the world: Portugal and New Zealand. If you do buy the fish whole, use the "frame" or skeleton to make an extraordinarily rich Fumet de Poisson (see page 213). The flesh of this odd-looking fish is rich and unctuous and has a particular affinity for artichokes. Florida pompano would be the closest substitute for John Dory.

.... SERVICE FOR 6 ....

Preparing the Artichokes

Have ready a bowl of cold water with the lemon juice added. Using a stainless steel knife, slice off the stems of the artichokes. Slice off the top 1½ inches of the artichokes. (You can also use a pair of scissors to snip off the leaf ends.) Turn the artichokes upside down. Working in a spiral direction, grasp one leaf at a time, bending it back until it breaks it off at the point where it meets the artichoke bottom. Be sure to remove all the leaves. Using a sharp paring knife, pare away all the dark green outer skin from the artichoke bottom. (You should have only tender, light green flesh left.) As you finish trimming each artichoke, place it in the lemon water. Using a melon baller or a heavy stainless steel teaspoon, scrape out and discard the inner "choke" (the hairy portion in the center of each artichoke, which is inedible). Slice each artichoke into ⅛-inch thick slices and set aside in lemon water until ready to cook.

Making the Sauce

Place shallots, mushrooms, Fumet de Poisson, Jus de Moules, and lemon juice in a saucepan and bring to a boil. Reduce the sauce by three quarters. Whisk in the butter and the sesame oil, then season to taste. Strain sauce through a fine sieve and keep warm. Just before serving, beat the sauce with a hand-held blender to lighten.

Preparing the John Dory

Sprinkle the fish with salt and pepper. In a large non-stick sauté pan, heat 1 tablespoon each of butter and oil until sizzling. Add the fish and brown 1 minute on each side. Remove fish from pan and keep warm. Add the remaining 1 tablespoon each of butter and oil and heat again until sizzling. Add the reserved artichoke slices to the pan and brown well, shaking pan to cook evenly for about 5 minutes.

Divide the artichokes into 6 portions and place in the center of each of 6 large dinner plates. Place a John Dory fillet on each plate over the artichokes. Pour the sauce around fish and sprinkle with coriander leaves and serve.

THE ARTICHOKES

Juice of 1 lemon

6 large fresh artichokes

THE SAUCE BEURRE LEGER

3 shallots, peeled and finely chopped

2 mushrooms, cleaned and finely chopped

½ cup Fumet de Poisson (see page 213)

1 cup Jus de Moules (see page 213)

Juice of 1 lemon

1 pound (4 sticks) unsalted butter,
*   cut into bits*

2 tablespoons Japanese sesame oil

Salt and white pepper

THE JOHN DORY

Six 6-ounce John Dory fillets

Salt and white pepper

2 tablespoons olive oil

2 tablespoons unsalted butter

1 tablespoon chopped fresh young
*   coriander leaves*

With this dish **Muscat d'Alsace** would be nice, or an aromatic white wine from the middle **Loire**, like a dry **Chéverny** or a **Vouvray**.

Pavé de Loup au Caviar, Petite Nage à l'Orange

Black Sea Bass with Caviar, in Orange-Scented Broth

avé comes from a word that means paving block in French. For this dish, I trim the fish into a rectangular shape. A Nage is a well-flavored broth used for seafood. Like all good chefs, I run an efficient kitchen, but I never stint on ingredients. Beluga caviar is certainly a luxury ingredient. Here its tangy, salt flavor and extraordinary mouthfeel (texture) serve as a perfect counterpoint to the light, fresh fish in broth.

.... SERVICE FOR 4 ....

THE NAGE

1 leek (white part only),
*   cut into ½-inch rings*

1½ ribs celery, coarsely chopped

½ onion, coarsely chopped

1 red bell pepper, coarsely chopped

1 carrot, peeled and coarsely chopped

1 orange, scrubbed

¼ bunch fresh Italian parsley

¼ bunch fresh thyme

½ clove garlic

2 tablespoons cognac

¼ cup dry white wine

1 quart (4 cups) water

THE SEA BASS AND THE SAUCE

Two 2-pound sea bass, scaled, filleted,
*   skin and pin bones removed*

Salt and white pepper

2 tablespoons olive oil

4 tablespoons unsalted butter

1 tablespoon finely snipped fresh chives

1 tablespoon each finely diced carrots,
*   zucchini, and celery (blanched*
*   and then refreshed in ice water)*

2 ounces best-quality caviar,
*   preferably beluga*

Preparing the Nage

Place the leeks in a bowl of cold water and swish around to release any sand. Remove the leeks, leaving behind any sand. Combine the leeks, celery, onion, pepper, carrot, orange, herbs, cognac, and wine in a stockpot and cover with 1 quart of water. Bring to a boil and simmer for 30 minutes. Puree in a blender then place back in the pot and simmer for 15 minutes longer. Strain through a fine sieve, reserving the liquid only.

Preparing the Sea Bass

Trim the sea bass fillets into rectangular shapes, discarding the scraps. Season the fillets with salt and pepper. In a large sauté pan, heat the olive oil and 2 tablespoons of butter until sizzling hot. Sauté the fish fillets on both sides until barely cooked through. Drain on paper towels and keep warm.

Making the Sauce and Assembling the Dish

Reduce the reserved Nage to ½ cup of liquid. Whisk in 2 tablespoons butter, then strain the sauce. Using a hand-held blender, beat the sauce until emulsified (creamy looking). Stir in the chives and the blanched, diced vegetables. Place 1 sea bass fillet on each of 4 large dinner plates, flesh-side up. Spread ½ ounce of caviar on top of each fillet. Ladle the sauce around each fillet and serve.

❧ *Chef's Truc* ❧

BUYING BELUGA CAVIAR: I use the best beluga caviar for this dish because it's so rich and extraordinarily appealing. Buy caviar from a reputable purveyor that knows the product. Keep the caviar well sealed and icy cold. If unopened, it will keep a month, though I surely can't keep it around that long.

With this dish serve a delicate **Chardonnay** from the **Côte de Beaune** such as "Les Caillerets" from **Guy Amiot**, or a **Blanc de Blanc Champagne** such as that of **Diebolt-Vallois**.

Filet de Lotte Farcie aux Épices Chinoises

Stuffed Fillet of Monkfish with Chinese Spices

Monkfish has only become accepted in finer restaurants in the United States in the past ten years. It has been long appreciated in France where it is known as lotte. The firm, white flesh of monkfish makes it a perfect candidate for stuffing, as in this recipe. Try to find a large fish for this recipe because it will hold its shape better when stuffed. Have your fishmonger trim and clean the membrane off the monkfish.

.... SERVICE FOR 4 ....

THE STUFFING

8 *freshly shucked littleneck clams,*
   juices reserved
2 *tablespoons olive oil*
½ *pound large sea scallops*
¼ *cup finely diced white mushrooms*
¼ *cup chopped fresh Italian parsley*
Salt and white pepper

THE MONKFISH

One 1½-*pound piece (center-cut) monkfish,*
   trimmed and cleaned
Salt and white pepper
1 *tablespoon Chinese five-spice powder*
½ *cup cornstarch*
¼ *cup olive oil*

THE SAFFRON TOMATO SAUCE

2 *shallots, peeled and chopped*
2 *mushrooms, cleaned and chopped*
1 *cup Fumet de Poisson (see page 213)*
½ *cup dry white wine*
2 *tablespoons dry white vermouth*
Generous pinch of saffron threads
½ *pound (2 sticks) unsalted butter*
½ *cup Tomates Concassées (see page 217)*
1 *tablespoon finely snipped fresh chives*

Preparing the Stuffing

In a small pan, poach the clams in their own juices, cooking until just firm, 2 to 3 minutes. Remove from the pan and let the clams cool in their cooking juices. Remove the hard adductor muscle from the side of each scallop, reserving these trimmings for the sauce. Dice the scallops. Heat 1 tablespoon olive oil in a sauté pan and brown the scallops over high heat. Remove from the pan and set aside. Add the remaining tablespoon olive oil to the pan and brown the diced mushrooms over high heat. Dice the clams and mix with the scallops, mushrooms, and parsley. Season with salt and pepper. Chill the stuffing while preparing the monkfish.

Preparing the Monkfish

Using a sharpening steel and paralleling the length of the fish, poke a hole through the center of the monkfish. Using your fingers, open up the hole slightly and stuff the monkfish. Chill until ready to cook. Combine the salt, pepper, Chinese five-spice powder, and cornstarch and set aside.

Preparing the Sauce and Finishing the Dish

Preheat the oven to 350°F. Dust the fish with the cornstarch-spice mix, shaking off any excess. In an ovenproof casserole, heat the ¼ cup olive oil on top of the stove until it just begins to smoke, then brown the fish on all sides. Pour off any excess fat, then add the shallots, mushrooms, Fumet, wine, vermouth, and saffron to the pan. Place in the oven to braise for 15 minutes, basting every few minutes with the liquid in the pan.

   Remove the fish from the pan and keep warm. Whisk the butter into the pan juices, then strain through a sieve into a small pot. Add the tomato and chives and gently rewarm. Using an electric or very sharp knife, slice the stuffed monkfish into 3 rounds per portion. Serve the monkfish on heated dinner plates with Saffron-Tomato Sauce drizzled over top and sprinkled with chives.

With this dish I would serve an aromatic, barely-sweet **Gewurtztraminer** from California's Anderson Valley like **Navarro's 1995**, or from **Alsace** like **Blank's 1994**.

Gratin de Macaroni et Homard

Baked Penne Pasta with Lobster

A gratin is cooked and served in its own special dish so it will make plenty of a crusty surface, both top and bottom. This lobster gratin is the best thing I can think of to eat after a Sunday afternoon football game! Make it ahead and put it in a hot oven near the end of the game. If the dish has been made ahead and chilled, reduce the oven temperature to 375°F and bake for an extra fifteen minutes or until it's bubbling hot through and through.

.... SERVICE FOR 4 ....

Preparing the Gratin

Grip the lobster on the back of its thorax, or main body shell. Look for the place where two sections of shell meet. Plunge the point of a sharp chef's knife between the shell sections. (This kills the lobster instantly.) Split the lobsters lengthwise from head to tail. Separate the two halves. Remove the "sand sac" or small bag, from each side of the head and discard. Remove any dark green roe sacs and set aside.

Cut off both claws and break the claw shells by hitting with a meat pounder. Heat a large sauté pan with 2 tablespoons olive oil, until just beginning to smoke. Sear the lobster body pieces at high heat until they turn bright red. Add vegetables and bouquet garni. Cook together for 3 minutes. Add cognac and port to pan and heat slightly. Keeping your face away from the flame, *flambé* (ignite with a long match). When the flames subside, add heavy cream and cook for 3 more minutes. Remove lobster pieces and cool.

Remove meat from the shells. Cut the lobster meat into large chunks and set aside. Return the shells to the liquid and simmer for about 30 minutes, or until the sauce is somewhat thickened. Strain through a sieve and thicken with beurre manié, using only as much as necessary. Season the sauce with salt and pepper to taste and set aside. The sauce should be *fluide*, light enough to be readily absorbed by the half-cooked penne.

Finishing the Gratin

Preheat the oven to 425°F. Bring a large pot of lightly salted water to a boil, then add the penne. Bring back to a boil and cook 3 to 4 minutes or until the pasta is half-cooked. Drain the pasta and toss immediately with the sauce and cut-up lobster meat. Spoon into a shallow gratin dish and sprinkle with the bread crumbs. Place the gratin dish in a second pan and fill halfway with hot water to make a bain-marie or water bath. Bake at 425°F for 15 minutes or until browned. Serve directly from the gratin dish.

THE GRATIN

Two 1½-pound lobsters, preferably female (see Chef's Truc page 25)

2 tablespoons olive oil

2 carrots, peeled and chopped

3 ribs celery, sliced

1 onion, peeled and chopped

Bouquet garni (1 sprig each thyme and tarragon, 2 bay leaves)

¼ cup port

2 tablespoons cognac

1 quart (4 cups) heavy cream

1 tablespoon Beurre Manié (see page 216)

½ pound penne (preferably imported Italian)

¼ cup fresh, soft bread crumbs

This dish needs a rich white wine like the **Pinot Blanc Auxerrois of Barmès Buecher 1995** or a **Riesling** from **Mendocino** like the wine of **Greenwood Ridge**. The delicious **Pinot Grigio 1995** from **Chaddsford Winery** in **Southeastern Pennsylvania**, one of the loveliest wines ever made there, works well too.

ROUGET ZINFANDEL À LA MOELLE

EUROPEAN RED MULLET IN RED ZINFANDEL WITH VEAL MARROW

I love the robust flavor and deep color of red Zinfandel wine. Here I pair a rich red wine sauce with the incomparable Rouget Barbet, a crimson-colored Mediterranean fish. Rouget was prized by both the Greeks and the Romans who were so obsessed with it, that they drove its price to absurd heights. Ours come to us from Portugal and France. If you can't get imported Rouget, use American red snapper.

SERVICE FOR 4

THE MARROW

Two 2-inch-long veal marrow bones

1 tablespoon finely snipped fresh chives

*1 tablespoon finely chopped fresh
    Italian parsley*

THE ZINFANDEL SAUCE

¼ cup Demi-Glace (see page 212)

1 bottle (25 ounces) red Zinfandel

6 whole black peppercorns, slightly crushed

2 shallots, peeled and coarsely chopped

1 sprig fresh thyme

*1 pound (4 sticks) unsalted butter,
    slightly softened and cut into bits*

Salt

THE ROUGET

*Eight 3-ounce fillets European red mullet
    (or four 6-ounce fillets American red
    snapper), skin-on, pin bones removed*

Salt and white pepper

2 tablespoons unsalted butter

2 tablespoons olive oil

Soaking the Marrow

Soak the bones in tepid water for about 2 hours. Push the softened marrow out from inside the bone and discard the bones. Soak the marrow overnight in a bowl of ice water in the refrigerator. (This will extract any blood, resulting in pure white marrow.) Cut the soaked marrow into ½-inch thick slices and set aside.

Making the Zinfandel Sauce

In a small nonstick saucepan, reduce the Demi-Glace to 2 tablespoons liquid, cooking carefully so the thickened sauce doesn't stick and burn. Using a rubber spatula, transfer the reduced Demi-Glace (now a Glace de Viande) into a small saucepot. Add the wine, peppercorns, shallots, and thyme and bring to a boil. Reduce until thick and syrupy, stirring occasionally. When the sauce is nearly fully reduced, stir constantly so it won't stick and burn. Remove from the heat and whisk in the butter, using a hand-held blender if possible. Strain the sauce through a fine sieve, then season to taste with salt. Set the sauce aside, keeping it warm.

Preparing the Rouget and Poaching the Marrow

Season the fish fillets with salt and pepper. Heat the butter and olive oil in a large nonstick sauté pan until sizzling hot. Place the fish skin-side down and cook over medium-high heat for 2 minutes, then turn the fish over and finish cooking for 2 minutes longer. Drain the fish on paper towels before serving.

Bring a small pan of water to a boil. Poach the marrow slices 1 to 2 minutes, then drain. Season with salt, chives, and parsley and set aside.

Serving the Rouget

Place the fish fillets in the centers of the 4 heated dinner plates. Ladle the Zinfandel Sauce around the fish and top with a slice of reserved marrow.

With this dish serve a **Sancerre Rouge** like **Dominique Roger's 1995** or a **California Zinfandel** in the medium-bodied **Bordelaise** style, like those of **Steve Storrs's**.

Loup sur sa Peau Croustillante à l'Orientale

Black Sea Bass Cooked on its Crispy Skin, Asian Style

The ginger and soy marinade and the method of cooking the crispy skin are both Chinese. I like to fillet my own fish to insure its absolute freshness, but you may also purchase the fish filleted for ease of preparation. I buy black sea bass in season from day-boats that fish off the Jersey coast. Because the fish have been caught the same day I get them, they lose none of their sparkling clarity. We make our own Moroccan-style salt-cured lemons at Le Bec-Fin (see Chef's Truc page 73), but you can also buy this ready-made.

.... SERVICE FOR 4 ....

THE BLACK BASS

2 black sea bass (about 2 pounds each),
    filleted and pin bones removed, skin on

1 cup dry white wine

1 cup soy sauce

1 cup water

1 tablespoon grated gingerroot

Salt and white pepper

½ cup cornstarch (for dusting)

2 tablespoons unsalted butter

2 tablespoons olive oil

THE SAUCE

¼ pound (1 stick) unsalted butter

¾ cup soy sauce

¼ cup balsamic vinegar

Juice of 1 lime

¼ teaspoon Tabasco

Marinating the Sea Bass

Inspect the fish fillets for any remaining scales or small pin bones. In a 2-quart bowl, combine the wine, soy, water, and gingerroot. Place the fillets in marinade and refrigerate for 4 hours.

Making the Sauce

Place the butter into a heavy-bottomed saucepan and cook over low heat until medium brown in color and nutty smelling. (Be careful not to burn the butter—when it starts to brown, it browns quickly.) Pour off and set aside the clear butterfat, and discard the milk solids remaining in the pot.

In another pan, combine the soy, vinegar, lime juice, and Tabasco. Warm over low heat. When hot, using a hand-held blender, slowly add ⅓ cup of the browned butter. (Or place soy/vinegar mixture in a blender and slowly pour in the butter.) Return to the pan and keep warm.

Preparing the Asian Vegetables

Using a channel knife, cut lengthwise grooves around the outside of the carrots (this step is optional). Cut the carrots crosswise into thin discs. They should resemble flowers.

Cut the scallions on the diagonal into 1-inch lengths. In a small sauté pan, combine the water, butter, and sesame oil. Bring to a boil over high heat and add the carrots, turnips, snow peas, and scallions. Cook over high heat until the liquid evaporates, and the vegetables are glossy and crispy, about 2 minutes. Set aside.

Cooking the Fish

Remove the fish from the marinade and pat dry with paper towels. Season with salt and pepper and dust the skin side with cornstarch.

In a large non-stick sauté pan, heat the oil and butter until sizzling hot. Place the fish fillets, skin-side down into the pan. Sauté over high heat. Turn fish over after about 2 minutes and cook about 2 minutes longer. The fish should be crispy and brown, but still juicy.

Finishing the Dish

Have ready 4 large, heated dinner plates. Place one-quarter of the vegetables in the center. Top with one portion of fish, skin-side up, then ladle the sauce around the fish. Garnish with the Moroccan preserved lemon rind and chopped parsley.

❧ *Chef's Truc* ❧

MAKING MOROCCAN PRESERVED LEMON: Under hot water, scrub 6 to 8 whole lemons using a brush. Cut them lengthwise into quarters. Place in a large bowl and toss with a liberal amount of kosher salt (or coarse salt). Spread the lemon quarters out on a baker's wire cooling rack set over a pan to catch the drips. Refrigerate for 3 days, turning once or twice. Sterilize several glass jars by boiling in water. Ladle the lemons into the jars. Divide the salty drippings from the pan among the jars, then add enough boiling hot water to cover the lemons. Process the jars to seal and preserve, cooking them in a large pot of boiling water for 20 minutes. Cool and leave the lemons to cure for 1 week before using. Scoop out and discard the lemon pulp, using only the preserved lemon rind.

THE ASIAN VEGETABLES

4 baby turnips (Tokyo turnips),
    peeled and thinly sliced

2 carrots, peeled

1 cup snow peas or sugar snap peas,
    strings removed

1 bunch scallions (white part only)

¼ cup water

1 tablespoon unsalted butter

Several drops of Japanese sesame oil

Salt and white pepper

THE GARNISH

1 teaspoon Moroccan preserved lemon rind,
    diced (homemade or purchased)

1 tablespoon chopped fresh Italian parsley

This dish deserves a good, direct white from the southern **Rhône** like the **Châteauneuf du Pape** of **La Nerthe 1994**, or a **Côteaux du Languedoc** like the **Château des Hospitaliers 1995**.

ARC-EN-CIEL DE COQUILLES ROYALES, VINAIGRETTE DE TRUFFES

"RAINBOW" OF DIVER SCALLOPS AND VEAL SWEETBREAD WITH TRUFFLE VINAIGRETTE

Any dish described with the word royale must be made with luxurious ingredients. Here I serve a rainbow of scallop slices surrounding a nest of diced sweetbreads. The dish is finished with a Truffle Vinaigrette made with four different forms of truffle: concentrated truffle paste, chunky chopped black truffles, flavorful truffle juice, and aromatic truffle oil. This recipe will make two cups of Truffle Vinaigrette, enough to use for other dishes like grilled fish or steamed asparagus. We like to alternate the scallops with paper-thin cucumber rings and a garnish of bright red lobster roe for a sophisticated presentation.

.... SERVICE FOR 4 ....

THE SWEETBREAD

1 veal sweetbread (about ½ pound)

THE TRUFFLE VINAIGRETTE

1 teaspoon Dijon mustard

1 egg yolk

1 teaspoon chopped canned black truffles

1 teaspoon truffle paste

1 tablespoon red wine vinegar

1 tablespoon white truffle oil

½ cup truffle juice (from canned truffles)

2 cups extra-virgin olive oil

Salt and white pepper

THE SCALLOPS

1 large Yukon gold potato, peeled and diced

1 cup olive oil

2 large white mushroom caps,
      cleaned and ⅛-inch diced

1 tablespoon sherry vinegar

8 jumbo diver sea scallops, muscle removed

½ cup arrowroot (for coating the scallops)

Preparing the Sweetbread

Soak the sweetbread overnight in a bowl of cold water to remove the blood. Bring a small pot of water to a boil. Add the drained, soaked sweetbread, bring back to a boil and simmer 20 minutes. Remove the sweetbread and refresh under ice water. Peel off and discard the outer membrane. Wrap in a towel and place between two pans (such as the bottoms of springform cake pans). Cover with a heavy weight (such as a tomato can) to flatten it and refrigerate like this overnight. The next day, remove the weight and pans and cut the sweetbread into ⅛-inch dice. Set aside.

Making the Truffle Vinaigrette

Place the mustard, egg yolk, black truffle, and truffle paste in a bowl. Whisk in the vinegar. Slowly pour in the truffle oil, whisking vigorously. Continuing to whisk, add one-fourth of the truffle juice and one-fourth of the olive oil, alternating until both are completely incorporated. Season with salt and pepper to taste and warm over low heat in a small pot. Set aside.

Cooking the Sweetbread and Scallops

Place the diced potato in a small pot, cover with ¾ cup olive oil and gently cook for 45 minutes. Strain the potatoes and keep them warm.

In a small sauté pan, heat 2 tablespoons of the olive oil and brown the diced sweetbread until golden. Remove the sweetbread from the pan and set aside. Sauté the diced mushroom in the same pan. Deglaze the pan with the sherry vinegar and pour over the sweetbreads. Combine the sweetbreads, mushrooms, and potatoes and season to taste with salt and pepper.

Dust the scallops with the arrowroot, shaking off any excess. In another large, nonstick sauté pan, heat the remaining olive oil and sauté the scallops at high heat until well browned on both sides.

With this dish I would serve a ripe white with low acidity like a good **Graves** or a **Pancherenc de Vic Bilh sec**.

Serving the Dish

Place a spoonful of the sweetbread mixture in the center of each of 4 large, heated dinner plates. Using an electric or very sharp knife, slice each scallop horizontally into 4 rounds. Surround the sweetbread mixture with 8 slices of scallop per plate in a fan shape. Drizzle the warm Truffle Vinaigrette over the scallops and serve.

❧ *Chef's Truc* ❧

SAUCE PÉRIGUEUX: In my restaurant, we add a tablespoonful of Sauce Périgueux (a Demi-Glace-based Madeira Sauce enriched with truffles) to the vinaigrette to enrich the sauce and give it extra body.

HOMARD À LA DAVID LETTERMAN

LOBSTER WITH ARTICHOKES, FAVA BEANS, AND CHANTERELLES

David Letterman inspired this luxurious dish of shelled lobster meat with a garnish of vegetable delicacies; I created this dish for my first appearance on his show. The zest of lime scattered over the top just before serving lights up the dish with a pungent, lively perfume. Sometimes one ingredient is what makes the dish. Here the lime zest truly sets it apart. I like to decorate this creation with dots of brilliant red lobster roe.

.... SERVICE FOR 4 ....

Cooking the Lobsters

Bring a large pot of water to a boil. Cook lobsters in boiling water for 2 minutes. Using a pair of tongs, remove the lobsters and place on a tray to cool. When cool enough to handle, remove the claw and tail meat from shell. Cut each tail into 6 slices and set aside both the claw meat and the tail meat for the sauce.

Cooking the Chanterelles

In a small pot with a lid, melt 2 tablespoons of the butter and cover. Cook the chanterelles over medium heat for 5 to 6 minutes, or until they release their juices. (Take care not to boil away the liquid released by the mushrooms; it is the base of the sauce.) Remove the lid and stir in the remaining butter. Season to taste with salt and pepper and set aside in a warm place.

Preparing the Artichokes

Using a mandoline or Benriner cutter, julienne the artichoke bottoms. Toss the julienned artichoke with the curry powder and salt and white pepper to taste. Sauté the artichokes in the butter over medium-high heat for 2 to 3 minutes or until lightly browned, stirring frequently. Set aside, keeping warm.

Finishing the Dish

Sauté the lobster meat in 1 tablespoon each of butter and olive oil in a large sauté pan until thoroughly heated. Add the fava beans and Tomates Concassées, then *flambé* (ignite with a long match) with the cognac. Add the reserved chanterelles and their juices and whisk in the remaining butter. Season with salt and pepper to taste.

To serve, place the julienned artichoke in the center of each of 4 large dinner plates, surround with lobster pieces. Spoon the mushroom mixture over top. Sprinkle each plate with grated lime zest and chopped parsley. Serve immediately.

For this dish I suggest a **Tokay d'Alsace (Pinot Gris)** or a fine **California Chardonnay** from a low-yield site like **Babcock's Mt. Carmel Vineyard**.

THE LOBSTERS

Four 1½-pound lobsters

THE CHANTRELLES

1 pound chanterelles, cleaned
    and quartered (if large)
4 tablespoons unsalted butter
Salt and white pepper

THE ARTICHOKES

2 artichoke bottoms (see page 65)
1 teaspoon curry powder
Salt and white pepper
2 tablespoons unsalted butter

THE LOBSTER AND GARNISHES

1 tablespoon olive oil
6 tablespoons unsalted butter
1 cup shelled fava beans
    (see Chef's Truc page 60)
1 cup Tomates Concassées
2 tablespoons cognac
Salt and white pepper
Grated zest of 2 limes
    (see Chef's Truc page 150)
1 tablespoons chopped fresh Italian parsley

COQUILLES ST. JACQUES EN CROÛTE DE POLENTA ET SON BOUILLON DE SAFRAN

SCALLOPS IN POLENTA CRUST WITH SAFFRON BROTH

Here I use polenta, a finely ground cornmeal from Italy, to give these scallops their crispy crust. I love the crunchy scallops, juicy on the inside, bathed in a saffron-tinted broth. I like to serve it topped with a mesclun salad which adds color, texture and a lightness to the overall composition of the dish. Mesclun is the Provençal name for a mixture of baby mixed salad greens, often sold in the United States as "spring mix." Dress the salad simply with raspberry vinegar and hazelnut oil.

.... SERVICE FOR 4 ....

THE SAFFRON BOUILLON

1 leek (white part only), cleaned and chopped

4 white mushrooms, cleaned and chopped

1 ripe tomato, chopped

1 tablespoon peeled and chopped ginger root

2 tablespoons olive oil

Large pinch of saffron threads

½ cup dry white vermouth

*1 quart (4 cups) Fond Blanc de Volaille
   (see page 214)*

1 cup Fumet de Poisson (see page 213)

2 tablespoons fresh lime juice

1 teaspoon chopped fresh thyme leaves

2 tablespoons unsalted butter, cut into bits

Salt and white pepper

THE SCALLOPS

Juice and grated zest of 1 lime

½ cup imported polenta

1 tablespoon chopped fresh thyme leaves

8 large sea scallops, muscle removed

Salt and white pepper

2 egg yolks, lightly beaten

2 tablespoons olive oil

20 nonpareil capers, rinsed and drained

Preparing the Saffron Bouillon

In a medium stockpot, place the leeks, mushrooms, tomato, ginger, oil, and most of the saffron. Cook the vegetables until translucent. Pour in the vermouth, then add the Fond Blanc de Volaille and the Fumet de Poisson. Simmer over low heat for 2 hours, skimming occasionally. Strain through a fine sieve into a small saucepan. When ready to serve, reduce the bouillon by three-quarters. Stir in lime juice, thyme, and remaining saffron. Whisk in the butter, and season with salt and pepper to taste. Set aside.

Cooking the Scallops

In a small bowl, combine the lime juice, lime zest, polenta, and thyme. Add enough water to make a liquidy paste. Pat the scallops dry, season with salt and pepper and dip one side only, first into the egg yolk and then into the polenta paste.

In a large nonstick sauté pan, heat the olive oil until just beginning to smoke. Place the scallops in the pan, polenta-side down and sauté 1 minute. Turn the scallops over and sauté 1 minute longer. Drain on paper towels, and set aside.

Finishing the Dish

Divide the scallops among 4 large, shallow room temperature bowls. Place the scallops in each plate, polenta-side up. Spoon 2 tablespoons of the reserved Saffron Bouillon around each portion and sprinkle with capers. Serve with a mesclun salad if you like.

A dry white wine from the middle **Loire**, like the **Savennieres "Clos de la Coulée de Sérrant**," goes well with this dish.

Savarin de Coquilles et de Homard

Individual Molded Scallop Mousses filled with Lobster

I have long prided myself on the lightness and delicacy of my fish mousses. If you follow my explicit directions, you can achieve the same ethereal results. You will need eight to ten individual Savarin molds. These ring-shaped round molds are named after the famed author of La Physiologie du Goût, Brillat-Savarin. You may also make this recipe in a large single Savarin mold. You will need to steam the larger mold for about forty-five minutes.

················· SERVICE FOR 8 TO 10 ·················

THE SCALLOP MOUSSELINE

2 pounds sea scallops, muscles removed
    and reserved

2 whole eggs

1 egg yolk

2 cups heavy cream, chilled

Salt and white pepper

1 carrot, peeled and cut into ⅛-inch dice,
    blanched and then refreshed in
    ice water)

1 zucchini, cut into ⅛-inch dice,
    blanched then refreshed in ice water

2 tablespoons softened butter (for the molds)

THE SAUCE

2 shallots, peeled and chopped

2 mushrooms, cleaned and chopped

2 tablespoons dry white wine

2 tablespoons dry white vermouth

1½ cups bottled clam juice
    (or Jus de Moules, see page 213)

1 cup Fumet de Poisson
    (see page 213)

1 cup heavy cream

½ pound (2 sticks) butter, cut into bits

Salt and pepper

Preparing the Scallop Mousseline

Place exactly 22 ounces of the scallops in a food processor with the blade and place in the freezer to chill for 30 minutes.

    Remove the bowl from freezer and begin processing the scallops. One at a time, add the whole eggs and the egg yolk. Process until smooth and shiny. Remove the bowl and place back into the freezer. After 30 minutes, or when very cold, remove the bowl and begin processing again. Slowly pour in 2 cups of the heavy cream and salt and pepper to taste. Process only until smooth and shiny.

    Preheat the oven to 350°F. Transfer the mousse to a stainless steel bowl and fold in the drained vegetables. Brush the Savarin molds with the softened butter. Carefully ladle the mousse into the molds. Place the molds in a *bain-marie* (a panful of hot water) and cover lightly with foil, poking several holes in the foil for steam to escape. Bake for 15 minutes, then check every 5 minutes, cooking until the molds are barely firm. They should jiggle but not be liquidy inside.

Making the Sauce

In a medium pot, combine the scallop muscle trimmings, shallots, mushrooms, wine, vermouth, clam juice, and Fumet de Poisson. Bring to a boil, then cook over high heat until reduced by half. Stir in the heavy cream and reduce again until the sauce lightly coats the back of a wooden spoon. Whisk in the ½ pound of butter piece by piece. Season with salt and pepper to taste and strain through a fine sieve. Use a hand-held blender to whip and lighten the sauce. Keep it warm.

Preparing the Garnish

Dice the remaining 10 ounces of scallops. In a sauté pan, heat 2 tablespoons butter over medium heat. Sauté the diced scallops until barely cooked through (opaque). Add the lobster meat and cook 1 minute longer or until thoroughly heated. Remove the scallops and lobster from the pan. Heat the remaining tablespoon of butter, then add the diced tomato and gently heat. Remove from the pan and fold into scallop-lobster mix.

Serving the Savarins

Carefully invert the Savarins onto heated individual serving plates (See *Chef's Truc*

THE GARNISH

Reserved 10 ounces scallops

3 tablespoons butter

One 1½-pound lobster, cooked and diced
  (see page 24)

2 cups Tomates Concassées (see page 217)

Salt and white pepper

2 tablespoons cooked lobster roe
  (or 2 tablespoons finely
  snipped chives)

below). Fill the centers with the scallop-lobster mixture. Ladle sauce around the Savarins. Sprinkle with lobster roe if available (or substitute chives) and serve piping hot.

❧ *Chef's Truc* ❧

MAKING SAVARINS AHEAD: If you make the Savarins ahead you can reheat them perfectly. Place the unmolded Savarins on a ceramic or glass tray and cover with plastic wrap, poking a few holes in the top to allow steam to escape. Heat for 1 minute in the microwave, then check. Heat for 1 minute more, checking again. Heat only until steaming hot. Don't overcook or the Savarins can get rubbery.

For this dish there is a wide variety of finely structured, delicately aromatic white wines from which to choose. I might choose an **Alsace Riesling** from **Léon Beyer** or **Mittnacht-Klack**.

Palourdes dans leur Sauce au Curry

Cockle Clams in Curry Sauce

We get our cockle clams flown in fresh from New Zealand. Tiny, sweet-tasting and clean, cockles are delicious. Our more common American Quahog or hardshell clams make a good substitute, but only if you choose small clams. The larger ones are too tough and strong in flavor for my taste. Curry is one of my favorite seasonings. As in this dish of clams with curry, I use it where the flavor of the meat is strong enough not to be overpowered by the curry.

.... SERVICE FOR 4 ....

Preparing the Clams

Soak the scrubbed clams in a sinkful of cold water for 20 minutes. Remove and keep cold until ready to use. Place an empty 4-quart pot fitted with a lid over medium heat until hot. Place the clams, shallots, wine, vermouth and water in the pot. Cover and steam the clams open over high heat. When almost all the clams have opened, remove them from the heat. Pry open any clams that haven't fully opened. (Note: a clam that won't open at all might be dead, so discard if it doesn't smell sweet.) Strain the cooking juices through a paper coffee filter to remove any sand and set aside.

Preparing the Sauce

Place the strained cooking juices and the curry powder into a small pan. Bring to a boil, then reduce the liquid by half. Stir in the butter and the Thai red curry paste. Season with salt and pepper, and blend the sauce to lighten, using a hand blender.

Finishing the Dish

Twist off and discard the top shell of each clam. Divide the clams on their half shells among each of 4 shallow soup plates. Drizzle the sauce over the clams, sprinkle with the parsley, and serve immediately.

Chef's Truc

THAI CURRY PASTE: Thai curry paste comes in green, red, and yellow versions, all quite potent. We use the red curry paste here, which is not as fiery hot as some of the others. Because it's so concentrated, use only what will fit onto the tip of a knife.

THE CLAMS

40 cockle clams, scrubbed well

2 shallots, peeled and chopped

¼ cup dry white wine

2 tablespoons dry white vermouth

½ cup water

THE SAUCE

¼ teaspoon Madras curry powder

4 tablespoons unsalted butter

A scant ⅛ teaspoon Thai red curry paste
 (see Chef's Truc below)

Salt and white pepper

THE GARNISH

1 tablespoon fresh Italian parsley, chopped

For this dish I would choose a dry white **Gaillac** or **Jurançon** with honey aromatics and good acidity. The **Domaine des Terrisses** makes very good wine.

TRESSE DE SAUMON ET DE SOLE AUX PÂTES VERTES

BRAID OF SALMON AND SOLE WITH SPINACH PASTA

I created this dish for Princess Grace of Monaco on the occasion of her visit to my restaurant. Inspired by her signature braided hairstyle, it became one of my most popular creations. A pretty dish, the pink and white fish braid contrasts with its nest of bright-green fresh spinach pasta. The sauce is a lovely shade of rosy pink, fit for a princess. The tresse is perfect for a party because the fish just needs to be steamed at the last minute before serving.

SERVICE FOR 4

THE TRESSE

1 Dover sole, cut into 4 fillets
   (2 from each side of the fish)
1 pound (center-cut) salmon fillet,
   skinned, pin bones removed
Salt and white pepper

THE BEURRE DE TOMATES

2 shallots, peeled and coarsely chopped
2 mushrooms, cleaned and coarsely chopped
2 large ripe tomatoes, quartered
1½ cups Jus de Moules (see page 213)
1 cup Fumet de Poisson (see page 213)
½ cup dry white wine
2 tablespoons dry white vermouth
1 cup heavy cream
1 pound (4 sticks) unsalted butter,
   cut into bits
Salt and white pepper

THE SPINACH PASTA

½ pound Pâte aux Epinards
   (see page 215), cut into fettuccine
1 tablespoon unsalted butter
Salt and white pepper

Preparing the Tresse

Cut each sole fillet into two lengthwise strips. Cut the salmon into eight equal lengthwise strips of the same size as the sole. Divide into four portions, with two strips of each fish per portion (four strips in all). Arrange the sole and salmon in alternating order. Attach one end of the four strips of fish together using a toothpick. Begin to braid the strips by taking the left-hand strip and crossing it over the two center strips, then take the right-hand strip and cross it over the left-hand strip. Repeat, working from the left and going over two strips, then from the right, going over the one strip. You should have an even braid that lays flat. Toothpick the ends to secure them. Repeat until you have four braids. Chill.

Making the Beurre de Tomates

Place the shallots and mushrooms in a stainless steel or enamel saucepan and add the tomatoes, Jus de Moules, Fumet de Poisson, wine, and vermouth. Bring to a boil, then reduce liquid by half. Add heavy cream and reduce again until the sauce lightly coats the back of a wooden spoon. Slowly whisk in the butter, then season with salt and pepper to taste. Strain through a fine sieve and keep warm.

Finishing the Dish

Bring a large pot of lightly salted water to a boil. Add the pasta, bring back to a boil and cook until al dente. Drain well, then toss with the butter and salt and pepper to taste. Twirl the pasta into nest shapes on each of 4 large dinner plates.

Meanwhile, bring a large, shallow pan of water to a boil. Reduce the heat. Place the fish braids on a lightly oiled wire rack set over the steaming water and cover with foil. Steam 3 to 4 minutes or until firm to the touch but still juicy. Lift the cooked braids off the rack using a spatula. Remove the toothpicks and gently lay the braids over the pasta nests. Ladle a small amount of the Beurre de Tomates around the nests and serve immediately.

This dish deserves an elegant white **Burgundy** such as "La Pièce sous le Bois" from the **Domaine Robert Ampeau**, or a **Cavollion** from **Domaine Leflaive**.

QUENELLES DE BROCHET À L'AMÉRICAINE

FEATHER-LIGHT PIKE DUMPLINGS IN LOBSTER SAUCE

I learned this recipe while working at La Pyramide, the famed restaurant of the legendary chef, Fernand Point. A specialty of Lyon where I grew up, these quenelles were my greatest signature dish of the 1970s. Craig Claiborne and Pierre Franey, then of the New York Times, heard of my quenelles and came to Philadelphia to taste them. Because of that, Claiborne wrote about me and helped to establish my reputation nationally. While quenelles are less in fashion these days, they still make a wonderful dish. To make them, you must use pike, a freshwater fish that's in season in colder months. Though ideal for quenelles because it is so gelatinous, pike is extremely bony. However, the tiny bones disintegrate when cooked and pureed. Technique is everything here. The ingredients are inexpensive; the results sublime.

.... SERVICE FOR 10 ....

THE QUENELLES

2 cups whole milk

Salt and white pepper

1 pound (4 sticks) unsalted butter,
        slightly softened

½ pound bread flour, sifted

10 eggs, at room temperature

1 pound pike fillet, skinned and boned

4 egg whites

5 egg yolks

Pinch of cayenne pepper

2 tablespoons vegetable oil

THE SAUCE

4 cups Sauce Américaine (see page 24–25)

2 cups heavy cream

4 tablespoons unsalted butter, cut into bits

Preparing the Quenelles

In a large heavy-bottomed pot (preferably copper), place the milk, 6 tablespoons of the butter and a pinch of salt and pepper. Slowly heat the milk and butter until it comes to a boil. (The butter should be completely melted just as the milk comes to a boil.) Remove the pot from the heat and immediately pour in all the flour, stirring vigorously with a wooden spoon. (This may be easier for two people: one to hold the pot, one to stir.) When the flour is fully combined, return the pot to the heat. Mix with a wooden spoon for 3 minutes until the mixture becomes a thick paste and pulls away from the sides of the pot.

Place the pot over a flame tamer, reduce the heat to the lowest possible setting and leave this *panade* (paste) to dry for 1 hour. Stir every 3 to 4 minutes during the drying process, or it will scorch on the bottom. Once the *panade* becomes stiff and completely dry, transfer to the bowl of a mixer.

Finishing the Quenelle Mixture

Using a flat paddle, beat the hot *panade* on high speed for 1 minute. Turn the mixer to low speed and add the whole eggs, one at a time, making sure to scrape the sides of the bowl often. When the eggs are completely incorporated, transfer the mixture to another bowl, cover, and refrigerate until cool.

Meanwhile, chill the pike fillets, the meat grinder, the mixer bowl, and the flat beater in the refrigerator for 30 minutes. Then, using the finest grinder plate, grind the fish and place in the cold mixer bowl. Mix on high speed until the fish is firm and shiny. Reduce the speed and scrape the fish off the sides of the bowl. Add the egg whites 1 at a time, and beat until incorporated, scraping the sides of the bowl occasionally.

Increase the speed to high and add the remaining butter. When the butter has been completely incorporated, turn the mixer to medium speed and add the reserved *panade*. Beat in the 5 egg yolks, mixing on high speed for 1 minute. Add salt, pepper, and cayenne to taste. Refrigerate the mixture until thoroughly chilled.

Poaching the Quenelles

Lightly dust a large wooden counter or board with flour. Using 2 spoons, form egg shapes of the chilled quenelle mixture. Then, on the floured surface, gently roll the egg-shaped quenelles into cylinders, larger at the top than the bottom. Chill the formed quenelles for 20 minutes.

Meanwhile, bring a large pot of salted water to a boil. Add the oil and quenelles and poach 20 minutes (the water must not boil, just gently simmer), turning once while poaching. Skim the poached quenelles from the water and gently place them into a large bowl of ice water to stop the cooking. Drain on paper towels and refrigerate until ready to use.

Finishing the Sauce

Reduce the Sauce Américaine by half, add the cream and reduce again by half. Whisk in the butter, season with salt and pepper to taste and keep warm.

Serving the Quenelles

You have two choices to finish the dish: either on top of the stove or in the oven. To cook on top of the stove, bring a large pot of lightly salted water to a boil. Poach the quenelles until doubled in size. (Here the liquid must be boiling.) Using a slotted spoon, remove the quenelles and drain on a towel. Arrange the quenelles on the serving plates and ladle the hot sauce on top.

As was done at **Fernand Point's** "**La Pyramide**" in **Vienne**, I would serve a **Côte du Rhône** like the one made by **Georges Vernay**.

To cook in the oven (an easier method for the home cook), preheat the oven to 400°F. Ladle ½ cup of the sauce into a large gratin dish. Arrange the quenelles over the sauce. Cover with the remaining sauce and bake in the hot oven until the quenelles are puffy and the sauce is bubbling, about 15 minutes. Serve immediately.

❧ *Chef's Truc* ❧

MAKING QUENELLES AHEAD: You can poach the quenelles 2 to 3 days ahead of time. If you cover them tightly, they will keep perfectly in the refrigerator until you're ready to reheat them (in water or in the oven).

SOLE GRILLÉE AUX DEUX SAUCES:
COULIS DE POIVRONS JAUNES ET JUS DE PERSIL

GRILLED DOVER SOLE WITH GOLDEN PEPPER COULIS AND PARSLEY ESSENCE

Dover sole, a king of fish in the culinary world, is only fished on the European side of the Atlantic, particularly in the North Atlantic waters of England, France, Belgium, and Holland. Its firm, succulent flesh makes it an incomparable eating fish and a chef's favorite. I serve fresh Dover sole year round, no matter what the price.

.... SERVICE FOR 4 ....

THE GOLDEN PEPPER COULIS

3 yellow bell peppers, roasted,
*   peeled, and seeded*

3 tablespoons olive oil

3 tablespoons Fond Blanc de Volaille
*   (see page 214)*

3 tablespoons sherry vinegar

Salt and white pepper

THE JUS DE PERSIL

1 clove garlic, peeled

1 shallot, peeled

1 quart (4 cups) water

2 bunches Italian parsley, stems removed

¼ cup extra-virgin olive oil

Salt and white pepper

THE DOVER SOLE AND PASTA

2 tablespoons extra virgin olive oil

¼ cup chopped fresh fine herbs
*   (tarragon, thyme, chives, chervil)*

Salt and white pepper

8 fillets of fresh Dover sole

1 pound fresh angel hair pasta (purchased)

2 tablespoons unsalted butter

Preparing the Golden Pepper Coulis

Place the peppers in a blender along with the Fond Blanc de Volaille and vinegar. Blend until smooth, then, with the machine still running, add the remaining olive oil and salt and pepper to taste. This sauce should be served at room temperature.

Preparing the Jus de Persil

Lightly oil the garlic and shallot. Roast 15 minutes at 400°F or until browned. Remove from the oven and set aside. In a medium pot, bring the water and 1 tablespoon salt to a boil. Blanch the parsley leaves in boiling water for 5 minutes. Refresh in ice water to set the color. Drain off any excess water. In a blender, blend the roasted garlic and shallot along with the parsley leaves and olive oil until very smooth. Season with salt and pepper to taste. Set aside.

Preparing the Dover Sole and Pasta

Combine the olive oil, herbs, salt and pepper and rub over the sole fillets. Marinate while heating the grill to red-hot. Season the grill by wiping with an oiled cloth several times. Grill the fillets on both sides, until they are opaque but barely cooked. Transfer to a platter and keep warm.

Meanwhile, bring a large pot of salted water to a boil. Cook the pasta until al dente. Drain and toss with butter.

Serving the Dish

On each of 4 large, heated dinner plates, twirl a nest of angel hair pasta in the center. Place 1 fillet of sole on either side of the pasta. Then place 2 tablespoons of each sauce on opposite sides of each plate. Serve immediately.

This dish calls for a wine as fine as the dish itself. Choose a white **Burgundy**, perhaps a **Puligny** from **Sauzet** or a **Meursault** from **Ampeau**.

Les Plats de Résistance

MEAT COURSE

CÔTE DE VEAU AU JUS ET PETITS POIS

VEAL RIB CHOP WITH NATURAL JUICES AND FRESH BABY PEAS

Good pale pink veal is a basic in fine cuisine. I choose my veal with great care, looking for light color and bright white fat, indicating that the meat is freshly cut. When you have such a beautiful cut of meat, why make it complicated? Serve it in the simplest of dishes, like this one. It really is worth the trouble of shelling fresh garden peas. The exquisite sweet tenderness of young fresh peas is a gift of spring. I serve the veal with my Potato Puree flavored with hazelnut oil (see page 123). For a wintertime version of this dish that is extraordinaire, accompany the veal with Potato Puree flavored with truffle juice and fresh truffle.

.... SERVICE FOR 4 ....

THE VEAL

4 thick-cut veal chops (about 1 pound each)

Salt and white pepper

2 tablespoons unsalted butter

4 carrots, peeled and coarsely chopped

1 onion, peeled and coarsely chopped

¼ cup dry white vermouth

¼ cup Madeira

2 cups Jus de Veau (see page 212)

Salt and freshly ground black pepper

THE PEAS

2 pounds tender garden peas, shelled
    (or 1 pound sugar snap peas, trimmed)

2 tablespoons unsalted butter

¼ cup water

Salt and white pepper

Roasting the Veal

Preheat the oven to 450°F. Preheat a roasting pan on the stovetop. Season the veal chops with salt and pepper. Over medium-high heat, sear the veal chops on both sides in the butter. Add the carrots and onions to the pan. Place the browned chops and the vegetables in the oven and roast for 20 minutes, basting once or twice. Remove the veal from the oven. The meat should test medium-rare (135°F). Remove the meat from the roasting pan and set aside. Pour off and discard the fat.

Place the pan on the stovetop over medium-high heat and deglaze with the vermouth and Madeira, scraping up the browned bits and vegetables with a wooden spoon. Add the Jus de Veau and bring to a boil. Pour the liquid into a small pot and simmer 20 minutes or until it is slightly thickened and reduced. Season with salt and pepper and strain through a fine sieve. Reheat the veal chops in a 350°F oven for 5 minutes. Arrange 1 veal chop on each of 4 large heated dinner plates, with the bone facing away from the center of the plate. Carve into slices if desired. Serve with the natural juices and a spoonful of peas.

Cooking the Peas

If the peas are truly young and tender, they won't need any pre-cooking. Heat the butter in a small sauté pan, then add the shelled peas and water, and season with salt and pepper. Bring the liquid to a rapid boil. Cook over high heat for 3 to 4 minutes, or until the peas are bright green and tender and the cooking juices have reduced to a syrupy glaze.

With this dish I would serve the finest and most complex wine possible, such as a great red **Burgundy** from the **Côte de Beaune** like those made by **Madame Gaunoux** in **Pommard** or **Hubert de Montille** in **Volnay**. A good substitute would be a **California Pinot Noir** like the **Talley 1994**.

ENTRECÔTE DE BOEUF AU POIVRE BLANC

SIRLOIN OF AGED BEEF WITH WHITE PEPPERCORNS

I am extremely particular about the beef I buy, which comes from the special Angus breed of cattle. I prefer the old-fashioned dry-aged sirloin of beef because it has the most highly developed flavor and is never tough. Because dry-aging takes time (five weeks for my orders) and the meat shrinks in size as it ages, this adds to the cost of an already high-priced cut. I believe, if you're going to eat beef, eat the best.

.... SERVICE FOR 4 ....

THE BEEF

2 tablespoons white peppercorns

Four 8-ounce New York strip sirloin steaks,
    completely trimmed of fat

3 tablespoons unsalted butter

1 tablespoon olive oil

2 ounces cognac

2 ounces Madeira

2 cups Demi-Glace (see page 212),
    or Fond Gibier (see Chef's Truc below)

Salt

If I had my wish, I'd serve **Jean-Louis Chave's Hermitage 1979** with this dish. Otherwise I would choose among the red wines of **Bordeaux**, the **Rhône**, **Cahors**, or **Chinon**.

Sautéing the Steaks

Using a meat mallet or other heavy object (such as the bottom of a saucepan) crush the white peppercorns so that they're still chunky. Place the crushed peppercorns in a fine sieve and shake out the fine pepper dust, reserving for another use. (You should have only crushed peppercorn chunks left.) Pat the peppercorns firmly onto the steaks. Heat one tablespoon butter and oil until sizzling hot. Brown the steaks on both sides.

Add the cognac and Madeira to the pan and heat slightly. *Flambé* (ignite with a long match). Allow the flames to subside. Remove the steaks from the pan and keep warm. (The steaks should test medium-rare, about 145°F: the pink juices from inside the steak will form beads on top when they're ready.) Add the Demi-Glace to the pan, reduce the liquid by one-third, then whisk in the remaining butter. Season to taste with salt. Serve the steaks on heated dinner plates with the sauce poured over top.

❧ *Chef's Truc* ❧

USING FOND GIBIER: In a restaurant setting, I prefer to use a Fond Gibier, a game stock based on bones from pigeons and other game birds. The complex wild game flavor of this stock adds depth to my sauces. At home, I would use Demi-Glace, unless you're lucky enough to have access to game meat.

EVENTAIL D'AGNEAU AU CURRY AVEC SON CHUTNEY DE COURGETTES

FANNED LOIN OF LAMB WITH CURRY AND ZUCCHINI CHUTNEY

One of my signature dishes, here I was inspired by the North Indian, or Moghul, marriage of lamb with curry. In my version, I use boneless loin of lamb with a creamy curry sauce. I make a quick-cooked chutney of zucchini and apples to serve with it. Once you have done your prep, the dish takes only minutes to prepare.

.... SERVICE FOR 4 ....

Preparing the Chutney

Slice ¼-inch-thick lengthwise strips of the zucchini skin and set aside, discarding the core. Cut the strips into ¼-inch dice. Combine with the apple, vinegar, allspice, salt, and cayenne in a small, heavy saucepan. Cook until the vegetables are tender, about 5 minutes.

Searing the Lamb

Season the lamb with salt and pepper. Heat one tablespoon of the oil until extremely hot in a heavy cast-iron or steel skillet. Sear the lamb loins on all sides, browning well and evenly. Remove the lamb and set aside. Pour off the fat and deglaze the pan with vermouth. Add the curry and Jus d'Agneau and bring to a boil. Reduce the liquid by half. Add the cream, bring to a boil again and reduce until the sauce lightly coats the back of a wooden spoon.

To finish the sauce, whisk in the butter, season with salt and pepper and strain. Stir in the diced tomato and chives and keep warm. Heat a sauté pan with the remaining tablespoon olive oil and finish cooking the lamb loins, about 1 minute on each side. Remove the lamb loins from the pan and keep warm. (The lamb should register about 145°F on a meat thermometer.) Allow the lamb to rest for 10 minutes, then slice thinly and arrange in a fan shape surrounding the chutney.

Chef's Truc

LETTING ROASTED MEAT REST: Always let the meat rest after roasting. A large roast should sit about 15 minutes before carving. This allows the juices of the meat to distribute more evenly and to be reabsorbed into the muscle fibers. If you cut the meat too soon, the juices will run out, making for a less succulent dish.

THE CHUTNEY

2 zucchini

1 Granny Smith apple,
    peeled, cored, and diced

2 tablespoons red wine vinegar

1 teaspoon ground allspice

¼ cup sugar

⅛ teaspoon cayenne pepper

THE LAMB

2 boneless lamb loins

Salt and white pepper

2 tablespoons olive oil

¼ cup dry white vermouth

2 teaspoon Madras curry powder

3 cups Jus d'Agneau (see page 212)

1 cup heavy cream

1 tablespoon unsalted butter

1 ripe tomato, peeled, seeded, and diced

1 tablespoon finely snipped fresh chives

I like an exotic wine with this exotic dish. Choose a **Pomerol** or a **St. Emilion**. An excellent alternative is a firmly structured **California Merlot** like the **Russian River** wine of **Keith Mietz**.

AGNEAU PRINTANIER AU THYM ET LÉGUMES CARAMÉLISÉS

SPRING LAMB WITH THYME AND CARAMELIZED VEGETABLES

or this dish of lamb garnished with primeurs, the first tender vegetables of spring, I like to use an imported rack of baby lamb from New Zealand. This lamb comes completely trimmed and pan-ready—a break for the cook. The light color and mild flavor of this lamb are appropriate here. Because it is smaller in size than domestic lamb, you'll need to roast it at higher heat for a shorter time. Be careful not to overcook the lamb.

SERVICE FOR 4

THE LAMB SAUCE

2 pounds lamb shanks,
    cut into 1-inch pieces

1 tablespoon olive oil

1 carrot, peeled and coarsely chopped

1 rib celery, coarsely chopped

2 white mushrooms, cleaned and chopped

1 bay leaf

5 black peppercorns

2 sprigs fresh thyme

1 ripe whole tomato, coarsely chopped

¼ cup dry white wine

1 quart (4 cups) Jus d'Agneau
    (see page 212)

Salt and white pepper

THE VEGETABLES AND LEGUMES

4 scallions (white part only),
    split lengthwise

2 large carrots, peeled and sliced

10 baby turnips, peeled and sliced

1 tablespoon plus 1 teaspoon unsalted butter

½ teaspoon sugar

Salt and white pepper

1 cup shelled and skinned fava beans
    (see Chef's Truc page 60)

1 cup fresh shelled garden peas

Preparing the Lamb Sauce

Preheat the oven to 450°F. Roast the lamb shanks about 25 minutes, or until well browned on all sides. Meanwhile, in a large pot, sauté the carrots, celery and mushrooms in the olive oil until transparent. Add the bay leaf, peppercorns, thyme, and tomato. Add the white wine, the Jus d'Agneau, and the roasted lamb shanks. Bring to a boil, skimming as necessary. Reduce the heat and simmer 1 hour, then strain and reduce the liquid by three quarters. Season the sauce with salt and pepper to taste and set aside.

Preparing the Vegetables and Legumes

Sauté the carrots, turnips, scallions, and sugar in 1 tablespoon butter until lightly browned. Season to taste with salt and pepper.

In a separate small pot, bring to a boil ¼ cup of water with the remaining teaspoon of butter. Add the fava beans and peas and cook over high heat until they are hot and glossy looking. Set aside.

THE LAMB

2 baby New Zealand racks of lamb

Salt and white pepper

¼ cup dry white wine

1 tablespoon unsalted butter

¼ cup Tomates Concassées (see page 217)

1 teaspoon finely chopped fresh thyme leaves

This delicate baby lamb would be very good with **de de Villaine's Mercurey "les Montots" 1992**, or **Joguet's Chinon Jeunes Vignes 1992.**

Roasting the Lamb

Heat a roasting pan on top of the stove over medium heat. Season the racks of lamb with salt and pepper, then sear on all sides. Roast for 10 to 15 minutes in the oven. Remove the lamb (which should have an internal temperature of 140 to 145°F) from the roasting pan and pour off the fat. Allow the lamb to rest 5 minutes before cutting. To finish the sauce, deglaze the pan with the wine, add the reserved Lamb Sauce and bring to a boil. Whisk in the butter and strain the sauce through a fine sieve and set aside.

Finishing the Dish

Stir the chopped thyme and the Tomates Concassées into the sauce and season with salt and pepper to taste. Just before serving, combine the fava beans and peas with the caramelized vegetables, seasoning to taste. Carve the lamb into individual chops. Make a mound of the vegetables in the center of each of 4 large, heated dinner plates. Surround the vegetables with the lamb chops. Ladle the sauce over top and serve immediately.

MAGRET DE CANARD AUX NAVETS

SLICED EUROPEAN DUCK BREAST WITH TURNIPS

Moullard ducks are specially fattened for foie gras. In keeping with the inherent frugality of good French cooks, each part of the duck is prepared in the way most suited to it. The magret or breasts are cooked quickly and served rare, like a steak. The legs and fat are transformed into confit similar to my Pigeon Confit (see Chef's Truc page 106). I like to accompany this time-honored pairing of duck and turnips with bowtie pasta, tossed with my Confit of Cabbage (see page 104).

.... SERVICE FOR 4 ....

Preparing the Sauce

Preheat the oven to 375°F. Roast the duck bones until well browned, about 45 minutes. Pour off the excess fat from the roasting pan. Deglaze the pan with Fond Blanc de Volaille. Bring the liquid to a boil, scraping up the browned bits using a wooden spoon. Transfer the bones and liquid to a stockpot. Cover with cold water, bring to a boil and skim as necessary. Lower the heat to a simmer and cook for 1 hour.

Heat the mirepoix and butter together in a heavy pan. Cook until the onions and celery are translucent. Add the sugar, red wine and bouquet garni. Heat together, then *flambé* (ignite with a long match), and allow the alcohol to burn off. Add to the stockpot and continue to cook on low heat for 2 hours. Strain the sauce, return to the heat, and reduce slightly until the liquid is syrupy. Whisk in the beurre manié (a little at a time) to thicken the sauce (enough to lightly coat a spoon). Set aside.

Preparing the Turnips

Trim off the tops and bottoms of the turnips so they lay flat. If the turnips are large, trim them into *tourné* (seven-sided barrels). If small, cook whole. In a heavy skillet, large enough to hold the turnips in 1 layer, melt the butter until sizzling. Brown the turnips in the butter. Add the sugar to the pan to caramelize the turnips. Set aside.

Preparing the Magret

Preheat the oven to 350°F. Season the breasts with salt and pepper. Place them skin-side down in a preheated oven-proof skillet. Cook over medium heat until the skin is crisp. Pour off the fat from the pan and turn the breasts over. Place the skillet in the oven and roast for 10 to 15 minutes or until rare (140°F). Remove from the oven and allow the meat to rest 5 minutes. Using a sharp knife, carve the duck on the angle into thin, even slices, paralleling the length of the breasts. Arrange on 4 large, heated dinner plates and coat with the sauce. Garnish with the glazed turnips.

This dish from the Southwest of France deserves a wine that shares its origin, like a red **Madiran** or **Cahors**.

THE SAUCE

Bones and necks of 2 ducks

*2 quarts (8 cups) Fond Blanc de Volaille
(see page 214)*

1½ cup mirepoix (see page 217)

1 cup turnips, coarsely chopped

2 tablespoons unsalted butter

1 teaspoon sugar

½ cup dry red wine

*Bouquet garni (1 sprig fresh thyme,
1 bay leaf, 6 black peppercorns)*

1 tablespoon Beurre Manié (see page 216)

THE TURNIPS

*1 pound baby white turnips,
peeled and blanched*

2 tablespoons unsalted butter

2 teaspoons sugar

THE MAGRET

*4 boneless breasts of Moullard ducks
(see Sources page 219)*

Salt and white pepper

Médaillons de Veau aux Morilles

Medallions of Veal with Wild Morel Mushrooms

*H*ere I quickly sauté medallions of veal cut from the loin. The mild but juicy veal is topped with a morel mushroom sauce. It's relatively easy, though a bit expensive, to buy dried morels, and in terms of flavor, they are a good substitute for the fresh. If you are substituting dried morels use one-quarter pound and cover them with cold water and soak for one hour before proceeding with the recipe. Strain the mushroom "liquor" (soaking liquid) through a coffee filter or cheesecloth. Simmer half with the trimmed stems and reserve for the sauce. Save the remaining half to add to a mushroom soup or sauce (such as the Mushroom Ravioli, see page 44).

.... SERVICE FOR 4 ....

THE MORELS AND VEAL

1 pound fresh morels,
　　stems trimmed and reserved

1 quart (4 cups) water

2 large shallots, finely chopped

2 tablespoons Madeira

3 tablespoons unsalted butter

1 pound boneless loin of veal,
　　cut into 8 medallions

1 cup flour (for dusting)

1 tablespoon olive oil

2 tablespoons dry white vermouth

¼ cup Jus de Veau (see page 212)

Salt and white pepper

With this dish I would serve as fine a red **Burgundy** as possible. I recommend the **Blagny 1995** of **Robert Ampeau**. **Patrice Rion**, of **Domaine Daniel Rion** makes excellent wine too.

Preparing the Morels

Place the morels in a large bowl filled with cold water. Soak for 10 minutes. Remove the morels from the water, reserving both the mushrooms and the water. Strain the water through a coffee filter or cheesecloth to remove any sand. Cut off the stems of the morels and combine with the strained mushroom water. Bring to a boil and cook until the liquid has reduced to 2 tablespoons.

Rub the morel caps with your fingers. If you feel any sand, wash again in cold water. Cut the morel caps lengthwise into halves. Sauté the shallots in 1 tablespoon butter until soft. Add the morels, their reduced cooking juices and the Madeira. Cook, covered, over medium heat, for 6 to 7 minutes, until plump. Remove from the heat and keep warm.

Preparing the Veal

Dust the veal medallions in flour, shaking off the excess. In a large sauté pan, heat 1 tablespoon of butter and the oil until sizzling. Sauté the veal on both sides until well browned. (Do not crowd the pan with veal. Cook in two batches if necessary.) Remove the medallions from the pan and keep warm. Pour off the fat from the pan and deglaze with the vermouth. Add the morels and Jus de Veau to the pan and bring to a boil. Cook to reduce the liquid slightly. Season with salt and pepper. Return the veal medallions to the pan to heat. Swirl the remaining 1 tablespoon of butter into the sauce to finish. Arrange the veal medallions on 4 large, heated dinner plates. Ladle the sauce and a portion of morels over each serving of veal.

❧ Chef's True ❧

FLOURING MEATS AND FISH: Flouring is done to meats and fish before sautéing to provide a dry surface that will brown well. The small amount of flour will also help to thicken the sauce. For best results, flour just before sautéing. Dust evenly and shake off all the excess just before immediately sautéing in a hot pan.

DINDE FARCIE AUX MARRONS,
SAUCE AUX AIRELLES ET GRAND MARNIER

POACHED THEN ROASTED TURKEY WITH CHESTNUT STUFFING
AND CRANBERRY-GRAND MARNIER SAUCE

I make a marvelous roast turkey. The secret? I poach the bird first in a court-bouillon, a lightly flavored quick-cooked broth. This gets rid of all the fat and gives the meat a fine texture. You'll need a large (4 to 5 gallon) pot to poach the turkey. I then roast the bird at high heat for a short time to maximize the flavor. The skin comes out crispy; the meat succulent. Try my way. You may never go back. In a marvelous complement to the turkey, I stud my stuffing with nuggets of sweet marrons, chestnuts, and spike it with cognac. Fresh chestnuts, in season in late fall and winter, come into this country from Europe, mostly Italy. They are graded A, AA, or AAA, the largest and fanciest.

.... SERVICE FOR 12 TO 15 ....

THE CRANBERRY-GRAND MARNIER SAUCE

2 cups fresh cranberries (one 12-ounce bag)

Grated zest and juice of 2 oranges

½ cup sugar

¼ cup Grand Marnier

THE COURT-BOUILLON

1 large carrot, peeled and coarsely chopped

1 head celery, coarsely chopped

1 whole peeled onion studded with 3 cloves

Bouquet garni (1 sprig fresh thyme,
    1 sprig fresh parsley, 1 bay leaf,
    and 6 peppercorns)

Making the Cranberry-Grand Marnier Sauce

The day before serving, place the cranberries, zest, juice, sugar, and Grand Marnier in a food processor. Finely chop, then chill overnight to ripen the flavors.

Making the Court-Bouillon

Place the carrot, celery, onion, and bouquet garni in a stockpot large enough to hold the turkey. Add enough cold water to half-fill the pot. Bring the liquid to a boil, then simmer 2 hours. Strain and set aside while you stuff the turkey.

Preparing the Stuffing

Start this dish early in the day. Allow about 6 hours from start to finish.

Remove the neck and giblets from inside the turkey and set aside for the sauce. (Reserve the turkey liver for another use.) Heat the olive oil in a large sauté pan.

Add the veal, pork, and shallots. Cook for 10 minutes, but do not brown the meat.

Meanwhile, soak the bread in the milk until soft, then squeeze out and discard the excess milk. Combine the veal and pork along with their pan juices and the soaked bread. Put the mixture through the fine-holed cutter on a meat grinder. Beat in the egg, cognac, parsley, and seasonings. Gently mix in the whole chestnuts.

Stuffing and Poaching the Turkey

Season the turkey inside and out with salt and pepper. Stuff the large cavity, then sew closed using a large needle and cotton string. Truss the turkey as desired, leaving enough string from the trussed drumsticks to tie onto the handle of the pot. Place the turkey in the *court-bouillon*. Add enough cold water to cover and bring the liquid to a boil, skimming as necessary. Cover, bring back to a simmer, reduce the heat as low as possible, and poach for 1½ hours. The liquid should never boil, rather it should *frémir*, or tremble, with just an occasional bubble coming to the surface. To remove from the *court-bouillon*, insert a carving fork into the underside of the turkey while carefully pulling up on the string. Place the turkey in a roasting pan along with the giblets and neck. (If you like, reserve the *court-bouillon* for soup.)

Roasting the Turkey

Preheat the oven to 450°F. Roast the turkey until evenly browned, about 30 minutes. Remove the giblets and neck from the pan, chop the meat finely and set aside for the sauce.

Using a bulb baster, remove and discard the excess fat from the roasting pan. With the turkey still in the pan, add the cognac, Madeira, and Demi-Glace to the pan to deglaze, then reduce the oven temperature to 350°F. Cover the turkey with foil and continue to roast for about 2 hours. Baste the turkey every 10 to 15 minutes with its cooking juices. It's done when a meat thermometer inserted into the thigh joint measures 165 to 170°F and the juices run clear.

Finishing the Dish

Remove the turkey from the roasting pan and keep it warm. Pour the liquid through a strainer into a small pan and bring to a boil. Reduce over high heat until slightly thickened. Season with salt and pepper and then whisk in the butter. Strain and, if desired, add the reserved chopped giblets. Serve with the carved turkey. Accompany with a sauceboat of the Cranberry-Grand Marnier Sauce.

☙ *Chef's Truc* ☞

USING FRESH CHESTNUTS: Choose heavy, hard chestnuts with shiny brown skins. To peel, use a small, sharp knife to make cross-cut slits on the domed side of the chestnut. Bring a pot of water to a boil. Blanch the chestnuts for 5 minutes. Remove from the water, cool slightly and pull off both the outer shell and the inner skin. If the inner skin won't come off, place the shelled chestnuts back in the boiling water for 2 or 3 minutes, then rub off the skin. The chestnuts should be plump and whole with the inner skin completely removed, including any skin between the walls where the nut splits. Cut away and discard any moldy spots.

THE STUFFING

1 tablespoon olive oil

½ pound veal stew meat,
cut into 1-inch cubes

½ pound pork butt (fatty cut),
cut into 1-inch cubes

2 shallots, finely chopped

9 slices firm white bread

1 cup milk

1 egg

¼ cup cognac

1 tablespoon chopped fresh Italian parsley

Salt and white pepper

1 pound fresh chestnuts, peeled and skinned,
or whole, unsweetened bottled chestnuts
(see Chef's Truc below)

THE TURKEY AND SAUCE

One 15-pound fresh turkey
(hens are juicier than toms)

Salt and white pepper

¼ cup cognac

½ cup Madeira (or white wine)

2 cups Demi-Glace (see page 212)

1 tablespoon unsalted butter

The most underappreciated great white wines of **France** are from **Vouvray**, and it would be hard to find a wine that works better with turkey. The **Clos Baudoin 1993** would be excellent.

Pigeon Rôti et Cannelloni de Champignons au Jus et Choux Confits

Roast Pigeon with Mushroom Cannelloni
and Confit of Cabbage

My favorite bird is pigeon, with its dark, gamy, slightly livery flavor. Like other red meats (magret of duck, lamb, venison and beef), pigeon should be served medium rare for juiciness. Americans are not accustomed to eating pigeon though it's common in France. In this dish, I combine roasted pigeon, sweet savoy cabbage and tiny cannelloni enclosing a rich stuffing of mushrooms and foie gras. To make this dish the way I like to serve it, you'll need to turn the tough but tasty pigeon legs into confit, a preserved meat. See the Chef's Truc following this recipe. It's a complicated dish but worth the effort.

.... SERVICE FOR 4 ....

THE CANNELLONI

1 ounce diced fresh foie gras
    (substitute 1 ounce Mousse de Foie
    Gras, but don't cook it in the pan)
2 cups mixed, cleaned and
    chopped mushrooms
1 tablespoon unsalted butter
2 tablespoons Madeira
Salt and pepper
Four 2-inch squares of Pâte aux Oeufs
    (see page 215)
½ cup Fond Blanc de Volaille
    (see page 214)
1 tablespoon grated Parmesan

THE SAVOY CABBAGE CONFIT

1 head savoy cabbage,
    quartered and cored
2 tablespoons diced bacon
2 tablespoons duck fat
    (see Chef's Truc page 106)
Salt and white pepper

Making the Cannelloni

Heat a dry, small, heavy skillet until very hot. Sear the fresh foie gras and set aside in the fat left in the pan. In another pan, cook the mushrooms in the butter until their juices have completely evaporated and have become a *duxelles* (dry paste). Add the Madeira and chill the mixture. Combine the *duxelles* with the reserved foie gras and reserved fat and season with salt and pepper. Spread the filling across the center of each pasta square. Roll up and set aside.

Preparing the Savoy Cabbage Confit

Bring a large pot of salted water to a boil. Blanch the cabbage for 5 minutes, then drain and set aside. In a large sauté pan cook the bacon cubes until lightly browned, then add the duck fat, cabbage, and season with salt and pepper. Cook on low heat for 20 minutes. Strain the cabbage in a colander to drain off the fat. Pat the cabbage dry on paper towels and set aside.

To Roast the Pigeons

Preheat the oven to 400°F. Sprinkle the pigeons with salt and pepper. Heat the olive oil in an oven-proof casserole on top of the stove. Sear the pigeons until brown on all sides. Transfer to the oven and roast for 10 minutes, then remove from the oven. Allow the meat to rest 5 minutes then cut off the breasts of the pigeon (which should be rare, 135°F). Cut off the leg-thigh portions and set aside. Reserve the carcasses.

Finishing the Sauce

Cook the mirepoix and bouquet garni in 1 tablespoon butter in a saucepan. Deglaze with the red wine. Add the pigeon carcasses to the pot along with the Demi-Glace. Bring to a boil and simmer for 1 hour. Strain the liquid through a fine sieve and reduce until slightly thickened.

THE PIGEONS

1 tablespoon olive oil

4 whole pigeons

1 cup mirepoix (see page 217)

Bouquet garni (1 sprig fresh thyme,
*   1 bay leaf, 1 sprig fresh parsley,*
*   6 black peppercorns)*

1 tablespoon unsalted butter

½ cup dry red wine

½ cup Demi-Glace (see page 212)

Salt and white pepper

With this dish I'd serve a country
wine with a strong nose from the
southwest like **St. Chinian Chateau
des Lauzes 1994.**

Finishing the Dish

Preheat the oven to 350°F. Place the cannelloni and the Fond Blanc de Volaille in a
small gratin dish and sprinkle with the Parmesan. Bake about 15 minutes or until
lightly browned. Reheat the cabbage confit in a small pan. Reheat the pigeon breasts
(and legs, if using) in a little of the sauce. If you made the confit of legs, rewarm for
10 minutes in a 350°F oven or until browned and crispy.

On each of 4 large, heated dinner plates, arrange the cabbage confit in the
center. At the six o'clock position, place the cannelloni. Cut each breast into thin
slices and divide in half. Place one half on either side of the cabbage confit, at nine
and at three o'clock. Place the 2 legs at the twelve o'clock position. Lightly coat with
the sauce and serve immediately.

❧ *Chef's Truc* ❧

MAKING CONFIT OF PIGEON LEGS: Cut the legs off the birds.
Remove the thighbone, reserving for the sauce if desired. Lightly salt the leg meat
and chill overnight. The next day, cover the legs with melted duck fat. Add 8
unpeeled cloves garlic, 1 bay leaf, 1 sprig thyme and 6 peppercorns. Bake slowly in
a 250°F oven for about 2 hours. Remove and allow the confit to cool. The confit will
keep in the refrigerator for several weeks if completely covered by its own fat. When
ready to serve, drain the fat off the legs and heat them until browned and crispy.

Foie de Veau Sauté au Vinaigre de Cassis

Sautéed Calf's Liver with Black Currant Vinegar

ood liver is a dish I can eat again and again. It's so rare that I find it prepared properly. The liver must be pale pink and absolutely fresh. Also, it must be cut into very thin scallops. The best, sweetest-tasting liver comes from kosher calves. Because of the method of slaughter, these livers contain the least amount of blood. Cook liver at high heat, very quickly, so it's still pink on the inside. Serve with Purée de Pommes de Terre (see page 123) or Gratin Dauphinois (see page 124).

SERVICE FOR 4

Cooking the Calf's Liver

In a large nonstick sauté pan, over a high flame, heat the olive oil and butter. When the pan is very hot, but not smoking, sauté the liver for 1 minute on each side. Remove from the pan and keep warm on a plate. Cook the shallots in the same pan until soft but not browned. Pour in the vinegar. Add the Demi-Glace and bring to a boil. Cook several minutes, or until the pan sauce is syrupy. At the last minute stir in the chives and parsley and season with salt and pepper to taste. Arrange the liver on 4 large, heated dinner plates and ladle the sauce on top.

THE CALF'S LIVER

1 tablespoon olive oil

1 tablespoon butter

1 pound calf's liver, skin removed,
     cut into ¼-inch slices

2 shallots, peeled and finely chopped

3 tablespoons black currant vinegar

¼ cup Demi-Glace (see page 212)

2 teaspoons finely snipped fresh chives

2 teaspoons finely chopped fresh parsley

Salt and white pepper

For this dish the best choice would be low-acid, ripe vintage reds from **Bordeaux**, **Côte du Rhône**, or other southern **French** wine. I especially recommend a **Pic St. Loup** from **Jean Orliac 1994**.

Suprême de Poulet Farci Parfumé au Vinaigre de Cidre

Stuffed Breast of Chicken Perfumed with Cider Vinegar

Here, a lovely combination of flavors is achieved using an interesting technique. First, I cut the chicken halves away from the rib cage. Then, I remove the legs and thighs from each chicken half, leaving behind the entire skin. I butterfly the breast meat, using it to cover the whole skin. I stuff the breasts with fruits and vegetables, roll them up and tie them into neat packages. When roasted and sliced, you'll get chicken rings enclosing a bright apricot stuffing surrounded by green spinach. By adding caramelized sugar and vinegar, the sauce become a gastrique, a flavor enhancement, often combined with poultry.

.... SERVICE FOR 8 ....

THE SPINACH

1 pound spinach leaves, stems removed

THE STUFFING

½ cup dried apricots (see
   Chef's Truc page 110)

¼ cup golden raisins

2 tablespoons unsalted butter

5 white mushrooms, cleaned and
   cut into ¼-inch cubes

1 cup Tomates Concassées (see page 217)

Salt and white pepper

THE CHICKEN BREASTS

Four 3½-pound whole chickens

Salt and white pepper

1 tablespoon unsalted butter

THE SAUCE

¼ cup sliced shallots

2 tablespoons unsalted butter

3 tablespoons sugar

¼ cup cider vinegar

1 quart (4 cups) Jus de Poulet
   (see page 214)

Salt and white pepper

Preparing the Spinach

Wash the spinach leaves three times in cold water baths to remove any sand. In a sauté pan, cook the wet spinach until wilted. Drain and spread out to cool. Gently squeeze out some of the water and set the spinach aside.

Preparing the Stuffing

Soak the apricots and raisins in hot water for 15 minutes. Drain. Slice the apricots in ¼-inch strips and set aside with the raisins. Sauté the mushrooms in butter until cooked, but not brown. Add the Tomates Concassées and cook until almost dry. Add the apricots and raisins and sauté for 2 minutes longer. Season with salt and pepper and let cool.

Stuffing the Chicken Breasts

Cut each chicken half (with skin) away from the rib cage. Without tearing the skin, pull out and remove the thigh and drumstick from each side of the chicken, leaving the breast and wing portion attached to the skin. You should have the chicken breast and wing and the skin from the whole side of the chicken intact. Place the chicken breasts, skin-side down, on a cutting board. "Butterfly" the chicken breast meat, covering the skin in an even layer and leaving the tenderloin portion intact.

Preheat the oven to 425°F. Season the chicken with salt and pepper. Lay the steamed spinach over the butterflied breast meat. Divide the stuffing into 8 portions. Place 1 portion of stuffing on each breast, opposite the wing. Roll up each breast, starting from the stuffed end, forming oblong packets wrapped in their skin. Tie each rolled breast with string as you would a roast.

Brown the chicken breasts in the remaining butter. Transfer to the oven and roast for 20 minutes, or until cooked through. Remove the chicken breasts from the pan, let cool slightly, then remove the string. Allow the chicken to rest 5 minutes longer, then cut into 4 or 5 slices. The last slice will be connected to the first wing joint.

Making the Sauce

Sauté the shallots in 1 tablespoon of the butter until they start to brown. Add the sugar and stir, cooking until caramelized. Add the vinegar and cook 2 minutes. Add the Jus de Poulet and bring to a boil. Reduce the liquid to 1½ cups. Whisk in the remaining tablespoon butter and season with salt and pepper to taste. Strain the sauce through a fine sieve and serve over the sliced chicken breast.

Chef's Truc

CHOOSING APRICOTS: If you can find them, use California apricots. The more common, and rather bland, apricots are imported from Turkey. These whole dried fruits are light in color and have leathery skins. Domestic apricots, grown exclusively in California, are more expensive but worth every penny. These deep orange fruit halves are velvety on the outside and intensely apricot-flavored.

Viennoise de Ris de Veau

Sweetbreads in Brioche Crust Served Two Ways

We French do love to eat organ meats. To us variety meats are simply another delicious thing to eat and we excel at cooking them. I've always been known for my foie de veau (calf's liver), rognons (kidneys), and ris de veau (sweetbreads). I give two options for these sweetbreads. You can serve them as an appetizer over a mesclun salad or drizzle them with a light lemon and caper sauce. The key here is the pre-cooking and weighting of the sweetbreads. Using this technique you'll get firm, delicately flavored sweetbreads. When cooked, they'll be crusty on the outside from the brioche crumbs and creamy on the inside.

.... SERVICE FOR 4 ....

Preparing the Sweetbreads

The day before serving, bring the water to a boil along with the bay leaf and the lemon. Add the sweetbreads and bring them back to a boil. Simmer 5 minutes, or until the sweetbreads are firm. Remove them from the broth, discarding the broth. Pull off and discard the outer membrane. Wrap in plastic wrap and refrigerate the sweetbreads covered with a weight, such as a brick or a can, to flatten them. The next day, slice the sweetbreads lengthwise into ½-inch thick slices.

Place the bread in a food processor and process until you have fine white crumbs. Have ready three bowls: one with flour, one with egg, and one with the crumbs. Dust the sweetbread medallions with flour, shaking off the excess. Then, dip in the egg and coat on both sides with the brioche crumbs, patting so the crumbs adhere. Heat the butter and olive oil to sizzling. Cooking at moderate heat, browning the sweetbreads evenly on both sides. Drain on paper towels and keep warm.

1. The Salad

Toss the mesclun with the vinaigrette, seasoning with salt and pepper to taste. Divide among 4 cold salad plates. Top with the sweetbreads and serve immediately.

2. The Sauce aux Câpres

Bring the Fond Blanc de Volaille (or water) to a boil, adding the lemon juice. Bring back to a rapid boil and whisk in the butter. The sauce should be emulsified (creamy looking). Whisk in the chervil, chives, and capers, season to taste with salt and pepper and serve over the sweetbreads.

If you're serving the sweetbreads with the Sauce aux Câpres, try a complex, earthy white like **Vouvray**. With the salad, serve a simple, direct white wine like a **Chasselas** from the **Loire** or a **Pinot Blanc** of **Alsace**.

THE SWEETBREADS

1 quart (4 cups) water

1 bay leaf

1 lemon, cut into quarters

1 pound fresh sweetbreads

2 eggs

One 1-pound loaf brioche bread, crust removed, cubed

½ cup flour (for dusting the sweetbreads)

2 tablespoons unsalted butter

2 tablespoons olive oil

1. THE SALAD

½ pound mesclun greens

½ cup Vinaigrette Maison (see page 216)

Salt and white pepper

2. THE SAUCE AUX CÂPRES

½ cup Fond Blanc de Volaille (or water)

Juice of 1 lemon

¼ pound (1 stick) unsalted butter

Salt and white pepper

1 tablespoon finely snipped fresh chervil

1 tablespoon finely snipped fresh chives

2 tablespoon nonpareil capers

TOURNEDOS DE BOEUF, SAUCE MÉDOC
FILLET OF BEEF IN BORDEAUX WINE SAUCE

Highly prized tournedos are cut from the center of a tenderloin of beef. This cut deserves a good wine—use good wine and you'll get a good sauce, because cooking accentuates the intrinsic qualities of the wine. In this preparation I use a Médoc from Bordeaux. Of course, you'll want to serve a fine Bordeaux wine with the beef. This is a classic that I've served for many years, a truly satisfying dish. For an elegant presentation, serve topped with a round of poached veal marrow (see page 70).

.... SERVICE FOR 4 ....

THE SAUCE MÉDOC

1 tablespoon unsalted butter

1 tablespoon olive oil

10 shallots, peeled and sliced

2 ribs celery, sliced

1 bay leaf

5 mushrooms, cleaned and sliced

3 sprigs fresh thyme

½ teaspoon crushed black peppercorns

½ bottle (1½ cups) red Bordeaux wine

½ teaspoon sugar

2 cups Demi-Glace (see page 212)

THE FILLET OF BEEF

1 tablespoon olive oil

3 tablespoons unsalted butter

Four 7-ounce center-cut fillets of beef

Salt and white pepper

¼ cup red Bordeaux wine

Making the Sauce Médoc

Heat the butter and olive oil in a large, heavy saucepan. Add the shallots, celery, bay leaf, mushrooms, thyme, and crushed peppercorns. Sauté together until browned. Add the wine and sugar and heat slightly. *Flambé* (ignite with a long match). When the flames subside, add the Demi-Glace and cook until the sauce is reduced by half. Strain the sauce through a fine sieve and set aside.

Preparing the Fillet of Beef

In a heavy sauté pan, heat the olive oil and 1 tablespoon butter until sizzling. Sprinkle the beef with salt and pepper. Sauté until well-browned on both sides. Remove the fillets from the pan, keeping them warm on a plate. Pour off the fat from the pan and deglaze with the red wine. Add the Sauce Médoc and allow the liquid to reduce until it lightly coats the spoon. Beat in the remaining butter and season with salt and pepper to taste. Pour any juices on the plate from the fillets back into the sauce. Arrange the fillets in the center of 4 large, heated dinner plates and ladle the sauce around. Serve immediately.

❧ *Chef's Truc* ☙

IDENTIFYING MEDIUM-RARE BEEF: When the beef is medium-rare, beads of red juice from inside the fillet will appear on the surface—that's the time to remove the beef from the pan. Remember, as with all meats, it will continue to cook even off the heat.

The best choice for this dish is red **Bordeaux**, specifically of the region just north of the city on the left bank of the **Gironde**, which is known as the **Médoc**. This dish merits the best bottle possible: a **Margaux 1953** or a **Pichon Lalande 1982**.

PINTADE AUX CITRONS CONFITS

ROAST GUINEA HEN WITH CONFIT OF LEMON

I don't know why Guinea Hen has never really caught on in the United States. Europeans, especially the French and the Italians, adore them. Guinea Hen is a truly tasty meat, most comparable to a quail or a pheasant, with flesh that's between light and dark. Because it's a lean bird, be sure to baste often. Here, I garnish the birds with a sprinkle of candied lemon zest.

SERVICE FOR 4

THE LEMON CONFIT

3 lemons

1 tablespoon sugar

THE PAPRIKA BUTTER AND MUSHROOMS

3 tablespoons butter

2 tablespoons sweet paprika

1 shallot, peeled

1 clove garlic, peeled

Salt and white pepper

2 cups dried mixed mushrooms,

1 quart (4 cups) cold water

THE GUINEA HENS

2 Guinea hens

Salt and white pepper

2 tablespoons unsalted butter

2 tablespoons cognac

1 quart (4 cups) Jus de Poulet
   (see page 214)

½ cup Demi-Glace (see page 212)

Salt and white pepper

The most beautiful wine I've tasted with this dish was a **Beaune "Vigne Franche" 1985** from **François Germain**. I would also serve a fine **Burgundy** from the **Côte de Beaune**.

Preparing the Lemon Confit

Using a carrot peeler, remove the zest of the lemons in strips being careful not to remove any of the bitter white pith. Trim the edges of the strips straight, then julienne. Bring a small pot of water to a boil. Add the lemon zest and return to a boil. Blanch for 2 minutes. Drain and rinse.

Bring 2 cups water to a boil in a medium pot and add the sugar, stirring to dissolve. Add the blanched lemon zest and bring to a boil over high heat. Continue to cook, stirring constantly, until the water has evaporated and the zest is coated with sugar. Remove the zest from the pan and set aside.

Preparing the Paprika Butter and the Mushrooms

Combine the butter, paprika, shallot, garlic and salt and pepper to taste in the bowl of a food processor. Process until smooth and set aside.

Soak the mushrooms in the water for 1 hour. Scoop out the rehydrated mushrooms and examine each individually for any dirt, especially near the stem end. Soak longer if necessary. Strain the mushroom "liquor" through a coffee filter or cheesecloth and set aside both the mushrooms and strained liquor.

Preparing the Guinea Hens

Preheat the oven to 450°F. Season the hens inside and outside with salt and pepper. Heat a roasting pan on top of the stove and brown the hens on all sides. Brush with the Paprika Butter. Roast the hens in the oven for 25 minutes, basting every 5 minutes. The hens are ready when the juices in the cavity run clear, not pink.

Preparing the Sauce and Finishing the Dish

Remove the hens from the roasting pan and let them rest for 10 minutes. Cut the breasts off the bone and cut off the leg-thigh joints. Keep the hen pieces warm on a platter. Pour off the fat from the pan. Add 1 tablespoon butter and the mushrooms to the pan. Sauté 1 minute. Pour in the cognac and *flambé* (ignite with a long match). When the flames subside, add 1 cup of the reserved mushroom liquor, the Jus de Poulet, and the Demi-Glace. Reduce by three-quarters or until the sauce thickens. Season with salt and pepper then whisk in the remaining tablespoon of butter. Reheat the hens in a 400°F oven for 5 minutes. Strain the sauce through a sieve and pour over the hens. Sprinkle each portion with a teaspoon of the Lemon Confit.

Poussin Rôti aux Endives à l'Orientale

Roasted Cornish Hen with Braised Belgian Endive

I discovered Cornish game hens in the United States. In France we do have Poussin, or baby chicken, which is also delicious prepared this way. The flavor combination of chicken with bittersweet endive is a little unexpected, but pleasing to the palate. I finish the sauce with a bit of Japanese dark roasted sesame oil, for a hint of the flavors of Asia.

.... SERVICE FOR 6 ....

Preparing the Cornish Hens

Preheat the oven to 400°F. Season the hens inside and out with salt and pepper. Place 1 sprig each of rosemary and thyme in the cavity of each hen. Heat the butter and oil in a large heavy sauté pan. Brown the hens on all sides then transfer to a roasting pan, add the garlic and roast until cooked through, about 45 minutes. Remove the hens from roasting pan and keep warm on a platter.

Preparing the Sauce and the Endive

Pour off the fat from the roasting pan and place on the stove top. Pour the wine in the roasting pan to deglaze, scraping any browned bits with a wooden spoon. Add Jus de Poulet and Demi-Glace and cook slowly to reduce by half. Strain the liquid through a sieve. Add the Tomates Concassées, sesame oil, chives, and parsley.

In a medium sauté pan, cook the endive in butter, lemon juice, sugar, and seasonings for about 20 minutes, or until the liquid is syrupy and lightly browned. Place a bed of endive in the center of 6 large, heated dinner plates. Top with the hens and the sauce.

❧ *Chef's Truc* ❧

KEEPING ENDIVE WHITE: Like all white vegetables (celery root, artichoke, salsify), endive will discolor if cut and then exposed to the air. If you cut the endive ahead of time, be sure to keep it in a bowl of water with the juice of ½ a lemon added.

For this dish I would choose a light middle **Loire** red like the **Chinon Vieille Vigne** of **Sourdais 1993** or a **Burgundy** from a lighter vintage like **1987**, **1989**, or **1992**. If you prefer a white wine, choose a fairly earthy, lower acid one like **Shoffit's Chasselas 1995** or a **Jurançon** sec from **Domaine Cauhape**.

THE CORNISH HENS

6 Cornish game hens

Salt and white pepper

6 sprigs fresh rosemary

6 sprigs fresh thyme

1 tablespoon unsalted butter

2 tablespoons vegetable oil

3 cloves garlic, unpeeled

THE SAUCE AND THE ENDIVE

½ cup dry white wine

1 cup Jus de Poulet (see page 214)

1 cup Demi-Glace (see page 212)

1 cup Tomates Concassées (see page 217)

½ teaspoon dark roasted sesame oil

1 teaspoon finely snipped fresh chives

1 teaspoon chopped fresh Italian parsley

2 pounds Belgian endive, cored and cut into 1-inch slices

2 tablespoons unsalted butter

Juice of ½ lemon

1 teaspoon sugar

Salt and white pepper

Poulet Riesling et Spaetzle aux Épinards

Chicken in Riesling Wine Sauce with Spinach Dumplings

In this dish, the herbal acidity of the Riesling provides the perfect balance of flavors for the sauce. Try it and you'll see just how apparent the right wine is in this dish. Of course, you'll want to serve the same type of wine to accompany the dish. The spaetzle, Alsatian dumplings, are a very old type of pasta pushed through a special form and dropped directly into boiling water.

.... SERVICE FOR 4 ....

THE SPINACH SPAETZLE

1 pound spinach leaves, stems removed

2½ cups all-purpose flour, sifted

1 teaspoon salt

¼ teaspoon baking powder

2 eggs

4 tablespoons unsalted butter, softened

THE CHICKEN

2 tablespoons olive oil

4 chicken breasts, rib bones removed,
first wing joint attached

Salt and white pepper

1 onion, peeled and sliced

4 mushrooms, cleaned and sliced

½ bottle (1½ cups) Riesling

½ cup Tomates Concassées

2 sprigs fresh thyme

¾ cup heavy cream

Preparing the Spinach Spaetzle

Wash the spinach three times in cold water baths to remove any sand. Place the wet spinach in a large pot. Heat just until wilted, then refresh under running cold water. Drain, squeezing out and reserving the liquid. Add enough water to the reserved liquid to make ½ cup. Puree the spinach, the liquid, and the eggs in a food processor. Transfer to a mixer. Add the flour, salt, and baking powder. Beat with the paddle attachment until you have a soft dough, almost a batter.

Bring a large saucepan of salted water to a boil. Reduce the heat to a simmer. Using a spaetzle press (or a colander with large holes), press the dough into the simmering water. The spaetzle dumplings will rise to the surface. Let them cook a few minutes longer, or until they appear light and fluffy. Remove from the water using a slotted spoon or skimmer and refresh in a bowl of ice water. Drain, then set aside. Repeat procedure with any remaining batter. (You can cook the dumplings up to 2 days ahead.)

In a small pan cook the butter over low heat until it begins to turn light brown and smells nutty. Pour off and set aside the butterfat, discarding the browned bits stuck to the bottom of the pan. Toss the spaetzle with the browned butter.

Cooking the Chicken

Sprinkle the chicken breasts with salt and pepper. In a large heavy-bottomed skillet (cast-iron or steel), heat the olive oil. Lightly brown the chicken breasts on all sides. Add the onions and mushrooms to the pan and lightly brown. Add the Tomates Concassées, thyme, and wine. Simmer until the chicken breasts are firm and cooked through. Remove the breasts from the pan and remove and discard the skin. Keep warm.

Continue cooking the pan juices until reduced to 1 cup. Add the heavy cream and reduce the liquid by half, or until the sauce is thick enough to coat the back of a wooden spoon. Strain the sauce through a fine sieve and season to taste. Rewarm the chicken breasts in the sauce. Serve on heated dinner plates accompanied by a mound of Spinach Spaetzle in brown butter.

Les Légumes

SIDE DISHES

ASPERGES SAUCE MOUSSELINE

ASPARAGUS WITH LIGHT MOUSSELINE SAUCE

This is one of the many dishes I learned from my mother and still love to eat. It's a quick and easy way to get a light sauce without making hollandaise. It will taste best if made with our homemade mayonnaise. I know there is increasing concern about using raw eggs. To minimize any problems, use the freshest eggs possible.

.... SERVICE FOR 4 ....

THE ASPARAGUS AND THE SAUCE

1 pound fresh asparagus

½ cup Sauce Mayonnaise

(see page 216)

Juice of 1 lemon

Salt and white pepper

1 tablespoon chopped, mixed fresh fine herbs (chives, parsley, chervil, tarragon, and thyme)

Cooking the Asparagus

Cut the asparagus into 4-inch-long spears, then peel them with a swivel-type peeler. Place 1 to 2 inches of lightly salted water in a large sauté pan and bring to a boil. Cook the spears until they turn bright green, about 2 to 3 minutes. Using a pair of tongs, remove them from the pan, reserving the cooking liquid. Refresh the asparagus spears under cold, running water and set aside.

Finishing the Sauce

Combine the Sauce Mayonnaise and lemon juice. Stir in about 3 tablespoons reserved asparagus cooking juice. Add a little more juice if necessary to get a smooth, light sauce. Season with salt and pepper to taste. When ready to serve, reheat the asparagus by steaming or by dropping them into a pan of boiling water for 1 minute. Heat the sauce slowly over low heat and stir in the herbs. Ladle over the asparagus.

❧ *Chef's True* ❧

CHOOSING ASPARAGUS: When choosing asparagus, size is not very important. Pay attention to both the growing season and the freshness of the cut. The asparagus stalks should be green almost to the bottom of the stalks. Too much white at the bottom means the spears will be tough and stringy. Because the tips deteriorate fastest, examine them before buying. They should be firm, closed, and dry, and have a pale violet color.

COMPOTE DE FENOUIL

BRAISED FLORENCE FENNEL

f you're not familiar with this superb vegetable, here's a good introduction. Fennel has a clean licorice flavor and a crisp, biting texture. It is equally good sliced paper thin and added to a green salad or cooked slowly till meltingly tender, as in this recipe. Fennel is in season in the United States in the cold weather months, but hot house fennel bulbs imported from Holland may be found at other times of the year.

.... SERVICE FOR 8 ....

Preparing the Fennel

Trim off a slice from bottom portion of each bulb so that it lays flat. Peel off and discard any tough looking outer layers. Place each bulb on its flat bottom, then using a sharp knife, cut down, making thin, even slices. You can also use a mandoline, Benriner slicer, or any other sharp vegetable slicer.

Braising the Fennel

In a large sauté pan, melt the butter over high heat. Add the fennel and sauté until tender when pierced with a fork. Add the sugar, Fond Blanc de Volaille, and lemon juice. Reduce heat and simmer, stirring occasionally, for 20 minutes. Season to taste with salt and pepper. Serve warm.

THE FENNEL

3 large bulbs Florence fennel

3 tablespoons unsalted butter

3 tablespoons sugar

1 cup Fond Blanc de Volaille

   (see page 214)

Juice of 1 lemon

Salt and white pepper

❧ *Chef's Truc* ❧

BUYING DOMESTIC FENNEL: Domestically grown fennel will often be sold complete with its large, feathery stalks. Cut these off on the diagonal, at the point where the bulb enlarges. You can chop off and reserve the fine, inner leaves for garnish. Discard the stringy stalks.

GALETTES DE MAÏS

SWEET CORN CAKES

*H*ere in the United States, we take for granted the right to sweet corn in season. This delicacy is almost unknown in Europe, where corn is grown strictly as animal fodder. My tiny corn pancakes are delicious served as an hors d'oeuvre topped with smoked salmon or other smoked fish, or garnished with caviar.

·· SERVICE FOR 6 TO 8 ··

THE CORN PANCAKES

2 cups corn kernels

½ cup all-purpose flour

1 teaspoon sugar

1 teaspoon baking powder

Salt and white pepper

1 egg yolk

1 whole egg

1 cup heavy cream

1 apple, peeled, cored, and diced

1 teaspoon grated orange zest

1 tablespoon unsalted butter

1 tablespoon olive oil

Making the Corn Pancake Batter

Place 1½ cups of corn kernels in the food processor and puree. Strain through a fine sieve into a bowl to remove hulls, pressing firmly with the back of a ladle to extract all the liquid. Discard the remaining pulp.

In a bowl, whisk together the flour, sugar, baking powder, salt and pepper. Add the strained corn puree, egg yolk, and whole egg, and whisk smooth with a wire whisk. Add the heavy cream. (The mixture should have the consistency of pancake batter.) Stir in the apple, the orange zest, and the remaining ½ cup whole corn kernels. Let the batter rest for 30 minutes in the refrigerator.

Cooking the Pancakes

Heat a griddle (preferably nonstick) with the butter and oil until sizzling. Ladle on 2 tablespoon rounds of batter. Cook over low to medium heat until bubbles appear all over the surface, then flip over and cook 1 minute more. Serve immediately.

Chef's Truc

USING FRESH CORN: In season, make this recipe with fresh corn kernels. Cut off enough corn for 2 cups, scraping against the cut cobs with the edge of a knife to remove all the "corn milk." In winter, substitute frozen corn.

Purée de Pommes de Terre

Potato Puree

When French chefs come to visit the United States, they often cart home souvenir bags of our fine Idaho Russet potatoes. Only these potatoes contain a high enough proportion of starch to make the lightest of potato purees. In recent years, I've started to incorporate golden varieties like Yukon Golds and Yellow Finnish potatoes. Besides their color, they add an almost buttery taste of their own. The hazelnut oil is my own variation. I use it for its rich nutty flavor and indescribable aroma.

SERVICE FOR 6

Preparing the Potato Puree

Place the potatoes in a pot and cover with cold water. Cook until quite soft when pierced with a fork. Strain off the water, and return the potatoes to the pot. Cook the potatoes over medium heat until dry, 3 to 4 minutes, stirring constantly with a spoon. Meanwhile, heat the cream to scalding. Using a potato ricer (or a *tamis*, a French flat wire sieve), press the potatoes into fine strands. Alternatively, pass the potatoes through a food mill. Return the riced potatoes to a pot and whisk in the hot heavy cream, butter, and oil. Season with salt and pepper to taste. Serve hot.

Chef's Truc

STEAMING POTATOES: If you steam potatoes instead of boiling them, you won't need to dry them out. For the lightest and fluffiest of potatoes, always work with hot potatoes and hot liquid.

THE POTATO PUREE

4 large Yukon Gold or
    Yellow Finnish potatoes,
    peeled and coarsely chopped

2 large Idaho potatoes,
    peeled and coarsely chopped

1 cup heavy cream

4 tablespoons unsalted butter, softened

4 tablespoons hazelnut oil

Salt and white pepper

GRATIN DAUPHINOIS

GRATIN OF POTATOES WITH CREAM AND GARLIC

For my Gratin Dauphinois, I never use cheese, because it destroys the purity of the dish. A gratin dauphinois is sublime if made properly. I've been making it ever since I opened my restaurant. My customers and I both still love it. Follow my recipe and you will be able to enjoy this meltingly creamy dish in your own kitchen.

.... SERVICE FOR 4 TO 6 ....

THE GRATIN

4 Idaho potatoes, well-aged
    (see Chef's Truc below) and peeled
2 cloves garlic, peeled and cut in half
2 tablespoons butter, softened
1 quart (4 cups) heavy cream
Salt and white pepper

Baking the Gratin

Slice the potatoes into ⅛-inch thick rounds. They should be evenly cut and thick enough not to bend, but thin enough to cook through when baking. (You may need to experiment with different thicknesses before the dish is a perfect success.) Rub the garlic cloves over the surface of a stoneware gratin dish that's just large enough to hold the potatoes. Generously butter the dish.

Preheat the oven to 350°F.

Place one-third of the potatoes in an even layer on the bottom of the dish. Add enough heavy cream to cover the potatoes and season to taste with salt and pepper. Repeat twice more, ending with a layer of cream. Cover the dish with aluminum foil and place it in a *bain-marie*, or water bath. Bake for 1 hour. Remove the foil and finish baking until top is browned and potatoes are cooked through, about 10 minutes. Serve bubbling hot.

☙ *Chef's Truc* ❧

USING AGED IDAHO POTATOES: For best results, use firm, well-aged Idaho potatoes for this dish and never wash them once they're sliced. The aging distributes the starch evenly throughout the potato. True Idaho-grown Russets are best. Because the ingredients are few, pay careful attention to using the best potatoes.

SALADE DE HARICOTS VERTS
AUX AMANDES GRILLÉES AU SEL
SALAD OF PENCIL-THIN GREEN BEANS AND SALT-GRILLED ALMONDS

A t Le Bec-Fin we buy hand-picked haricots verts specially grown for us by a Bucks County organic farmer. He picks these pencil-thin green beans daily to meet our standards. These velvety, snappy beans tossed with little bits of roasted red pepper and grilled almonds are a true delicacy.

.... SERVICE FOR 4 ....

THE SALAD

1 cup blanched, sliced almonds

2 teaspoons salt

2 tablespoons unsalted butter

8 ounces fresh haricots verts

8 ounces large white mushrooms, cleaned

1 teaspoon lemon juice

1 red bell pepper

1 tablespoon extra-virgin olive oil

1 tablespoon walnut oil

1 tablespoon sherry vinegar

Salt and white pepper

1 tablespoon fresh chervil sprigs

Preparing the Almonds

Preheat the oven to 275°F. Wet the almonds and toss with the salt, then toss with the melted butter (The salt will stick to the wet almonds.) Spread the almonds on a baking sheet in a single layer and roast for 10 to 12 minutes, shaking the pan every 3 or 4 minutes. The almonds should be nutty-smelling and evenly golden brown, about 10 minutes. Take care as they burn easily. You will have more almonds than you need, so set aside the remainder for another use.

Preparing the Salad

Using a sharp paring knife, slice off the tips and ends of the beans. Soak the beans in a bowl of ice water for 1 hour. Bring a large pot of salted water to a boil. Drain the beans and cook until bright green and al dente. Refresh the beans under ice water to stop the cooking.

Cut three ⅛-inch slices off the top of each mushrooms. (You only want to use the white of the mushrooms; the brown "gills" on the under side can be used for another dish.) Julienne the slices of mushrooms and toss in the lemon juice to keep them white.

Roast the red pepper over an open flame, such as a grill, a gas burner, or a broiler, until the skin is blackened. Cool, then peel and seed. Cut into ⅛-inch dice and set aside.

Serving the Salad

Toss the beans, mushrooms, red pepper and 2 tablespoons of the almonds with the olive oil, walnut oil, and the vinegar. Season to taste and serve mounded in the center of 4 chilled salad plates. Sprinkle each plate with the chervil sprigs and serve.

❧ *Chef's Truc* ❧

BUYING HARICOTS VERTS: *Haricots verts* should be velvety on the outside and completely green. Their curling tips should be lively and pointed, not at all limp. For best appearance cut the beans on both ends into even lengths.

CHOU ROUGE AU GINGEMBRE

BRAISED RED CABBAGE WITH GINGEROOT

A wintertime tradition, this braised red cabbage dish has a note of ginger that sets it apart. This is one of the few vegetables that tastes good reheated. At the restaurant, I serve it as an accompaniment to salmon coated with a crispy polenta crust, which we prepare in a similar fashion to our Coquilles St. Jacques en Croûte de Polenta (see page 78).

.... SERVICE FOR 4 ....

Braising the Red Cabbage

Bring a large pot of salted water to a boil. Add the cabbage and cook until tender, about 5 minutes. Drain. Sauté the garlic and ginger in olive oil, and cook until barely starting to brown. Add the cabbage, thyme, and season with salt and pepper to taste. Cover and reduce the heat and braise for 10 minutes. Stir in the vinegar and simmer for 5 minutes more.

THE RED CABBAGE

1 small head red cabbage, quartered,
    cored, and finely shredded

1 clove garlic, peeled and finely chopped

1-inch length gingerroot,
    peeled and finely grated

2 tablespoons olive oil

2 teaspoons chopped fresh thyme

Salt and white pepper

1 tablespoon sherry vinegar

RISOTTO À LA MILANAISE À LA FEUILLE D'OR

RISOTTO MILANESE STYLE WITH GOLD LEAF

Is there anything better than a perfectly cooked risotto? I make a superb risotto—a dish I learned from Italian chefs. Be sure to buy the best quality imported Italian Arborio rice for this dish, or you'll never be able to achieve this proper texture. I cook my Risotto à la Milanaise in vegetable broth so as not to mask the saffron flavor. For a knockout presentation, gild the risotto with gold leaf. Although it adds no flavor because gold is inert, it ornaments the dish, echoing the golden saffron.

SERVICE FOR 4

THE RISOTTO MILANESE

2 cups Jus de Legumes (see page 213)

Pinch of saffron

2 shallots, finely chopped

2 tablespoons unsalted butter

½ cup Arborio rice

¼ cup dry white wine

½ cup fresh-shelled, blanched fava beans or peas (optional)

2 tablespoons freshly grated Parmigiano-Reggiano cheese

Salt and white pepper

Four 2-inch squares gold leaf (optional)

Cooking the Risotto Milanese

In a small pot (or using the microwave) heat the Jus de Legumes and saffron to scalding. Meanwhile, in a medium saucepan, cook the shallots in the butter until transparent, but not browned. Add the rice, stirring until it is shiny and translucent. Turn up the heat and add the wine. Cook over high heat until the wine evaporates. Turn the heat down so the rice just simmers.

Start adding the hot broth, one ladleful at a time. Keep simmering, stirring occasionally until the broth is absorbed, then add another ladleful. Continue until all the broth has been absorbed by the rice. Turn off the heat, stir in the fava beans and grated cheese. Season with salt and pepper to taste and let the rice sit a few minutes until the cheese melts. The risotto should consist of firm but cooked grains of rice suspended in a creamy liquid.

Divide the risotto between 4 heated appetizer-sized plates. If desired, decorate the top of each risotto portion with the gold leaf. Serve immediately.

Chef's Truc

MAKING RISOTTO AHEAD: Risotto is best made to order. However, in a restaurant setting, we pre-cook the risotto as follows. Cook the risotto with only two-thirds of the broth, removing it from the heat when the grains are still pearly and hard in the center. Spread the hot risotto out onto a large tray, making holes in the surface of the risotto to allow all the steam to escape. When somewhat cooled, chill the risotto on its tray in the refrigerator. When it's completely cold, transfer it to a covered container until ready to finish. When you want to serve the risotto, take about 1 cup per portion of the cold, cooked risotto and place it in a small pan. Separate the grains using a spoon. Measure ⅔ cup of the remaining broth per 1 cup portion of risotto. Bring the broth to a boil and stir in the risotto. Simmer 5 minutes or until the broth is absorbed. Then finish with cheese and season with salt and pepper. Serve immediately.

Risotto aux Truffes Blanches

Risotto with White Truffles

In winter, when the finest white truffles from Alba (the Savoy region of Northern Italy) are in season, I prepare this marrow-enriched risotto dish to show off these rare culinary gems. White truffles are always served raw to preserve their delicate flavor. At Le Bec-Fin we use a special truffle slicer to shave paper-thin slices over this risotto.

SERVICE FOR 4

THE RISOTTO WITH WHITE TRUFFLES

2 cups Fond Blanc de Volaille

    (see page 214)

2 shallots, peeled and finely chopped

1 tablespoon unsalted butter

1 tablespoon diced veal marrow,

    soaked but raw (see page 70)

½ cup Arborio rice

¼ cup dry white wine

2 tablespoons whipped heavy cream

2 tablespoons freshly grated

    Parmigiano-Reggiano cheese

Salt and white pepper

Fresh white truffle (for garnish)

Cooking the Risotto with White Truffles

In a small pot (or using the microwave) heat the chicken broth to scalding. Meanwhile, in a medium saucepan, cook the shallots in the butter until transparent, but not browned. Add the diced marrow and the rice, stirring until the rice is shiny and translucent. Turn up the heat and add the wine. Cook over high heat until the wine evaporates. Turn the heat down so the rice just simmers.

Start adding the hot broth, one ladleful at a time. Continue to cook, stirring occasionally until the broth is absorbed, then add another ladleful. Continue until all the broth has been absorbed by the rice. Turn off the heat, fold in the whipped heavy cream and the grated cheese. Season to taste and let the rice sit a few minutes until the cheese melts. The risotto should be consist of firm but cooked grains of rice suspended in a creamy liquid.

Divide the risotto among 4 heated appetizer-sized plates. Grate the fresh white truffle over each portion of risotto at the table.

RIZ BASMATIC AUX TRUFFES

BASMATI RICE PILAF WITH TRUFFLES

asmati rice is a fragrant long-grain rice from India. I've been serving it more frequently in my restaurant because I love its aroma. Here I accent its perfume with truffle peelings. Basmati rice is especially good served with delicate fish and poultry dishes. Because the rice is long-grain, it cooks into fluffy, separate grains. Don't overcook this rice. You must treat it with tender loving care.

SERVICE FOR 6

Preparing the Basmati Rice

In a medium saucepan cook the onion in the butter until translucent, then add the rice and stir until transparent. Bring the Fond Blanc de Volaille and water to a simmer in a small pan. Add the liquid and chopped truffle to the rice and bring to a boil. Cover and reduce the heat to very low and cook until al dente, but cooked through, about 10 minutes. Season with salt and pepper to taste.

Garnish the rice by stirring in the chopped truffles or the vegetable dice.

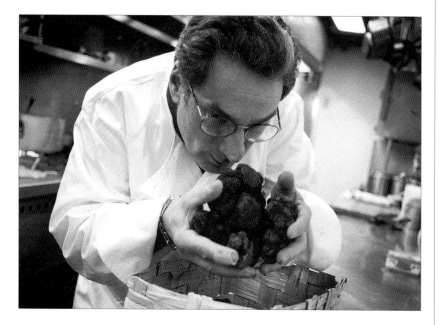

THE BASMATI RICE

2 tablespoons finely chopped onion

1 teaspoon unsalted butter

½ cup basmati rice

½ cup Fond Blanc de Volaille
    (see page 214)

½ cup water

1 teaspoon chopped black truffle

Salt and white pepper

THE GARNISHES

1 tablespoon chopped black truffles or

1 tablespoon each carrots and zucchini,
    cut into ⅛-inch dice and blanched

Mousse de Carottes

Carrot Mousse

owly carrots are transformed into a most elegant mousse here. At Le Bec-Fin we pipe this mousse through a pastry bag into decorative swirls on the plate. My customers love this dish, but most can't figure out the "secret" ingredient: it's the honey.

SERVICE FOR 4

THE CARROT MOUSSE

3 pounds large carrots,
    peeled and coarsely chopped

2½ cups heavy cream

4 tablespoons unsalted butter, softened

¼ cup honey

Salt and white pepper

Cooking the Carrots

Preheat the oven to 200°F.

Bring a large pot of salted water to a boil. Add the carrots and cook over medium heat until tender, about 5 minutes. Drain, then place on a baking pan and bake in the oven for 30 minutes to dry. Heat the heavy cream to scalding. Remove the carrots from the oven, then puree in a food processor until very smooth. With the machine running, add the scalded heavy cream, butter, and honey. Season with salt and pepper to taste.

Chef's Truc

PIPING CARROT MOUSSE: To pipe the mousse, you will first need to force the finished mouse through a food mill. This will ensure that no larger bits clog the pastry tip. Pipe through a medium-sized star tip. Be sure to wrap the bag in a towel while piping so you don't burn your hands.

ENDIVES BRAISÉES

BRAISED BELGIAN ENDIVE

My absolute favorite vegetable, refreshingly bitter and slightly sweet at the same time, braised Belgian endive melts in your mouth. I use an electric skillet to prepare this dish because I can control the temperature precisely.

SERVICE FOR 8

Braising the Endive

Pull off and discard any limp or bruised outer leaves. Using a sharp paring knife, cut out the cone-shaped bitter core from each endive. Sprinkle each endive with salt and pepper. In a large sauté pan over medium heat, melt the butter and oil, add the endive and cook until evenly browned on all sides. Cover the pan and reduce the heat to lowest possible setting. Cook the endive in their own juices for 1 hour, shaking the pan occasionally.

THE ENDIVE

8 heads Belgian endive

Salt and white pepper

4 tablespoons unsalted butter

1 tablespoon vegetable oil

Les Desserts

DESSERT COURSE

BLANCS EN NEIGE AUX FRAMBOISES DÉGUISÉES

FLOATING ISLANDS WITH CARAMELIZED RASPBERRIES

Poached meringue islands float in a sea of vanilla custard in this classic dessert. The surprise here are the raspberries in disguise—raspberries dipped in caramel. The raspberries stay whole, but the heat of the caramel almost liquefies them, so when you bite one you get an explosion of raspberry in your mouth. Caramelize the raspberries no more than one hour before you serve them.

························ SERVICE FOR 4 ························

THE CRÈME ANGLAISE

2 cups milk

1 vanilla bean, split lengthwise

6 egg yolks, at room temperature

6 tablespoons sugar

THE RASPBERRIES

1 ¼ cups sugar

1 tablespoon light corn syrup

½ cup water

24 extra-large red raspberries

THE FLOATING ISLANDS

8 egg whites

Pinch salt

¼ cup sugar

Preparing the Crème Anglaise

Place milk and vanilla bean in a small, heavy saucepan. Bring to a simmer over medium-low heat.

In a medium-sized bowl whisk together the egg yolks and sugar until light and thick. Gradually whisk half of the hot milk into the egg yolks until thoroughly blended. Return the mixture to the saucepan, and whisk to combine. Increase the heat to medium and cook, stirring constantly with a wooden spoon, until the sauce thickens slightly. (Do not let it boil.) When it's ready, the custard will reach 165 to 170°F. It should lightly coat the back of a wooden spoon and you should be able to see a clear trail when a finger is drawn across the surface. Strain the custard into a heatproof bowl. Scrape the seeds out of the vanilla bean and stir the seeds back into the custard. Cool the bowl over ice then cover with plastic and refrigerate until ready to use (see *Chef's Trucs* page 137). Can be prepared up to 1 day ahead.

Preparing the Raspberries

Lightly oil a baking sheet and set aside. In a small stainless steel or enamel, heavy-bottomed pot with a lid, combine the sugar, corn syrup, and ½ cup water. Stir together, then bring to a boil over medium heat. Boil until clear, then cover and continue to cook until the sugar becomes a light caramel color. Check often; it will burn easily once the sugar starts to turn brown. Keep the lid on so the steam will condense. This will help keep the caramel from crystallizing. (See *Chef's Truc* page 137.)

Have the 24 raspberries ready. Have a pan of cold water nearby. When the caramel is ready, carefully place the pot in the pan of cold water. Keep the pot in the water for about 30 seconds to stop further cooking, then remove from the water. Working quickly, place one raspberry at a time on the end of a long fork and dip into the caramel, swirling it around to get an even coat. Place the coated raspberries on the oiled baking sheet, without letting them touch each other. Let them set at room temperature.

Preparing the Floating Islands

Fill a wide sauté pan with water and bring to a boil. Reduce the heat so the water simmers. Meanwhile, beat the egg whites and the salt until soft peaks form. Add the sugar and beat until firm and shiny. Using 2 large soup spoons, shape the meringue into egg-shaped ovals. Place each oval into the simmering water. Poach until just firm, about 45 seconds each side. Using a skimmer, gently transfer the poached meringues to paper towels to drain.

Serving the Blancs en Neige

Pour ½ cup of the Crème Anglaise into each of 4 shallow-rimmed dessert plates. Arrange the poached meringues in a star pattern on the custard and place the raspberries around the meringues. Serve immediately.

❧ Chef's Trucs ❧

COOKING CARAMEL: If your caramel crystallizes, either start over or add more water to the pot, then reboil the mixture until it gets clear and brown. The pros dip their fingers in a bowl of ice water and use their icy-cold fingers to quickly wash off the sides of the pan. While this works, I don't recommend it for anyone not professionally trained, because the caramel is at about 350°F. and can easily burn you.

You'll get best results working with caramel on a day with low humidity. If the weather is hot and humid, the caramel coating won't harden properly on the berries.

• • •

PREVENTING A SKIN ON A SAUCE: To prevent a skin from forming on the sauce, let the sauce cool slightly, then dot the surface with butter. The butter will melt and spread out, forming a protective layer over the top. Another method is to first allow the sauce to cool slightly. Then, lay a piece of plastic wrap directly onto the surface of the sauce, gently pressing down so the plastic contacts the entire surface of the sauce.

• • •

COOKING CUSTARD SAUCES: This type of sauce, made with cream and thickened with cooked egg yolks, is actually a custard. The egg yolks must cook until they thicken, between 165°F and 170°F. Beyond that they will begin to curdle or separate. It's always important to "temper" a sauce like this. You must gradually heat the egg mixture by beating in a little hot liquid before combining it with the remaining broth. In this way, the yolks will heat and thicken gradually and smoothly hard, cooked with no lumps.

BÛCHE DE NOËL

CHRISTMAS LOG CAKE

This cake is a French Christmas classic. It's an edible representation of an ancient custom: burning a log in the hearth throughout Christmas Eve. French pâtissiers invented the cake about 125 years ago. The cake imitates a log complete with meringue mushrooms, chocolate trees, and sometimes even marzipan holly leaves. My version uses a Savoy cake brushed with kirsch-flavored syrup then filled and iced with a light chocolate-meringue buttercream. Because this recipe makes 2 cakes, you may wrap one and freeze it.

·········· SERVICE FOR 10 TO 12 (MAKES TWO 15-INCH JELLY ROLLS) ··········

THE MERINGUE MUSHROOMS

½ cup egg whites

Pinch of salt

½ cup sugar

¾ cup confectioners' sugar

2 ounces white chocolate,
    melted in double boiler

¼ cup Dutch process cocoa powder
    (for dusting)

THE SYRUP

½ cup sugar

½ cup water

¼ cup kirschwasser

THE CAKE

5 eggs, separated

9 tablespoons sugar

1 teaspoon vanilla extract

1¼ cups cake flour, sifted

Preparing the Meringue Mushrooms

Preheat the oven to 250°F. Line two baking sheets with parchment paper. Whip the egg whites with the salt on medium speed until they form soft peaks. Increase the speed to high, then slowly add the granulated sugar. Beat until firm and glossy. Remove from the mixer and gently fold in the confectioners' sugar.

On the first baking sheet, pipe cone shapes, which will become the stems. On the second sheet pipe rounds, which will become the caps. Bake 2 hours, then turn off the oven and allow the meringues to cool completely in the oven. (They should be very crisp.) Remove the caps and carve out a hole in each base to accommodate the stem. Dip the pointy end of the stems into the melted white chocolate. Attach the stems to the underside of the caps, placing the mushrooms back on a parchment-lined baking sheet to set.

Making the Syrup

Bring the sugar and water to a boil. When the syrup is clear, remove from the heat, then stir in kirschwasser. Cool the syrup to room temperature and set aside.

Making the Cake

Preheat the oven to 400°F. Prepare two parchment paper-lined jelly-roll pans. Sift the cake flour and set it aside. Using the whisk attachment, beat the egg yolks with 6 tablespoons of sugar until the mixture forms a light yellow ribbon. In a separate clean, dry bowl, whip the egg whites to a soft peak, then sprinkle in the remaining 3 tablespoons sugar and beat until firm and glossy.

Fold one-third of the whites into the yolk mixture, then stir in the vanilla. Fold in half the cake flour and one-third more of the whites. Finish batter by folding in the remaining cake flour and the remaining whites. Using a rubber spatula, divide the batter in two. Spread half the batter onto each jelly-roll pan, smoothing evenly with the spatula. Bake 8 to 10 minutes, or just until cake has set in the center and is golden brown on the edges.

Remove the cakes from the oven, then immediately pass the back of a metal spatula around the edges of the pans to release them. While still hot, invert the

THE BUTTERCREAM

½ pound bittersweet chocolate, chopped

1 cup egg whites

1 cup sugar

1½ pounds (6 sticks) unsalted butter,
    softened

cakes onto a parchment paper-lined baking tray. Let the cakes cool, then brush generously with the syrup and set aside.

Making the Chocolate Buttercream

Place the chocolate in a clean dry bowl, then slowly melt over steaming water. Remove the melted chocolate from the heat and let cool to room temperature.

Place the egg whites and the sugar in another clean, dry bowl and warm over the hot water while stirring constantly, until quite warm to the touch. (The sugar should melt and the liquid remain clear.) Transfer the warmed whites to a mixer bowl and beat on high speed until the mixture has cooled to room temperature. Reduce the speed and beat in the butter until completely incorporated. Increase the speed to high and beat until light and creamy. Reduce the speed to low, then pour in the chocolate and whip until completely incorporated.

Finishing the Cake

Spread a thin layer of the buttercream over each cake, then roll up tightly lengthwise (you should have a log-shaped roll). Spread the remaining buttercream on the outside of each bûche. Using a fork, make a rough barklike pattern to resemble a Yule log. From each cake, cut a 2-inch slice on the diagonal so that you end up with a wedge. Place on top of the cake to resemble a log. Refrigerate the cakes, but bring to room temperature before serving. Dust the tops of the meringue mushrooms with the cocoa and arrange around and on top of the logs.

Mousse au Chocolat Noir
Dark Chocolate Mousse

Mousse au Chocolat Blanc
White Chocolate Mousse

Back before Craig Claiborne and Julia Child revolutionized American thinking about French cuisine, American cooks still knew how to make at least one French dish: chocolate mousse. It's still delicious. My version comes from a recipe of my mother's. It's made without cream and flavored with espresso to make a black mousse. White chocolate isn't chocolate technically because the cocoa solids have been removed. However, we treat it like a rather finicky cousin of dark chocolate. Buy high-quality white chocolate made entirely with aromatic cocoa butter (the most expensive part of the chocolate) rather than any waxy vegetable fats.

SERVICE FOR 8

Preparing the Mousse Noir

Partially melt the chocolate, either in a dry bowl over steaming water or in the microwave. Add the butter and melt with the chocolate, stirring until smooth. Keep warm. Beat the egg yolks and the sugar until the mixture forms light yellow ribbons. Whip the egg whites to soft peaks only. (Don't whip any further or your mousse will be grainy.) Fold the egg yolk mixture and the espresso into the warm chocolate. Then gently fold in the egg whites. Pour immediately into individual serving dishes and refrigerate at least 2 hours or up to 24 hours.

Preparing the Mousse Blanc

In a chilled mixing bowl, and using a chilled beater, whip the cream to soft peaks and set aside in the refrigerator.

Meanwhile, bring the sugar and water to a boil. Cook to 250°F (firm-ball stage) on a candy thermometer.

When the sugar is just about ready, begin whipping the whites to soft peaks in a dry, clean bowl. Turn the mixer to medium speed and slowly pour in the sugar syrup. Beat on high speed for 1 minute, then on low speed until the meringue is warm, but not hot. Add the white chocolate and vanilla and continue beating for about 10 seconds. Ideally three-quarters of the white chocolate will melt into the meringue and one-quarter will remain in small grated pieces. Fold the white chocolate meringue into the cream. Pour into individual serving dishes and refrigerate 2 hours or up to 48 hours.

THE MOUSSE NOIR

9 ounces semisweet chocolate, chopped

7 ounces (14 tablespoons) unsalted butter

6 eggs, separated

¼ cup sugar

2 tablespoons strong, freshly brewed espresso

THE MOUSSE BLANC

2 cups heavy cream

2 teaspoons vanilla extract

1¼ cups sugar

¼ cup water

8 egg whites

10½ ounces white chocolate, grated

CRÈME BRÛLÉE

CUSTARD CREAM WITH A BURNT SUGAR TOPPING

Many restaurants make this pure and simple dessert that calls for only four ingredients. But, the simpler the dish, the more important the technique. Crème brûlée deserves to be served at its best. The custard should be barely set and at room temperature; the sugar topping thin and crackling hard. If you make the custard the day before, be sure to return it to room temperature before serving. Use plump, fragrant vanilla beans. In my opinion, you can't have too much real vanilla with its subtle whiff of the tropics.

.... SERVICE FOR 8 ....

THE CUSTARD

2 whole vanilla beans

1 quart (4 cups) heavy cream

1 cup sugar

7 egg yolks

Making the Custard

Preheat the oven to 325°F.

Using a small, sharp paring knife, split the vanilla beans lengthwise in two. Scald the cream with the split vanilla beans and ⅓ cup of the sugar. Whisk together the yolks and another ⅓ cup of the sugar. While whisking, pour the scalded cream over the yolk/sugar mixture. Keep whisking until combined. Remove the split vanilla beans. Scrape out the seeds into the custard mixture. Strain the custard through a fine sieve.

Ladle the custard into eight 4½ x ¾-inch shallow custard cups. Place the cups in a pan of hot water that comes halfway up the sides of the cups. Bake 30 to 40 minutes or until set. Cool to room temperature. When ready to serve, sprinkle the tops of the custards with a thin layer of the remaining ⅓ cup sugar. For best results use a salamander. Alternatively, preheat the broiler, then place the custards in a baking pan filled with crushed ice. Caramelize under the hot broiler, watching carefully so that the sugar bubbles and browns—but doesn't burn.

Chef's Trucs

CHOOSING CRÈME BRÛLÉE DISHES: You'll need 8 individual shallow custard dishes, about 4 inches in diameter and about ¾-inch deep. This will provide the right amount of surface to filling. If the cups are too deep, there won't be enough caramel for every bite.

. . .

USING A SALAMANDER: For best results, use an old-fashioned cast-iron salamander to burn the cream. Named after the legendary animal that resists fire, this simple iron (more elaborate ones are electric) will burn or brand the sugar without overcooking the underlying custard layer.

FONDANT AU CHOCOLAT

CHOCOLATE CREAM

My mother gave me this recipe many years ago. It's a wonderful, dense, rich chocolaty cream, almost a chocolate paté. Use best quality semisweet chocolate couverture. This is one place where the flavor of a good chocolate will really shine. Try serving it with a pistachio-flavored Crème Anglaise (see page 136) or a Raspberry Coulis (see page 156).

SERVICE FOR 8

Preparing the Fondant

Line the bottom and sides of a mini-sized (2-cup) loaf pan with parchment paper. Place the chopped chocolate in a clean, dry bowl. Melt over a pan of steaming hot water. Remove from the heat and stir in the espresso. Beat in the egg yolks, one at a time, until incorporated. Then, in a separate clean, dry bowl lightly beat the egg whites just until foamy. Beat into the chocolate mixture, then strain through a fine sieve.

Pour the fondant into the prepared pan, cover tightly and chill for 4 hours. Unmold by inverting onto a work surface. Remove and discard the parchment paper. Dust with cocoa. Serve in thin slices with Crème Anglaise or Raspberry Coulis if desired.

THE FONDANT

1 pound semisweet chocolate
   couverture, chopped

6 tablespoons strong, hot espresso

9 large eggs, separated

Dutch process cocoa powder (for dusting)

GÂTEAU AU CHOCOLAT LE BEC-FIN

SIGNATURE CHOCOLATE CAKE

*T*his is my most famous cake. Every year, thousands of customers just have to have a sliver of this cake. There are no secrets here, just careful handling of superb ingredients. We use a variety of chocolates, depending on the use. Valrhona has some wonderful blends or crus. Many pastry chefs depend on Callebaut from Belgium. Cocoa Barry is also good and reliable. El Rey, a newer company, uses only the finest Venezuelan cacao beans. Taste different brands of chocolate until you find one that suits your palate. My recipe makes three cakes, but they freeze perfectly.

······································ MAKES THREE 8-INCH CAKES ······································

THE CAKES

10 egg yolks

¾ cup sugar

1 tablespoon water

⅞ cup pastry flour

10 tablespoons Dutch process cocoa powder

2¼ teaspoons baking powder

10 egg whites

½ teaspoon cream of tartar

6 tablespoons sugar

THE SYRUP

2 cups sugar

2 cups water

1 cup dark rum

THE CHOCOLATE BUTTERCREAM

5 whole eggs

¾ cup sugar

¾ pound semisweet chocolate,
    melted and cooled

9 tablespoons (1 stick plus one tablespoon)
    unsalted butter, softened

Baking the Cakes

Preheat the oven to 350°F. Butter and flour three 8-inch cake pans. Combine the egg yolks, sugar and 1 tablespoon water and beat on high speed until light and pale yellow.

Sift together the flour, cocoa, and baking powder and set aside. In a clean, dry bowl, beat the egg whites and cream of tartar until soft peaks form. Sprinkle in the sugar, then beat again until stiff and glossy.

Fold half of the egg whites into the egg yolk mixture. Fold in the dry ingredients. Then fold in the remaining egg whites. Divide the batter among the 3 prepared pans. Bake for 30 minutes or until the cakes pull away from the sides of the pan. Let cool for 10 minutes then invert the cakes onto racks to cool completely.

Making the Syrup

In a small pan, bring the sugar and water to a boil. When clear, remove from the heat and stir in the rum. Let cool to room temperature.

Making the Chocolate Buttercream

Whisk eggs and sugar in the top of a double boiler set over simmering water until very warm. Then place in a mixer bowl and whip at high speed until cooled and light. Reduce the speed and pour in the melted chocolate. Increase the speed to medium and add the soft butter. Beat until light and fluffy. Set aside.

Making the Chocolate Fans

(I don't temper the chocolate here because I want it to be pliable.) Melt the chopped chocolate with the oil. Have ready 2 flat baking sheets. Warm them slightly in the oven, then remove. Using a flat metal spatula spread the chocolate thinly over the backs of both sheets, dividing it evenly. Refrigerate until set, about 15 minutes.

Remove one tray at a time from the refrigerator. Line another sheet with parchment paper. Allow the chocolate to warm slightly, about 3 minutes. Test the chocolate by scraping up one edge with a straight-edged metal spatula. The chocolate should form wavy fans. If the chocolate breaks instead of fanning, it's too cold. If it won't come off the tray, it's too warm.

THE CHOCOLATE FANS

6 ounces semisweet chocolate
couverture, finely chopped
1 tablespoon peanut oil
Confectioners' sugar (for dusting)
3 to 4 ounces shaved chocolate
(for garnish)

When ready, gently scrape up 3 to 4 inches of chocolate, using your free hand to lightly hold onto the edge of the fan. (This will encourage the other side to pleat freely.) As you finish each fan, place it on the parchment-lined baking sheet and refrigerate. (If storing, transfer to an air tight covered container and refrigerate for up to 2 days.)

Assembling the Cakes

Using a long serrated knife, split each cake into 3 layers each. For each cake, place 1 layer on a cardboard cake circle or a cake platter. Brush generously with the syrup. Spread a thin layer of chocolate buttercream over the cake, making sure to spread all the way to the edge. Top with a second cake layer, brush with syrup and spread with buttercream, repeating until all 3 layers are assembled. Coat the entire cake with buttercream and garnish the sides with shaved chocolate.

Arrange the fans with their pointed sides in to make a circle around the outside edge of the cake. Then, arrange more fans to make a second circle forming a point in the center of the cake. (The entire top of the cake should be covered with layered chocolate fans.) Dust the top of the cake with confectioners' sugar and serve.

❧ *Chef's Trucs* ❧

FREEZING FROSTED CAKES: This recipe makes 3 complete cakes. After the final buttercream coating, wrap extra cakes tightly and freeze them. To serve, remove from freezer 4 hours before serving and let sit at room temperature. Garnish with shaved chocolate and chocolate fans, if desired. The cakes keep well in the freezer for up to 1 month.

• • •

STORING CHOCOLATE FANS: If you keep the fans refrigerated too long, water will start to condense on them, destroying their sheen. When making the fans, don't get discouraged. It takes patience, practice, and dry weather.

Pain aux Noix et aux Fruits Secs

Walnut-Fruit Bread (to serve with Cheeses)

One of the hallmarks of a fine French restaurant is the care taken with the cheese course. Anyone who's eaten in France will remember the superb farm cheeses served there. We have more limits here on the types of cheeses we can serve, because we especially like the full-bodied flavor of French raw milk cheeses. But we always add slices of our homemade fruit bread to make a special memory.

.... MAKES TWO 9 x 5-INCH LOAVES ....

Making the Pain aux Fruits

Whisk together the bread flour, whole wheat flour, sugar, and salt. In a large mixing bowl, dissolve the yeast in the tepid water. When yeast is dissolved, add half of the flour mixture, then beat in the butter. Beat in the remaining flour mixture. Continue beating until the dough is shiny and elastic. Stir in the walnuts, pistachios, cherries, apricots, and figs. (Be careful not to overmix once the nuts and fruits have been added.) Divide the dough in half. Place half into each of two 9 x 5 x 3-inch loaf pans. Cover with a damp towel and allow to rise until the bread is doubled in size, about 1 hour (see *Chef's Truc* below).

Preheat the oven to 375°F.

Bake the loaves 10 minutes, then cover the bread with lightly oiled aluminum foil and bake for about 10 minutes. Remove the foil and bake 10 minutes more. Let cool for 30 minutes before slicing.

Chef's Trucs

RISING BREAD: If you have an electric oven, set the temperature as low as possible (about 100°F). Or preheat your oven for 3 minutes, then turn off the heat. Allow the bread to rise in the oven, covering first with a damp cloth.

• • •

TESTING BREAD: A good way to tell if your bread is fully cooked inside is to stick it at its thickest point with an instant-read meat thermometer. The temperature should read 190°F to 200°F.

• • •

DEFROSTING BREAD: This bread freezes well if wrapped tightly in plastic first. Remove from the freezer, discard the plastic, wrap in foil and bake at 300°F for about 20 minutes to reheat.

THE PAIN AUX FRUITS

4¼ cups bread flour

1 cup whole wheat flour

1 tablespoon sugar

2 teaspoons salt

1 tablespoon dry yeast

1½ cups tepid water

2 tablespoons unsalted butter,
melted and cooled

2 ounces walnuts, chopped

2 ounces pistachios, chopped

2 ounces dried cherries

2 ounces dried apricots, halved

7 ounces dried figs, stemmed and quartered

ANANAS AU GINGEMBRE

POACHED PINEAPPLE WITH GINGER

With our passion for ultra-rich desserts, we sometimes forget how good simple poached fruit can be. Often it's the only dessert I wish to eat after a meal. The important thing is to search out and fully ripen good quality in-season fruit. Don't bother if your fruit isn't good. It will just be a waste of time. Here I give my recipe for a personal favorite: poached pineapple perfumed with ginger.

.... SERVICE FOR 8 ....

THE PINEAPPLE WITH GINGER

1 large whole ripe pineapple, cored, and cut into 1-inch chunks

3 cups water

2 cups sugar

One 2-inch piece gingerroot, peeled and thinly sliced on the bias

Poaching the Pineapple with Ginger

Combine the pineapple, water, sugar, and ginger in a stainless steel or enamel heavy medium saucepan and bring to a boil. Reduce the heat to low and simmer for about 30 minutes, stirring once or twice. Remove from the heat and let the pineapple cool in its syrup. When cool, remove and discard the ginger slices. Serve the pineapple bathed in a little pool of its syrup.

✑ Chef's Truc ✑

CHOOSING PINEAPPLES: The best pineapples come from Hawaii by airplane. They are marked with a special tag that says "Jet-Fresh." These generally cost more because of the air freight. Because they're picked when ripe rather than when hard and green, they taste better. Recently we've been using the Costa Rican golden pineapples for this dish. They are sold fully ripe and their flesh is golden rather than creamy white.

PÊCHES AU SIROP DE CERISES

PEACHES IN SOUR CHERRY SYRUP

In early summer, when peaches and sour cherries are in season, try this rosy compote. In the fall, try poached pears with cinnamon stick, poached pineapple-scented quince with vanilla, or poached figs with Madeira.

SERVICE FOR 8

Poaching the Peaches in Sour Cherry Syrup

Combine the cherries with the water and bring to a boil. Reduce the heat and simmer 15 minutes, crushing the cherries as they cook with a potato masher. Remove from the heat and allow to cool in their syrup for 1 hour. Strain the clear syrup through a fine sieve. (Don't press the pulp; this will make your syrup cloudy.) Set aside the clear syrup. Stir in sugar and vanilla bean. (The sour cherry syrup can be made up to 1 week ahead.)

Bring a medium pot of water to a boil. Dip the peaches in boiling water for about 30 seconds, or until the skins loosen. (The riper the peach, the easier to peel.) Plunge the blanched peaches into a bowl of ice water then slip off their skins. Halve and pit the peaches.

Bring the reserved sour cherry syrup to a boil and add the peach halves. Return to a boil, then reduce the heat to low and simmer until soft and yielding when pricked with a skewer, about 10 minutes. Remove from the heat and let the peaches cool in their syrup. Serve the peaches bathed in a little pool of the cherry syrup.

Chef's Truc

USING FRESH SOUR CHERRIES: It's worthwhile to search out fresh sour cherries when they're in season in June. Their intense flavor will transfer to the peaches, combining the best of both worlds. Sweet cherries just won't have the same flavor. Make the syrup and freeze it for use when peaches are in season. Early in the peach season, you'll find clingstone peaches. The fruits are firm but have pits that are difficult to remove. Later in the season you'll find "freestone" peaches. When these peaches are fully ripened, you can easily twist out the pit without destroying the fruit.

THE PEACHES IN SOUR CHERRY SYRUP

2 pounds fresh sour cherries,
    stemmed and rinsed

2 quarts (8 cups) water

3 cups sugar

1 vanilla bean, cut in half lengthwise

6 ripe but firm freestone peaches

MILLE-FEUILLE DE FRAMBOISES

LAYERED COOKIE CRISPS WITH WHIPPED CREAM AND RASPBERRIES

ille-Feuille means a thousand leaves. It usually refers to puff pastry with its paper-thin layers of flaky dough. Here it is a simple but delicious dessert made from tuiles dentelles, or thin, crispy cookies filled with Chantilly Cream and fresh raspberries. Serve it with a Raspberry Coulis (see page 156), if you like.

SERVICE FOR 8

THE COOKIES

7 tablespoons unsalted butter, softened

1½ cups confectioners' sugar

7 tablespoons orange juice

⅓ cup all-purpose flour

2 cups crushed, sliced blanched almonds

Grated zest of 1 orange

THE CRÈME CHANTILLY
AND RASPBERRIES

2 cups heavy cream

¼ cup confectioners' sugar

2 teaspoons vanilla extract

*Three ½-pint containers
large firm raspberries*

Baking the Cookies

Preheat the oven to 400°F. Have ready at least 2 nonstick baking pans. Using a wooden spoon, combine the butter, confectioners' sugar, and orange juice. Stir in the flour, almonds, and orange zest. Drop the batter by teaspoons onto the pans, leaving a 1-inch border around each cookie. Bake for 10 minutes, or until evenly and lightly browned. Cool slightly then remove from pan. Cool to room temperature on a flat surface. Store in an air-tight container.

Whipping the Crème Chantilly

Put the cream in a chilled bowl and whip to a soft peak. Sprinkle in the confectioners' sugar and vanilla and beat again to stiff peaks. Place the cream in a pastry bag fitted with a medium-sized star tip.

Assembling the Mille-Feuilles

For each guest you will need 3 cookies. Arrange a cookie on each of 8 chilled dessert plates. Pipe a layer of Crème Chantilly onto each cookie, then sprinkle generously with raspberries. Top with another cookie and layer with Crème Chantilly and raspberries. Finish each serving by topping with a cookie, a rosette of Crème Chantilly, and a raspberry, then refrigerate and serve within the hour.

Chef's Truc

USING CITRUS ZEST: The zest, or outer colored skin of a citrus fruit contains all the volatile, aromatic oils of the fruit enclosed in tiny bubbles. The underlying white pith is bitter and undesirable for cooking. If you don't have a special zester, use a sharp potato peeler. You will then need to cut the long strips into fine shreds.

NOUGAT GLACÉ

FROZEN NOUGAT WITH PISTACHIOS, CANDIED ORANGE, AND BRANDIED CHERRIES

*N*ougat is a sweetmeat made with beaten egg white, nuts, and sugar or honey. The origins of nougat go back to Roman times, but the modern type came from Marseilles in the sixteenth century. It is one of the traditional Provençal Thirteen Desserts served at Christmas. My version is a frozen confection, called a parfait, that includes luxurious additions like pistachios and brandied cherries.

················· MAKES ONE 9 x 5 x 3-INCH LOAF ·················

THE GARNISH

¼ pound whole blanched almonds

¼ pound unsalted shelled pistachios

¼ pound Candied Orange Peel
     (see page 160, or purchase)

¼ pound brandied cherries, chopped
     (purchased)

THE PARFAIT

1 cup sugar

½ cup water

1 vanilla bean, split lengthwise

8 egg yolks

1 quart (4 cups) heavy cream

Preparing the Garnish

Preheat the oven to 350°F. Spread the nuts in a single layer in separate baking pans. Toast the nuts, shaking once or twice, until they just begin to color, about 6 minutes for the pistachios, 8 to 10 minutes for the almonds. Cool both nuts to room temperature, then chop. Toss the almonds, pistachios, orange peel and cherries together. Spread out on a parchment-lined baking pan and freeze for later. Line a 9 x 5 x 3-inch loaf pan with parchment paper.

Making the Parfait

In a small heavy-bottomed saucepan, stir together the sugar and water. Brush down the sides of the pan with a pastry brush dipped in water to wash away any sugar crystals. Cover, then heat at medium until the sugar syrup comes to a boil. Take off the cover and increase the heat. Cook until the syrup reaches 250°F (firm-ball stage) on a candy thermometer.

Scrape out the seed pulp from the vanilla bean and set aside. Place the egg yolks and vanilla bean seeds in a mixer with a whisk attachment. Beat the yolks at medium speed until light and fluffy. When the syrup reaches 250°F, with the mixer running, carefully and slowly pour the cooked sugar into the egg mixture. Increase the speed to high and beat until thick and cooled to room temperature.

Whip the heavy cream until soft peaks form. Fold into the egg mixture. Using a rubber spatula, fold in the frozen garnishes. Mold in the prepared loaf pan and freeze until firm, about 4 hours.

To remove the parfait from the mold, sharply rap the outsides of the pan against the counter and invert onto a serving tray. Slice with a wet, serrated knife.

❧ Chef's Trucs ❧

TESTING FOR FIRM-BALL STAGE: If not using a candy thermometer, you can also test sugar syrup for firm ball stage by dropping a teaspoonful of hot syrup into a small bowl of ice water. The sugar should form a ball that is firm and holds its shape. It should not caramelize.

• • •

TOASTING PISTACHIOS: I like to toast the pistachios to heighten their flavor, but pay extra attention while cooking them. They should be only lightly tinted with brown. You don't want to lose the beautiful bright green color. If you buy shelled pistachios in a Middle Eastern market, you will likely get a variety which is extra-green and firmer than domestic pistachios grown in California.

Mignardises "Le Bec-Fin"

Assorted Delicacies (Cookies, Chocolate Truffles)

Mignardises, friandises, and petits fours all refer to the tiny, delicate confections served at the end of the meal or at receptions. They provide the last taste memory of a meal at Le Bec-Fin. Our chef pâtissier, Robert Bennett, prides himself on the variety and delicacy of his mignardises. Here are the recipes for just a few of most requested specialités maison, including my grandmother's Truffes au Chocolate.

Cigarettes
Thin and Crispy Rolled Cookies
MAKES 3 TO 4 DOZEN

THE CIGARETTE COOKIES

½ cup sugar

½ cup pastry flour (¼ cup all-purpose,
  ¼ cup cake flour)

¼ pound (1 stick) unsalted butter,
  very soft but not melted

2 egg whites (¼ cup)

1 tablespoon water

1 teaspoon vanilla extract

Preparing the Cigarette Cookies

Preheat the oven to 400°F. Have ready a wooden dowel the diameter of a broom handle. Lightly butter a baking sheet. Sift together the sugar and pastry flour. Using a wooden spoon, work in the butter until well-combined. Beat in the egg whites, water, and vanilla just until smooth. Place teaspoonfuls of the batter, 4 inches apart, on the prepared baking sheet. Bake until lightly browned around the edges, about 6 to 8 minutes. While still warm, roll each cookie around the dowel to form "cigarettes." Cool to room temperature before storing in an airtight container.

Petits Fours aux Noisettes
Tiny Square Hazelnut Cookies
MAKES 12 DOZEN

THE NOISETTE COOKIES

6 ounces skinned hazelnuts,
  coarsely chopped

2 cups bread flour

7 ounces (14 tablespoons) unsalted butter

½ cup confectioners' sugar

2 tablespoons brown sugar

½ teaspoon vanilla

¼ teaspoon salt

Confectioners' sugar (for dusting)

Preparing the Noisette Cookies

Prepare one 10 x 15-inch jelly-roll pan and two baking sheets with parchment paper. Combine the flour and nuts in a food processor, and process to a fine powder.

Place the butter, confectioners' sugar, and brown sugar in a mixer. Beat with the flat paddle until well combined. Add the vanilla and salt and beat for 1 minute. Remove the bowl from the mixer and stir in the flour-nut mixture, using a wooden spoon.

Press the batter firmly and evenly into the prepared jelly-roll pan. Freeze until firm, about 30 minutes. Preheat the oven to 350°F. Turn out onto a cutting board. Using a heavy knife, cut the dough into even 1-inch squares. Arrange squares 1 inch apart on the prepared baking sheets and bake 20 minutes or until well browned. Cool to room temperature then coat with confectioners' sugar. Store in an airtight container.

MADELEINES

SHELL-SHAPED SPONGE CAKES

MAKES 2 DOZEN MINIATURE (OR 1 DOZEN REGULAR) MADELEINES

Making the Madeleines

Preheat the oven to 400°. Using a pastry brush, generously coat the Madeleine pans with softened butter. Combine the confectioners' sugar, almonds, and flour in a food processor and process to a fine powder. Add the egg whites, melted butter, honey, and orange zest and process again 1 minute to combine. Pour batter into the molds, filling each three-quarters full. Bake until golden and, ideally, there is a pronounced, split bulge in the middle of each cookie, about 7 minutes. These cookies don't keep well, so bake and serve the same day.

TRUFFES AU CHOCOLAT

CHOCOLATE TRUFFLES

MAKES ABOUT 4 DOZEN TRUFFLES

Making the Chocolate Truffles

Chop the chocolate into small bits. In a medium stainless steel or enamel pot, scald 1 cup of the heavy cream. Remove from the heat and stir in the chopped chocolate until completely melted. Transfer to a mixer bowl and let cool to room temperature. Using the paddle attachment, beat the chocolate cream on medium-high speed, while slowly pouring in the remaining chilled cream until light and fluffy. Refrigerate until set. Using a melon baller, scoop 48 small, round balls from the chocolate mixture. Then, using your hands, roll in cocoa. Refrigerate and serve within 3 days.

TUILES

ROOF-TILE SHAPED WAFER COOKIES

MAKES ABOUT 6 DOZEN COOKIES

Making the Tuiles

Preheat the oven to 400°. Prepare several baking sheets by lining with parchment paper or use nonstick baking pans. Lightly beat the egg whites and salt until foamy. Sift together the sugar and flour. Stir the egg whites into the sugar-flour mixture, using a wooden spoon. Stir in the melted butter, then stir in the almonds. Let the batter rest at room temperature for 20 minutes.

Using a fork dipped in water, spread 1 tablespoon of the batter into a 5-inch circle, leaving a 1-inch border around each cookie. Bake until evenly golden brown, 6 to 8 minutes. Remove from oven and cool slightly. While still warm, drape each cookie over a rolling pin to make a curved shape. Cool to room temperature, then store in an airtight container for up to 4 days. (For best results, don't make these on a humid day, as they will quickly lose their crispness.)

THE MADELEINE BATTER

Softened butter (for pans)

¾ cup confectioners' sugar

½ cup sliced, blanched almonds

⅓ cup all-purpose flour

3 egg whites (6 tablespoons)

7 tablespoons unsalted butter,
*   melted and cooled*

1 teaspoon honey

1 teaspoon grated orange zest

THE CHOCOLATE TRUFFLES

1¾ pounds semisweet chocolate

2 cups cold heavy cream

Dutch process cocoa powder (for dusting)

THE TUILES

6 egg whites (¾ cup) at room temperature

¼ teaspoon salt

1½ cups sugar

¾ cup all-purpose flour

¼ pound (1 stick) unsalted butter,
*   melted and cooled*

¼ pound sliced almonds

SOUFFLÉ GLACÉ GRAND MARNIER

FROZEN GRAND MARNIER SOUFFLÉ

Here is one of my all-time great desserts. I don't see how it can be improved, so I make it the same today as I did twenty-five years ago when I first opened my restaurant. You can also make individual frozen soufflés, which are a little more time-consuming, but work well for a dinner party. I like to serve this soufflé with a Raspberry Coulis or fresh raspberries.

SERVICE FOR 6 TO 8

THE SOUFFLÉ

Vegetable oil (for oiling dish)

1 cup sugar

½ cup water

8 egg yolks

5 tablespoons Grand Marnier

3 cups heavy cream

2 tablespoons Dutch process cocoa powder

Making the Soufflé

Wrap a 1-quart soufflé dish in aluminum foil to give it a 2-inch-high collar, then lightly oil the inside of the collar and the dish.

Combine the sugar and water in a small heavy-bottomed pot with a lid. Bring to a boil, stirring until the sugar is dissolved. Cover and continue to boil until the mixture reaches 250°F (firm-ball stage) on a candy thermometer.

Meanwhile, place the egg yolks in the bowl of a mixer. Using a wire whisk, beat the yolks lightly by hand just enough to liquefy them. Slowly pour the hot syrup into egg yolks while continuing to whisk vigorously by hand. (This method keeps the syrup off the sides of the mixing bowl.) When the syrup is incorporated, place the bowl on the mixer and beat at medium speed with the whisk attachment until cool and very thick, about 15 minutes. Stir in the Grand Marnier.

Beat the cream in a chilled bowl until soft peaks form. Fold the whipped cream into the egg yolk mixture. Pour into the prepared dish. For best appearance, the soufflé should come at least 1 inch above the rim. Freeze for at least 4 hours or up to 8 hours.

Just before serving, dust the surface with cocoa. Peel off the foil collar to give the effect of a soufflé and serve immediately.

Chef's Truc

MAKING RASPBERRY COULIS: To make a Raspberry Coulis from fresh raspberries, first make a simple syrup. Combine ¼ cup water with ¼ cup sugar and bring to a boil. Cool to room temperature. In the blender, puree 2 pints of raspberries along with the cooled simple syrup. Strain, first through a food mill, then strain again through a fine sieve to remove all the seeds. Or, defrost 1 container of frozen, sweetened raspberries, then blend and strain as above.

GÂTEAU ST. NIZIER

FLOURLESS CHOCOLATE CAKE

*M*y mother gave me the recipe for this simple French-style chocolate cake. It is named after her small hometown outside of Lyon. It is a cake for chocolate purists—no glaze, no filling, just rich, intense chocolate cake.

.... MAKES THREE 8-INCH CAKES ....

THE CAKE

10 ounces semisweet chocolate

10 ounces (2½ sticks) unsalted butter

9 eggs, separated

1½ cups sugar (divided in half)

3 tablespoons cornstarch

Dutch process cocoa powder (for dusting)

Making the Cake

Melt the chocolate and 10 ounces of the butter together in a dry bowl over hot water. Cool to room temperature.

Preheat the oven to 300°F. Butter three 8-inch cake pans. Then sprinkle with sugar to coat, shaking out any excess.

Beat the egg yolks with ¾ cup of the sugar until light and fluffy. Beat in the cornstarch and the cooled chocolate mixture.

In a separate dry, clean bowl, whip the egg whites until soft peaks form. Add the remaining sugar and beat until glossy but not stiff.

Fold one-quarter of the egg whites into the chocolate mixture. Fold the lightened chocolate mixture back into the remaining egg whites. Divide the batter among the 3 prepared pans. Bake for 1 hour or until set in the middle. Cool for 10 minutes. Invert 1 cake onto a serving platter, dust the top with cocoa and serve. Wrap the other cakes and freeze for up to 1 month.

ROULADE DE POTIRON

ROLLED PUMPKIN SPICE CAKE WITH CRANBERRY AND CHESTNUT FILLINGS

In creating this cake, I was inspired by American holiday traditions. The result: I've combined three American favorites (pumpkin, cranberry, and chestnuts) in one cake. The flavors are American; the techniques are French. It's a wonderful dessert for a holiday party and can be made a day ahead of time.

············· MAKES TWO 15-INCH JELLY ROLLS ·············

Preparing the Brandy Syrup

Bring the sugar and water to a boil. When the liquid is clear, remove it from the heat and stir in the brandy. Set aside.

Making the Cranberry Jam

Bring the sugar and water to a boil. Add cranberries, reduce the heat and simmer for 15 minutes, stirring occasionally. Cool slightly, then pass through a fine sieve and set aside to cool completely.

Making the Chestnut Cream

Combine heavy cream, Crème Fraîche, canned chestnut cream, and vanilla in the bowl of a mixer. Using the whisk attachment, beat until light and firm. Refrigerate until ready to use.

Preparing the Pumpkin Spice Cake

Preheat oven to 400°F. Line two 10 x 15-inch jelly-roll pans with parchment paper. Whisk together the flour, baking soda, spices, and salt.

Place the eggs and sugar in the bowl of a mixer. Beat with the whisk attachment on high speed until the mixture is pale yellow and fluffy. Reduce the mixer to low speed, and add the pumpkin. Fold in the dry ingredients.

Using a rubber spatula, divide the cake batter between the prepared jelly-roll pans. Bake 8 to 10 minutes or until the cake tests done in the middle. Remove the cakes immediately from the oven and invert onto parchment paper. Let cool. Brush each cake with the Brandy Syrup.

Assembling the Cakes

Spread half the Cranberry Jam evenly over each cake, leaving a 1-inch border on one long end of each layer. Top each cake layer with half the chestnut cream, leaving a 1-inch border on the same long end. Starting at the filled ends and rolling lengthwise, roll both cakes tightly, using the plain border for the seam. Place the cakes seam side down and refrigerate for at least an hour or overnight. Dust well with confectioners' sugar. Slice on the diagonal using a serrated knife, and serve.

THE BRANDY SYRUP

2 cups sugar

2 cups water

1 cup brandy

THE CRANBERRY JAM

1 cup sugar

¾ cup water

One 12-ounce bag cranberries

THE CHESTNUT CREAM

1½ cups heavy cream

¾ cup Crème Fraîche (see page 217)

¾ cup (6 ounces) canned chestnut cream

1 teaspoon vanilla

THE PUMPKIN SPICE CAKE

1 cup sifted cake flour

1 teaspoon baking soda

¾ teaspoon ground cinnamon

¼ teaspoon ground cloves

½ teaspoon ground ginger

¼ teaspoon ground nutmeg

¼ teaspoon salt

3 eggs

1 cup sugar

¾ cup canned pumpkin

Confectioners' sugar (for dusting)

PEAUX D'ORANGES GLACÉES

CANDIED ORANGE RIND

I find the combination of sweetened chewy, slightly bitter orange rind most refreshing to the palate. If you like, dip the ends of the candied rind into tempered chocolate for a classic accompaniment to a glass of after-dinner cognac or liqueur. You can use the same recipe and method to make a Candied Grapefruit Rind, a special favorite of mine.

.... MAKES ABOUT 12 OUNCES ....

THE ORANGE RIND

8 large, brightly colored navel oranges, well scrubbed

2 teaspoons salt

1 quart (4 cups) water

5 cups sugar

5 ounces light corn syrup

4 ounces semisweet chocolate couverture (optional), tempered (see Chef's Truc below)

Preparing the Orange Rinds

Score the orange skin into quarters, starting and ending at the stem. Repeat for each orange. Then peel. (Set aside the orange flesh for another use, such as the Salade d'Oranges au Cointreau on page 161) Cut each peel section into long, thin strips. Bring two separate one-gallon pots of water to a boil. Add the salt to the first pot and blanch the strips, cooking for 1 minute. Drain and refresh in ice water. Blanch the strips for 1 minute in the second pot of unsalted water, then drain and refresh again in ice water.

In another pot, bring the 1 quart of water and sugar to a boil. Add the blanched orange strips and simmer for 2 hours. Add the corn syrup, reduce the heat to very low and simmer for 15 minutes longer. Remove from the heat and allow the orange strips to cool in their cooking syrup overnight.

The next day, drain the strips. Arrange them on cooling racks set over baking pans to dry. Let dry for 24 hours. Dip both ends in semisweet chocolate *couverture*, if desired, or serve as is.

❧ *Chef's Truc* ❧

TEMPERING CHOCOLATE: When you temper chocolate, you melt and cool it in such a way as to encourage it to crystallize properly, making it hard and shiny. You must use a top quality chocolate *couverture*. This chocolate has a high percentage of pure cocoa fat crystals needed for tempering. Chop 6 ounces *couverture* into small bits. Place 4 ounces of the chopped chocolate in a small glass or plastic bowl into the microwave, heating for 30 seconds at a time, until completely liquid but not hot. Then add the remaining chocolate bits, stirring until smooth. The chocolate bits should be completely melted. Allow the chocolate to cool enough so that it starts to harden around the edges, then gently heat only enough to remelt. Use immediately for dipping.

Salade d'Oranges au Cointreau

Orange Salad with Cointreau Liqueur

implest is often best. When navel oranges are in season in the winter, use them. Even better and certainly spectacular looking are blood oranges, which you can prepare the same way. The oranges are cut à vif (to the quick), removing all the bitter white pith.

.... SERVICE FOR 4 ....

Preparing the Salad

Using a sharp knife, slice ½-inch off the tops and bottoms of the oranges. Place each orange on its flat bottom. Using a small, sharp paring knife, cut vertical ½-inch-wide strips through the orange skin. Peel off the orange outer skin, the white inner pith and the membrane covering the orange flesh itself. You should now have a bare orange with all the flesh visible. Trim away any remaining bits of pith. Cut ¼-inch thick slices crosswise through the oranges. Discard the top and bottom slices, which will be somewhat stringy. Combine the sugar and Cointreau in a medium bowl. Add the orange slices and gently toss to coat. Chill for 3 hours, then arrange the marinated slices on 4 individual chilled dessert plates and serve.

THE ORANGES

4 large, brightly colored navel oranges

3 tablespoons sugar

2 tablespoons Cointreau

Soupe de Fruits, Sauce Banane et Citron Vert

Summer Fruit Soup with Banana Lime Sauce

*M*y summer fruit soup is as lovely to look at as it is good to eat. This light dessert is served with a clear sauce that has a surprisingly intense flavor of banana and a bit of lime zest. I adapted this sauce from the Troisgros brothers. Any seasonal ripe fruits are appropriate here. Use your own favorites.

.... SERVICE FOR 4 ....

THE BANANA LIME SAUCE

2 cups water

1¼ cups sugar

Grated zest of 3 limes

Juice of 2 limes

2 large ripe but firm bananas,
    sliced into 1-inch rounds

1 tablespoon unflavored gelatin

¼ cup cold water

Grated zest of 1 lime for garnish

THE SUMMER FRUIT SOUP

2 kiwi fruit, peeled

½ pint large red raspberries

1 ripe but firm banana, peeled and sliced
    at the last minute

2 red, green, or black plums, thinly sliced

1 pint small red, ripe strawberries

½ pint large, firm blueberries,
    washed and drained, stems removed

½ pint fresh red currants (optional),
    with stems, rinsed

Making the Banana Lime Sauce

Bring the water and sugar to a boil in a small pot. Add the lime zest and juice and the bananas. Remove from the heat and cover. Cool to room temperature. Strain the sauce through a fine sieve. (Don't force the liquid through or your sauce will be cloudy.) Discard the bananas and zest. In a small bowl, soften the gelatin in the water, then heat over a pot of simmering water until clear. Set aside.

Reheat the banana sauce and stir in the gelatin. Strain again. Place the sauce in a bath of crushed ice and water. When cooled and thickened to a clear, thin jelly, stir in the remaining zest of 1 lime and set aside.

Making the Summer Fruit Soup

Cut ½-inch off the top and bottom of the kiwis and discard. Cut the kiwi into ¼-inch-thick rounds. Pick through the raspberries and discard any that aren't firm and whole.

Assembling the Fruit Soup

Divide the Banana Lime Sauce among 4 chilled shallow soup plates. Arrange the remaining fruits decoratively on top of the sauce. Serve immediately.

❧ *Chef's Truc* ☙

USING SHEET GELATIN: At Le Bec-Fin, we use sheet gelatin from Europe. Though more expensive, it is much easier to use than powdered gelatin. All you have to do is soak the sheet in cold water, then add it to hot liquid and it dissolves completely. Powdered gelatin must first be "bloomed" or soaked in liquid until the grains swell. After that it must be melted over very low heat until it is completely clear. A good way to do this is in the microwave. Don't boil the gelatin as this will diminish its strength; just melt it. Figure on substituting approximately 1 sheet of gelatin for 1 teaspoon granulated gelatin.

Soupe de Fruits, Sauce aux Poires

Winter Fruit Soup with Pear Sauce

In winter I make a different version of my fruit soup, appropriate to the season. I serve it with my very favorite sauce made from fragrant pear Eau de Vie. My philosophy is to keep your menu in tune with the seasons and keep it simple, Here, in my winter fruit soup, I combine tropical fruits with winter fruits.

.... SERVICE FOR 4 ....

THE PEAR SAUCE

One 15-ounce can poached pears
    with light syrup

2 tablespoons Eau de Vie Poire William

THE WINTER FRUIT SOUP

2 blood or navel oranges

2 kiwi fruit, peeled

2 tart, firm apples, peeled

2 ripe but firm bananas

1 ripe but firm mango, peeled (see page 48)
    and cut into cubes

2 very ripe persimmons (the flesh should be
    clear orange rather than opaque),
    cut into wedges and seeded

1 cup Ananas au Gingembre
    (see page 148)

Making the Pear Sauce

Place the pears and their syrup in a blender. Blend until smooth, then stir in the Eau de Vie. Strain through a fine sieve and refrigerate until needed.

Assembling the Winter Fruit Soup

Cut the blood oranges according to the instructions in the recipe for Salade d'Oranges (see page 161), but don't cut into slices. Cut in between the membrane and remove an orange section at a time.

Cut ½-inch off the top and bottom of the kiwis and discard. Cut the kiwi into ¼-inch-thick slices.

Just before serving the fruit soup, use a Japanese Benriner cutter or a French mandoline to cut the apple into thin julienne strips. Cut the bananas into ¼-inch-thick slices. Ladle the pear sauce into the bottom of each of 4 large shallow soup plates. Place a mound of apple julienne in the center of each plate, then surround with the remaining fruits and serve.

SORBET PAMPLEMOUSSE ET VERMOUTH

GRAPEFRUIT AND VERMOUTH SORBET

SORBET CASSIS

BLACK CURRANT SORBET

Sorbets have been around a long time. They are the most refreshing of desserts, full of ripe fruit aroma and flavor. Originally from Persia, sorbets started out as a combination of fruit, honey, and snow. At formal dinners we sometimes serve a sorbet containing alcohol, such as this grapefruit and vermouth sorbet, between the main courses to refresh the palate. As a dessert, a sorbet accompanied, perhaps, with several of our mignardises (see pages 154–155) is a beautiful thing to serve. Each fruit calls for a different amount of sugar, depending on its ripeness and percentage of solids. For example, a blood orange sorbet will require much more sugar syrup than a plum or peach sorbet. Home electric ice cream machines make it easy to serve sorbet. Try experimenting with your own versions.

.... SERVICE FOR 6 ....

Making the Grapefruit and Vermouth Sorbet

Stir together juice, sugar, and vermouth, until the sugar is completely dissolved. Freeze in your ice cream maker according to the manufacturer's instructions.

Making the Cassis Sorbet

Combine the black currant puree, corn syrup, and water. Strain, then freeze in an ice cream maker according to the manufacturer's instructions.

❧ *Chef's Truc* ❧

BUYING BLACK CURRANTS (CASSIS): Black currants are available in jars packed in syrup, imported from Poland. At Le Bec-Fin, we are lucky enough to be able to buy pure frozen black currant puree from France. If you can't find black currants, substitute blackberries for a similar result.

THE GRAPEFRUIT VERMOUTH SORBET

1 quart (4 cups) freshly squeezed grapefruit
    juice (Star Ruby or Marsh Ruby
    varieties are exceptional for sorbet)

1 cup sugar

1 cup dry white vermouth
    (such as Nouilly Prat)

THE CASSIS SORBET

2 cups black currant puree (see Chef's Truc)

½ cup light corn syrup

½ cup water

GÂTEAU DE FROMAGE FRAIS À LA CRÈME AIGRE

SOUR CREAM CHEESECAKE

My version of this American favorite is ultra-creamy and light. In the French style, we make a smaller cake that can be cut into thin slivers for a taste at the end of the meal. We serve our cheesecake atop a thin layer of Savoy sponge cake and decorate the outside with crystallized almonds.

MAKES TWO 8-INCH CAKES

THE SAVOY CAKE

5 eggs, separated

9 tablespoons sugar

1 teaspoon vanilla

1¼ cups cake flour, sifted

THE CRYSTALLIZED ALMONDS

1 cup sugar

1 cup water

2 cups sliced blanched almonds

THE CHEESECAKE FILLING

1 pound (16 ounces) cream cheese,
    at room temperature

1 cup sugar

1 tablespoon cornstarch

3 eggs

3 tablespoons freshly squeezed lemon juice

½ teaspoon vanilla

¼ teaspoon salt

3 cups sour cream

THE SOUR CREAM TOPPING

1 pint (2 cups) sour cream

2 tablespoons sugar

1 teaspoon vanilla

Baking the Savoy Cake

Preheat the oven to 350°F. Coat two 8-inch round cake pans with nonstick spray.

Using the wire whisk, beat the egg yolks with 6 tablespoons of the sugar until they become pale yellow and fluffy.

In a separate clean, dry bowl, beat the egg whites until soft peaks form. Sprinkle in the remaining 3 tablespoons sugar and beat until firm and glossy.

Fold one-third of the whites into the yolk mixture, then stir in the vanilla. Fold in half of the cake flour and one-third more of the egg whites. Fold in the remaining cake flour and the remaining egg whites. Divide the batter between the two pans. Bake for 20 minutes or until lightly browned. Let cool for 10 minutes, then remove and cool completely. Using a long serrated knife, slice off a ½-inch-thick layer from one of the cakes for the cheesecake base. (Reserve the remaining cake for another use—it will freeze perfectly.)

Preparing the Almonds

Preheat the oven to 350°F. Bring the sugar and water to a boil until the syrup is clear. Remove from heat. Toss the almonds in about half the sugar syrup, or enough to thoroughly coat and moisten the almonds. Spread the nuts on a baking sheet and bake, stirring once or twice, for about 15 minutes. Bake until the almonds are evenly browned and the sugar has melted and crystallized. Let cool, then coarsely chop by hand. Set aside.

Preparing the Cheesecake Filling

Preheat the oven to 350°F. Place the cream cheese in the bowl of a mixer. Beat, using the paddle attachment, until smooth, scraping down the sides of the bowl once or twice. Add the sugar and cornstarch and beat again until smooth, scraping down the sides. Beat in the eggs, one at a time. Beat in the lemon juice, vanilla, salt, and sour cream.

Pour the batter into the prepared pan and place in a larger pan. Fill the larger pan halfway with hot water. Bake until set (without cracks), about 45 minutes. Remove the cake from the oven and place on a rack to cool for an hour. Place the Savoy cake round directly on top the the cheesecake. Cover with an 8-inch cardboard round, then invert the cheesecake.

Reduce the oven to 325°F. Mix together the sour cream, sugar, and vanilla. Spread over the top of the cake, allowing the topping to drip over the sides. Bake for 5 minutes or until lightly set. Remove from the oven and let cool to room temperature. Coat the sides of the cheesecake with the caramelized almonds, then refrigerate for 1 hour before slicing.

Chef's True

SLICING CHEESECAKE: Have ready a sharp knife. Run the knife under the hot water, then dry with a towel and cut the cake into equal halves. Run the knife under hot water again to clean and heat. Dry again, then cut into quarters. Repeat, cutting each quarter into halves, for a total of 8 portions, or cut each quarter into thirds, for a total of 12 portions.

TARTE AU CITRON

LEMON TART

This lightest of lemon fillings makes a superb tart. My customers make sure I never take this dessert off my cart. Some recipes are difficult to cut down. This is one of them. The small amount of eggs makes enough filling for three small tarts. You may prepare the dough in a deeper American style pie because you'll have plenty of filling. This recipe also work well for individual tarts to serve at a sit-down dinner party. If you wish, decorate the tart with Crème Chantilly (see page 150) and Lemon Confit (see page 114).

.... MAKES THREE 8-INCH TARTS ....

THE PASTRY SHELLS

2 pounds (double recipe) Pâte Sablée

(see page 214)

THE LEMON FILLING

3 eggs

3 egg yolks

1 cup sugar

Juice of 6 lemons

Grated zest of 2 lemons

6 tablespoons unsalted butter, softened

Preparing the Pastry Shells

On a floured surface, roll out the dough. Cut out three 10-inch circles. Lay each circle of dough into an 8-inch tart pan with a removable bottom. Trim the edges so they are even to the edge of the pan. Chill 1 hour.

Preheat the oven to 400°F. Line the tart shells with heavy-duty foil and fill with dried beans or pie weights. Bake for 15 minutes. Remove the foil and weights. Bake until light golden, pricking the bottom with a fork if it bubbles up. Let cool to room temperature.

Making the Lemon Filling

In a medium stainless steel or enamel pan over medium heat, combine the eggs, egg yolks, sugar, lemon juice, and zest. Whisk until light and the whisk leaves tracks in the foam. Remove from the heat and whisk in the butter. Pour the filling into the prebaked shells. Chill before serving. Garnish as desired.

TARTE MERINGUÉE AUX AIRELLES

CRANBERRY-MERINGUE TART

I absolutely love cranberries, a taste I discovered in America. While we do have small cranberries in Europe, they aren't nearly as common or as good as American cranberries. Make this tart in winter, when cranberries are in season. What we do have in France are red currants. If these are in season in late summer, or if you grow your own, try this tart with currants. Both cranberries and red currants are mouth-puckering red berries. Their intense flavor contrasts well with the almond-meringue batter and the crispy, unsweetened tart shell.

MAKES ONE 10-INCH TART

THE PASTRY SHELL

1 pound Pâte Brisée (see page 214)

THE CRANBERRY MERINGUE FILLING

½ cup finely chopped blanched almonds

2 teaspoons cornstarch

¼ teaspoon ground cinnamon

3 egg whites

Pinch of salt

¾ cup sugar

½ teaspoon lemon juice

½ pound fresh cranberries,
    washed and drained

Confectioners' sugar (for dusting)

Baking the Pastry Shell

Preheat the oven to 400°F. On a floured surface, evenly roll out the dough, lightly dusting the rolling pin as needed. Place the dough in a 10-inch tart pan with a removable bottom and trim the edges even with the top. Chill for 20 minutes. Line the shell with heavy-duty foil and fill with beans or pie weights. Bake for 15 minutes, then remove the foil and weights and let cool.

Making the Cranberry-Meringue Filling

Reduce the oven to 350°F. Combine the almonds, cornstarch, and cinnamon in a small bowl and set aside. Beat the egg whites and the salt until soft peaks form. Sprinkle in the sugar and beat again until almost firm and glossy. Stir in the lemon juice and beat until firm and glossy. Gently fold the almond mixture and the cranberries into the meringue. Pour the filling into the pre-baked tart shell, smoothing out the surface with a rubber spatula. Dust with confectioners' sugar. Bake immediately on the lower rack of the oven for 30 minutes or until the filling has set and is no longer runny.

❧ Chef's Truc ❧

FREEZING CRANBERRIES: When cranberries are in season, buy several extra bags and freeze them right in their bag. Then you can make the tart whenever you want. Fold in the cranberries while still frozen.

TARTE AUX FIGUES

FIG-BUTTERMILK TART

I do adore fresh figs. Here I use dried figs for the cooked filling and quartered fresh figs on top for decoration. The buttermilk topping has a lovely faint sourness that doesn't overpower the evanescent flavor and aroma of fresh figs. Try to find black Mission or brown figs from California. Green Kadota figs can be good if they're ripe and sweet. Sometimes Kadotas have a leathery skin, which is better removed. You'll have extra of the wonderful fig filling. Blend it with heavy cream and make it into ice cream, spread it on toasted slices of our Pain aux Fruits, or thin it with Madeira and serve as a sauce with poached fruit.

MAKES ONE 10-INCH TART

Baking the Pastry Shell

On a lightly floured surface, roll out the dough and lay it into a 10-inch tart pan with removable bottom. Trim the edges even to the edge of the pan, then chill 1 hour.

Preheat the oven to 400°F. Line the tart shell with heavy-duty foil and fill with dried beans or pie weights. Bake 15 minutes, removing the foil and weights. Bake until light golden, pricking the bottom with a fork if it bubbles up, about 10 minutes more. Cool to room temperature.

Making the Fig Filling

Combine the dried figs and the water in a medium pan over low heat. Cover and simmer for 30 minutes, stirring occasionally. Add the sugar, lemon zest, and salt and simmer uncovered for another 30 minutes, stirring often. Transfer to a blender and puree until smooth. Let cool. (This will make ample filling for about 4 tarts. It will keep for 1 month in the refrigerator.)

Preparing the Buttermilk Topping

Place the butter, sugar, eggs, vanilla, buttermilk, flour, and lemon juice in a blender, and blend until smooth.

Finishing the Tart

Reduce the oven to 350°F. Spread a ¼-inch layer of the fig filling in the bottom of the prebaked shell and top with the buttermilk topping. Bake until set, about 20 minutes. Remove the tart from the oven and let cool to room temperature. Heat the apricot jam in a small saucepan until bubbling. Strain through a fine sieve to remove solids. Arrange the figs around the outside border of the tart, then brush the figs with the apricot glaze. Chill until set, about 1 hour. Serve the same day.

THE PASTRY SHELL

1 pound Pâte Sablée (see page 214)

THE FIG FILLING

1½ pounds plump dried figs, stemmed and halved

3½ cups water

⅔ cup sugar

Grated zest of 1 lemon

½ teaspoon salt

THE BUTTERMILK TOPPING

4 tablespoons butter, melted and cooled

½ cup sugar

2 eggs

1 teaspoon vanilla

¼ cup buttermilk

2 tablespoons all-purpose flour

2 teaspoons lemon juice

THE GARNISH

¼ cup apricot jam

4 to 6 ripe figs, stemmed and quartered

GÂTEAU AU CHOCOLAT VALRHONA

WARM INDIVIDUAL VALRHONA CHOCOLATE CAKES

This cake was developed by the top-of-the-line French chocolate company Valrhona. They produce a variety of fine chocolate crus, or blends. This one is made with their Caraïbe chocolate, an incredibly intense, dark-roasted chocolate. I would compare this chocolate to a dark-roasted espresso. You can, of course, use your own favorite bittersweet chocolate.

.... MAKES 8 INDIVIDUAL CAKES ....

THE CHOCOLATE CAKE

*½ pound Pur Caraïbe chocolate
(or other bittersweet chocolate
couverture), finely chopped*

½ pound (2 sticks) unsalted butter

5 eggs

5 egg yolks

6 tablespoons sugar

¾ cup sifted all-purpose flour

THE GARNISH

Crème Anglaise (see page 136)

Raspberries or fresh fruit puree

Baking the Cakes

Preheat the oven to 375°F. Brush eight 4-ounce ramekins with butter. Dust lightly and evenly with flour, shaking out any excess. In a medium bowl, barely melt the chocolate with the butter. The mixture should reach 104°F on a candy thermometer (only slightly warmer than body temperature).

In a mixer, beat the whole eggs, egg yolks, and the sugar using the whisk attachment until light and fluffy. Fold the egg mixture into the chocolate. Stir in the flour. Divide among the ramekins and bake for 5 to 7 minutes or until the cakes have puffed up. (The outsides should be cooked but the inside still liquid.) Remove from the oven, unmold each cake onto an individual dessert plate and serve immediately with Crème Anglaise and fresh raspberries or with a colorful homemade fresh fruit puree, such as mango.

La Cuisine du Bistro

BISTRO FOOD

FILET DE BOEUF À LA FICELLE, SAUCE BÉARNAISE

POACHED FILLET OF BEEF WITH BÉARNAISE SAUCE

This is a home-style dish, but so good. The beef is poached in a richly flavored broth and served with poached root vegetables, beef marrow, and my Béarnaise Sauce. Perfect for a gathering of good friends on a cold winter's day. I start with a savory beef broth made with gelatinous and flavorful—but tough—beef shin. I roast the shins first to intensify their flavor.

SERVICE FOR 4

THE BROTH

2 onions, peeled and studded with
   4 whole cloves, cut in half
4 center-cut beef shin bones,
   cut 2-inches thick
2 leeks (white part only), washed
   and coarsely chopped
1 bunch fresh Italian parsley
Bouquet garni (1 sprig fresh thyme,
   2 bay leaves, 1 teaspoon
   crushed peppercorns)

THE VEGETABLES AND BEEF FILLET

4 carrots, peeled
4 turnips, peeled
4 Idaho potatoes, peeled
1 bunch scallions (white part only)
1½ pound center-cut beef fillet
   (completely trimmed of
   all fat and silver skin)
Salt and white pepper

Cooking the Broth

Prepare the broth at least 1 day before serving. Preheat the oven to 400°F. Heat a cast-iron or steel skillet until smoking hot, then place the onions cut-side down in the skillet and sear until dark brown. Remove from heat. In a roasting pan, brown the beef shins in the oven for about 1 hour, or until well and evenly browned.

Place the beef shins and any browned bits from the pan, the onions, leeks, parsley, and bouquet garni in a stockpot. Cover with 4 inches of cold water and bring to a boil. Skim once, then reduce the heat to a simmer. Cook the broth for 4 hours, skimming occasionally. Strain through a fine sieve. Discard the vegetable solids. Remove the marrow bones from the beef shins and set aside. Cool the pot of broth in an ice bath, then refrigerate overnight. The next day, remove and discard any solidified white fat on top of the broth. (The broth may be made up to 4 days ahead of time.)

Poaching the Vegetables and Beef

Bring the broth to a boil, reduce the heat to a simmer and season with salt and pepper to taste. Prepare the carrots, turnips, and potatoes by cutting them into *tourné* (seven-sided barrel shapes). Trim off the tops and bottoms of the vegetables, then

THE BÉARNAISE SAUCE

1 pound (2 cups) Beurre Clarifié
     (see page 216)
1 tablespoon dry white wine
1 tablespoon chopped fresh tarragon leaves
2 large shallots, finely chopped
1 tablespoon finely chopped
     fresh Italian parsley
¼ teaspoon crushed black peppercorns
2 tablespoon red wine vinegar
4 egg yolks
2 tablespoons water
Salt

cut into 1-inch-diameter rough oblong shapes. Using a sharp paring knife, cut each oblong into a seven-sided cylinder. Cook the carrots, turnips, and potatoes for 5 minutes in the simmering broth. Add the scallions and cook for 5 minutes more. Remove the vegetables from the broth and set aside.

Tie the cotton string around the circumference of the fillet. (This will keep its shape and make the cooking even.) Lower it into the broth and simmer for about 20 to 25 minutes, or until medium-rare (140°F on a meat thermometer). Remove the beef from the broth, cut off the string and let cool for 5 minutes.

Making the Béarnaise Sauce

Warm the clarified butter. Place the white wine, tarragon, shallots, parsley, crushed pepper, and vinegar in a small stainless steel or enamel pot and cook until almost all the liquid is evaporated. Transfer to the top of a double boiler, along with the egg yolks and water. Whisk constantly over boiling water until the eggs are thickened and fluffy. Remove the pot from the heat and, while continuing to whisk, slowly drizzle in the warm clarified butter. Season to taste with salt and keep warm.

Serving the Beef

If you like, serve the broth as a separate first course. For the main course, slice the fillet into ¼-inch-thick rounds, then arrange in 4 shallow soup bowls with the vegetables and top each with 1 bone marrow. Moisten with a little of the cooking broth. Serve the Béarnaise Sauce on the side.

CARRÉ D'AGNEAU À LA MOUTARDE

ROASTED RACK OF LAMB IN MUSTARD CRUST

I use Colorado-raised domestic lamb for this dish. American corn-fed lamb has the mild grain-fed flavor and the large-sized "eye" of meat that I'm looking for in this dish. With that size, the seared meat can get browned and crispy on the outside while remaining pink and juicy on the inside. For the most elegant look, have the butcher prepare the rack "French style," completely trimming each rib bone.

SERVICE FOR 4

Preparing the Lamb

Preheat the oven to 450°F. Heat a roasting pan over high heat on the stovetop. Place the lamb racks, fat-side down (and any bones, such as the chine) in the pan. Brown the lamb on all sides on top of the stove. (The fat may splatter so take care.) Add the vegetables and herbs to the pan and turn the lamb fat-side up. Roast for 20 minutes. Remove from the oven and cool slightly. Pull off the first thick layer of fat. Return the lamb to the oven for 10 minutes longer. Remove the racks again and trim off all fat and connective tissue. You should have only the bare eye of the lamb racks resting on the bones. The meat should reach 125°F or "French Rare" on a meat thermometer and rest for 10 minutes before finishing.

Finishing the Lamb

Sprinkle the meat with salt and white pepper. Brush with the mustard. Combine the breadcrumbs and parsley and sprinkle over the lamb. Place 2 tablespoons of the butter on each lamb rack and roast about 10 minutes longer. The meat should test rare (140 to 145°F). Remove the meat from the roasting pan. Pour off and discard the fat. Pour in the wine, using a wooden spoon to scrape up the browned bits and vegetables. Transfer to a saucepan and reduce the liquid to a glaze. Add the water and reduce again to a glaze. Season the cooking juices with salt and pepper then strain through a fine sieve. Slice the lamb into individual chops. Arrange the chops on each of 4 large heated dinner plates, accompanied by the lamb juice.

❧ *Chef's Truc* ❧

COOKING LAMB: At Le Bec-Fin, we prepare the lamb ahead up to the point of covering it with the mustard crumbs. Then, when the guest is ready to be served, we finish the lamb in the oven. You can do the same at home. If you prepare the lamb this way, you won't need to let it rest long before carving, because it will have already had a chance to rest after the first cooking.

THE LAMB

One 7-to 8-pound rack of lamb, split into
2 racks, trimmed, chine-bone removed

3 cloves garlic, peeled

1 whole carrot

1 whole, unpeeled onion

3 whole ribs celery

1 sprig fresh thyme

1 bay leaf

Salt and white pepper

THE CRUST

2 tablespoons Dijon mustard

2 tablespoons dried bread crumbs

2 tablespoons finely chopped
fresh Italian parsley

4 tablespoons unsalted butter

¼ cup dry white wine

2 cups water

THON AU POIVRE AVEC SA SALADE DE CRABE

TUNA WITH PEPPERCORNS ACCOMPANIED BY CRAB SALAD

*T*una is one fish where absolute freshness is crucial. We buy "sushi-grade" tuna, caught on a line rather than in a net. The fish is light red in color, its flesh is firm, and it smells sweet and briny. Tuna are so large that they are sold in cuts similar to meat. Buy center-cut loin of tuna from a reputable fish store. Avoid dull or dry looking tuna. To keep it from overcooking, cook only the outside edges of the fish, never the cut ends. Like other red meats, tuna should rest before being sliced.

SERVICE FOR 6

THE RED PEPPER OIL

1 large red bell pepper

2 teaspoons Dijon mustard

½ cup olive oil

Salt and white pepper

THE TUNA

2 tablespoons black peppercorns,
    coarsely crushed

1 tablespoon finely chopped fresh thyme

1 pound center-cut tuna loin (in one piece)

1 tablespoon olive oil

THE CRAB SALAD

½ pound jumbo lump crabmeat,
    shells removed

1 Haas avocado (firm but ripe),
    peeled and cut into 1-inch cubes

¼ cup olive oil

1 teaspoon Madras curry powder

Salt and white pepper

½ English cucumber, peeled in
    alternating stripes, thinly sliced

Making the Red Pepper Oil

Roast the pepper directly over an open flame, turning until evenly blackened on the skin surface only. Cool, peel, and seed. Place the roasted pepper and mustard in a blender and blend until combined. With the motor running, drizzle in the olive oil and blend until emulsified. Strain, season with salt and pepper, and set aside, storing in a plastic squeeze bottle (see *Chef's Truc* below) if desired.

Cooking the Tuna

Preheat the oven to 400°F. Place the crushed peppercorns in a fine sieve and shake out the fine pepper dust, reserving for another use. (You should have only crushed peppercorn pieces left.) Combine the peppercorns with the thyme and place in a shallow bowl. Roll the tuna in the pepper-thyme mix, coating evenly on all sides.

Heat the olive oil in an ovenproof casserole. Sear the tuna on the outside edges—but not the cut ends. Transfer to the oven and roast about 5 minutes, or until medium-medium rare (about 135°F. on a meat thermometer). Remove from the oven and let the tuna rest 5 to 10 minutes before slicing.

Assembling the Salad

Have ready 6 large chilled plates, each with a 3-inch metal ring mold (see *Chef's Truc* page 36) in the center. Gently toss together the crab, avocado, olive oil, and curry powder. Season to taste with salt and pepper. Slice the tuna crosswise into ½-inch slices, using an electric or very sharp knife. Cut the cucumber slices into half moons. Line the molds with overlapping cucumber slices. Divide the crab salad into 6 portions and fill each mold. Carefully remove the mold. Arrange the tuna slices on plate surrounding crab salad. Drizzle the plates with Red Pepper Oil and serve.

❧ *Chef's Truc* ❧

PAINTING WITH SAUCE: To make those beautiful designs on the plates, we use the plastic squeeze bottles sold for hair coloring. Fill a brand-new clean bottle with the pepper oil, then snip off only enough from the tip so the vinaigrette can be squeezed out in a thin, even line. Cut a little at a time, until you have the right-sized opening.

BLANC DE DINDE EN POT-AU-FEU

POACHED TURKEY "POT-ON-THE-FIRE"

How much more basic can we get than Pot-au-Feu? This farmhouse standard is often made with a chicken or capon. In this version, I use a whole fresh turkey breast, which I've become familiar with here in the United States. The essence of French country cooking is all here in this dish: the good flavors from slow cooking; the simplicity of a one-pot dish.

.... SERVICE FOR 8 ....

THE CONSOMMÉ

1 onion, peeled and studded with 4 cloves
    and cut in half

5 pounds chicken bones (backs and necks)

2 carrots

2 leeks (white part only), cut in half
    lengthwise and washed

1 whole rib celery

¼ bunch fresh thyme

2 bay leaves

12 black peppercorns

1 teaspoon coarse salt

THE POT-AU-FEU

One 8-pound fresh turkey breast
    on the bone

2 pounds celery root, cleaned

3 English cucumbers, peeled,
    cut lengthwise and seeded

2 pounds butternut squash
    (or French red pumpkin,
    called potiron), split and seeded

1 tablespoon unsalted butter

½ cup Crème Frâiche (see page 217)

2 egg yolks

2 tablespoons port

Salt and white pepper

1 bunch fresh chervil sprigs (for garnish)

Making the Consommé

Cut the onion in half and cook the cut edge directly on a hot steel pan, cooking until the surface is dark brown. (This onion brulée adds golden color to the consommé.) Place the chicken bones, vegetables, broiled onion, herbs and seasonings in a large stockpot with 3 quarts cold water. Bring to a boil and skim off any foam. Reduce heat to a bare simmer and cook for 2½ hours. Strain the consommé into a clean pot. (You should about have 6 cups of liquid left; if you have less, add enough water to make 6 cups.)

Preparing the Pot-au-Feu

Submerge the turkey breast in the consommé. Return to a boil and reduce the heat again to a bare simmer, skimming off any foamy impurities as necessary. Poach for 1½ hours.

Pare the celery roots, trimming off any dirt remaining. Using a small Parisian scoop (a melon baller), scoop out 40 small round balls of each vegetable. (Alternatively, cut the vegetables into ¾-inch cubes.) Ladle 2 cups of the consommé into a small pot. Bring to a boil. Add the celery root balls and cook for 2 minutes. Add the squash and cook for 2 minutes. Add the cucumber balls and cook for 1 minute longer. Stir in the butter and keep warm.

Finishing the Pot-au-Feu

Remove the turkey breast from the consommé and cover with a damp cloth to keep warm. Cook the consommé until it's reduced to 2 cups. Beat together the egg yolks, port, and Crème Frâiche. Temper by beating in about ¼ cup of the consommé. Return the mixture to the pot and place over low heat, whisking constantly. Cook until the sauce thickens. (Do not allow the liquid to boil, or it will curdle and separate.) Season the sauce with salt and pepper to taste.

Slice the turkey breast and divide among 8 heated dinner plates. Divide the vegetables among the 8 plates. Coat with the sauce and sprinkle with the chervil sprigs.

COQ AU VIN

CHICKEN COOKED IN RED WINE

In the old days, this dish called for rooster. A rooster was killed only when it outlived its usefulness. Because these birds would be several years old, they needed long, slow braising to make them tender. But the older the bird, the stronger the flavor. In France, the combs and kidneys of the rooster would be served as a garnish. In the United States we normally use hens for this dish. I am extremely particular about the chickens I serve, insisting on specially raised organic, free-range birds from Pennsylvania.

SERVICE FOR 4

Cooking the Coq au Vin

Season the chicken with salt and pepper. In a heavy ovenproof casserole, sauté the bacon until browned. Remove the bacon bits from the pan and set aside. Add the chicken to the fat remaining in the pan, and brown on all sides. Remove the chicken and keep warm. Add the shallots and the garlic and cook for 3 minutes. Place the browned chicken back in the pan and stir in the flour.

Preheat the oven to 400°F.

Heat the wine and the ¼ teaspoon sugar in a small pot. *Flambé* (ignite with a long match) and let cook until the flames subside. Pour the red wine into the casserole with enough of the Jus de Poulet to cover. Bring to a boil on top of the stove and stir to loosen any cooked bits. Add the bouquet garni and bake in the oven, covered, for about 40 minutes, then remove the casserole from the oven.

Finishing the Coq au Vin

To finish the sauce, remove the chicken pieces from the pan and set aside. Strain the cooking juices through a fine sieve and set aside. Sauté the mushrooms in 2 tablespoons of the butter. Remove the mushrooms and heat the remaining 2 tablespoons butter. Brown the pearl onions, then stir in the remaining sugar, cooking until caramelized, about 3 to 4 minutes.

Return the chicken, mushrooms, and pearl onions to the reserved cooking juices. Divide among 4 heated dinner plates. Ladle the sauce over the top, then sprinkle each portion with parsley. Serve immediately.

Chef's Truc

SUBSTITUTING DEMI-GLACE: In a professional kitchen, we substitute Demi-Glace for the Jus de Poulet to add body and richness to the pan sauce. If you use Jus de Poulet, you may need to add a bit of beurre manié to slightly thicken the sauce.

THE COQ AU VIN

One 3½- to 4-pound free-range chicken,
    cut into quarters

Salt and white pepper

¼ pound smoked bacon, diced

3 shallots, peeled and sliced

1 clove garlic, peeled and minced

2 tablespoons all-purpose flour

2½ cups good-quality dry red wine

¼ teaspoon plus 1 tablespoon sugar

2 cups Jus de Poulet (see page 214)

Bouquet garni (2 parsley sprigs,
    1 bay leaf, 2 fresh thyme sprigs,
    6 crushed peppercorns)

½ pound white mushrooms,
    cleaned and quartered

4 tablespoons unsalted butter

1 pint pearl onions, peeled

2 tablespoons chopped fresh Italian parsley

GASPACHO AUX OLIVES NOIRES

GAZPACHO WITH BLACK OLIVES

There are almost as many recipes for gazpacho as there are chefs. Unlike most versions of this soup, my gazpacho is cooked. It's also a lovely shade of sunset orange-red because I use both red bell pepper and sweet Spanish paprika to intensify the color. Of all the culinary herbs, fresh basil is probably my favorite and so I include this non-traditional flavoring here. Serve the gazpacho icy cold with a garnish of finely-diced cucumber, red pepper, chopped jet-black olives, and tiny homemade croutons. My friend Jacques Pépin gave me the idea for the black olives when he was a guest chef at my restaurant during Philadelphia's Book and Cook festival.

.... SERVICE FOR 8 ....

THE GAZPACHO

2 large onions, peeled and chopped

3 red bell peppers, seeded and chopped

½ cup (8 tablespoons) olive oil

3 cloves garlic, peeled and crushed

6 ripe tomatoes, roughly chopped

2 cucumbers, peeled and sliced

1 bunch fresh basil, rinsed and
    stems removed

1 tablespoon paprika

2 cups water

¼ cup red wine vinegar

Salt and white pepper

THE GARNISHES

10 slices firm white sandwich bread, crusts
    removed and cut into 1-inch cubes

2 tablespoons olive oil

1 English cucumber, peeled, seeded,
    and finely diced

1 red bell pepper, seeded and finely diced

¼ cup oil-cured black olives,
    pitted and chopped

Making the Gazpacho

In a large, heavy-bottomed soup pot, slowly cook the onions and peppers in 2 tablespoons of the olive oil, until tender and translucent. Add the garlic and tomatoes and simmer for 10 minutes. Add the cucumbers, basil, paprika, and 2 cups water and simmer 5 minutes longer. Puree with a hand-held blender (see *Chef's Truc* below), while slowly pouring in the remaining 6 tablespoons oil and the vinegar. Season with salt and pepper to taste, then strain through a food mill and chill.

Preparing the Croutons

Preheat the oven to 325°F. Cut the crusts off the bread and discard. Toss the bread in a bowl with the olive oil. Spread in a single layer on a baking sheet. Bake, shaking once or twice, until golden brown, about 10 to 12 minutes. Cool.

Serving the Soup

Ladle the soup into chilled shallow soup bowls. Sprinkle each portion with about 1 teaspoon of each garnish, then top with the croutons. Serve immediately. If you serve the soup family-style from a tureen, pass small bowls of the garnishes for guests to add themselves.

Chef's Truc

USING A BLENDER: If you don't have a hand-held blender, blend the soup in a regular blender, strain through a food mill, then whisk in the olive oil by hand.

FRICASSÉE DE CREVETTES À LA PROVENÇALE

FRICASSEE OF SHRIMP PROVENÇAL STYLE

A fricassee is a very old term for a dish that originally meant a sort of stew of meat or poultry in a white or brown sauce. Here it refers to a quick sauté of shrimp in a sauce of garlic, tomato, and brandy. I like to accompany this dish with Purée de Pommes de Terre. Use extra-large sized shrimp. If you need to order them, they will be 16 to 20 count per pound, which means about one ounce per shrimp, or about a quarter pound of shrimp per person.

········· SERVICE FOR 4 ·········

THE SHRIMP

1 pound extra large shrimp,
    peeled and deveined

Salt and white pepper

1 tablespoon plus ½ pound (2 sticks)
    unsalted butter

1 tablespoon olive oil

1 tablespoon chopped garlic

1 cup Tomates Concassées (see page 217)

2 tablespoons brandy

2 tablespoons dry white vermouth

½ cup Fond Blanc de Volaille
    (see page 214)

3 tablespoons finely chopped
    fresh Italian parsley

Preparing the Shrimp

Season the shrimp with salt and pepper to taste. In a large sauté pan, heat 1 tablespoon of the butter and the oil until sizzling. Add the shrimp and sauté until just cooked through (pink and opaque). Remove the shrimp from the pan and keep warm. Add the garlic and sauté 15 seconds, stirring constantly to avoid browning. Stir in the Tomates Concassées.

Add the brandy and heat slightly. Then *flambé* (ignite with a long match). When the flames subside, add the vermouth and Fond Blanc de Volaille. Reduce the liquid until syrupy. Whisk in the remaining ½ pound butter in small pieces, then add the parsley. Return the shrimp to the pan to rewarm. Season with salt and pepper to taste.

To serve, surround a mound of Purée de Pommes de Terre (see page 123) with the shrimp and sauce.

Tempura de Coquilles St. Jacques, Sauce Aigre-Douce

Sea Scallop Tempura with Sweet and Sour Sauce

I do love curry, especially with these scallops that I serve as an appetizer on my Bar Lyonnais menu. I use an imported Madras curry powder. A little bit goes a long way, so don't overdo it. Fried food has a bad reputation because it's often done carelessly or with less than top-quality ingredients. I make a paper-thin Japanese style tempura batter for this dish. The Japanese learned the technique of tempura from the Portuguese method of frying brought to Japan by missionaries in the sixteenth century. Tempura was adapted by the Japanese and has been adopted by the West.

.... SERVICE FOR 4 ....

Preparing the Scallop Mixture

Combine the curry, paprika, cayenne, cornstarch, and salt in a bowl. Toss with the scallops. (The mixture should hold together.) Form the mixture into 1-inch balls and refrigerate until ready to cook.

Making the Sweet and Sour Dipping Sauce

Stir together the sugar, soy, and vinegar until the sugar dissolves. Stir in the tomatoes and chives and set aside.

Cooking the Tempura

Heat the oil in a large, heavy-bottomed pot to 360°F on a frying thermometer.

Meanwhile, quickly whisk together the ice water, flour, and baking powder. (The batter should have the consistency of heavy cream.) Dip the scallop balls into the batter, letting the excess batter drip off. Fry until golden brown, then drain on paper towels. Serve the tempura accompanied by a saucer of Dipping Sauce.

Chef's Truc

MAKING TEMPURA BATTER: For good tempura batter, the key is to use icy cold water, with a few ice cubes in the batter. A cold batter coats better without the need for excess flour, so you'll get a thinner, crispier coating.

THE SCALLOP MIXTURE

¼ cup cornstarch

1 teaspoon Madras curry powder

1 teaspoon paprika

¼ teaspoon cayenne pepper

Salt

½ pound fresh sea scallops, tough muscles removed, diced and patted dry

THE SWEET AND SOUR DIPPING SAUCE

½ cup sugar

¼ cup soy sauce

½ cup white vinegar

½ cup Tomates Concassées (see page 217)

2 tablespoons finely sliced fresh chives

THE TEMPURA

Peanut oil for frying

1½ cups ice-cold water with a few ice chips

1 cup all-purpose flour

1 teaspoon baking powder

Volaille au Vinaigre de Framboises à la Fernand Point

Chicken with Raspberry Vinegar in the Style of Fernand Point

Fernand Point, chef/proprietor of the renowned La Pyramide Restaurant in Lyon trained many of the famous chefs of our day. I worked in his restaurant as a young man and learned this recipe. Even though I never met him, I dedicate this dish to Fernand Point and to his widow, Madame Point, who carried on his philosophy.

.... SERVICE FOR 4 ....

THE CHICKEN

4 tablespoons unsalted butter

4 large boneless chicken breast halves,
    skin and first wing-joint on

2 sprigs fresh thyme

8 cloves garlic, unpeeled

Salt and white pepper

¼ cup raspberry vinegar

2 tablespoons white wine

1 tablespoon Dijon mustard

4 teaspoons tomato puree

4 teaspoons Worcestershire
    (Lea & Perrins brand preferred)

1 cup heavy cream

½ cup cognac

¼ cup Demi-Glace (see page 212)

½ pint fresh raspberries

Cooking the Chicken

Melt 2 tablespoons of the butter in a large nonstick skillet. When sizzling, add the chicken breasts, skin-side down. Then add the thyme and garlic cloves to the pan. Season the chicken with salt and pepper. Cover the pan and cook for 5 minutes on the skin side. Turn the breasts over, cover, and cook until the breasts are firm to the touch but not dry, about 15 to 20 minutes more. Remove the chicken from the pan and set aside.

Finishing the Dish

Pour off the excess fat from the pan and place back on the heat. Pour in the vinegar and wine and scrape the pan with a wooden spoon to release the browned bits and incorporate them into the sauce. Cook until the liquid is reduced by half. Add the mustard, tomato puree, Worcestershire, and heavy cream. Bring to a boil and stir in the cognac and Demi-Glace. Reduce again until the sauce coats the back of a wooden spoon, then stir in the remaining 2 tablespoons butter. Strain through a fine sieve, then season to taste with salt and pepper. Arrange the chicken on 4 plates and pour the sauce over, and sprinkle each dish with fresh raspberries.

Chef's True

CUTTING EUROPEAN-STYLE CHICKEN BREAST: This cut of chicken breast is known as a "European style" breast. Sometimes it's also called "airline cut" because it's been popularized in airline meal service. If you cut your chicken yourself, just separate and remove the first two joints of the chicken wing, leaving on the last joint. Pull out the wishbone (or collar bone) from the top of the breast, then cut away the rib cage.

GIGOT DE LOTTE RÔTI AUX NOUILLES FRAÎCHES

ROAST WHOLE FILLET OF MONKFISH WITH FRESH NOODLES

Served family-style, the carved roasted monkfish is a play on the traditional Sunday roast of meat. Gigot refers to a roast leg of meat, like lamb. The fresh, homemade noodles are served in a separate platter. Each guest helps himself to a slice of fish with its sauce and some of the noodles.

SERVICE FOR 6 TO 8

Roasting the Monkfish

Preheat oven to 400°F. Season the monkfish fillet with salt and pepper.

In a large ovenproof casserole, heat the oil. Sear the monkfish, browning well on all sides. Add carrots, onion, mushrooms, bouquet garni, and saffron and cook, while stirring vegetables for 5 minutes. Pour in the wine to deglaze, then add enough water or Fumet de Poisson to measure 1 inch up the sides of the fish. Cover and bake for 25 to 30 minutes, basting often. Remove the monkfish roast from the casserole and keep warm, reserving the casserole and its juices.

Making the Sauce

Scrape the sides and bottom of the casserole to loosen the bits of fish and strain the liquid through a sieve into a saucepan. Cook over medium heat until reduced to 1 cup. Using a hand-held blender, whisk in the butter. Adjust the seasoning and add the Tomates Concassées and the parsley to the sauce. Slice the monkfish and arrange on a large, heated serving platter. Ladle the sauce over the fish.

Cooking the Noodles

Bring a large pot of lightly salted water to a boil. Add the noodles, bring the water back to a boil and cook 3 to 4 minutes or until the noodles are cooked al dente. Drain then toss with the oil, and season to taste with salt and pepper. Place noodles on another large, heated serving platter and serve with the fish.

Chef's Truc

MAKING A BOUQUET GARNI: I combine 1 to 2 sprigs Italian parsley, 1 sprig fresh thyme, 1 bay leaf, and about 10 peppercorns. I roll these up in a small square of cheesecloth, tying it shut with long cotton string. This way, I can find and remove the bouquet easily.

THE MONKFISH

2 pounds whole monkfish fillet in one piece,
    cleaned and trimmed

Salt and white pepper

2 tablespoons olive oil

1 carrot, peeled and chopped

1 onion, peeled and chopped

5 white mushrooms, cleaned and chopped

Bouquet garni (2 sprigs parsley,
    1 sprig thyme, 1 bay leaf,
    10 black peppercorns)

Pinch of saffron threads

¾ cup dry white wine

THE SAUCE

3 tablespoons unsalted butter

1½ cups Tomates Concassées
    (see page 217)

1 tablespoon chopped fresh Italian parsley

THE NOODLES

½ pound Pâte aux Oeufs
    (see page 215), cut into fettucine

2 tablespoons olive oil

Salt and white pepper

MOUCLADE DE MOULES AU CURRY

MUSSELS IN WHITE WINE WITH CURRY

*M*ussels are becoming much more popular and well accepted, especially because cultivated mussels are now widely available. In France, we usually eat them steamed with wine. This regional dish is from the Charentais, near La Rochelle, the center of France's cultivated seafood industry in Normandy. Here, large, plump cultivated mussels are steamed with white wine. Then, they're coated with a sauce made from their tasty cooking juices thickened with cream. Sometimes saffron or turmeric is added. In my version, I add a touch of curry, which I love with seafood. I serve the mussels on a bed of spinach, to soak up the delicious sauce.

SERVICE FOR 4

THE SPINACH AND MUSSELS

1 pound spinach leaves, stems and
    tough ribs removed

4 tablespoons unsalted butter

2 shallots, peeled and chopped

1 teaspoon curry powder

½ cup dry white wine

4 pounds Prince Edward Island mussels
    (or other cultivated mussels), scrubbed

1 ½ cups heavy cream

2 tablespoons finely snipped fresh chives

Salt and white pepper

Cooking the Spinach

Wash three times in cold water baths, or until the water is clear. Place the wet spinach in a large pot. Heat quickly, stirring constantly, until wilted. Drain and then refresh under cold running water. Set aside.

Steaming the Mussels

Heat 1 tablespoon of the butter in the bottom of a large stockpot. Add the shallots and curry powder and cook for 2 minutes, stirring. Add the wine and cook 3 to 4 minutes longer. Add the mussels, cover, and cook over high heat. As the mussels open, remove them from the pot. Remove and discard the top half shell from each mussel and set them aside.

When all the mussels have been removed, strain their juices through a coffee filter or cheesecloth.

Transfer the strained mussel juice to a medium pot and reduce by half. Add the heavy cream and reduce again by half. Stir in the chives. Finish the sauce with 2 tablespoons butter, season to taste, and keep warm.

To serve, gently squeeze out excess water from the spinach. Heat the remaining tablespoon of butter in a pan and lightly sauté the spinach, cooking just enough to heat thoroughly. Divide the spinach among 4 deep bowls, top with the mussels and ladle sauce on top.

Chef's Truc

CLEANING MUSSELS: Buy the cultivated mussels that come in a net bag, usually 2 pounds for each bag. Pull off the hairy "beards." Sort the mussels. Look for any that aren't tightly closed. If they are just slightly open, try pressing their edges together. If the mussel closes up, it is alive and healthy. Discard any mussels with cracked or broken shells or any that gape open. Scrub the mussels with a brush, under cold, running water.

LAPIN SAUTÉ CHASSEUR

SAUTÉED RABBIT HUNTER'S STYLE

Another personal favorite, my mother often cooked this dish for Sunday dinner after church. In France, we eat a great deal of rabbit, a meat that really hasn't caught on here in the United States. If you've never cooked rabbit before, this is a good recipe to start with. Ideally, the rabbit should be wild for best flavor, but you can certainly use the more tender farm-raised rabbit.

.... SERVICE FOR 4 ....

THE RABBIT

One 2½- to 3-pound young wild rabbit

¼ pound smoked bacon, cubed

3 shallots, peeled and chopped

½ cup dry white wine

½ cup Jus de Poulet (see page 214)

1 cup Tomates Concassées (see page 217)

1 pound white mushrooms,
    cleaned and quartered

Bouquet garni (1 bunch fresh Italian
    parsley, 1 sprig fresh thyme, and
    1 bay leaf)

¼ cup pitted black oil-cured olives
    (see Chef's Truc)

Beurre Manie, if necessary
    (see page 216)

Salt and white pepper

Cooking the Rabbit

Sauté the bacon in a large heavy casserole. When half cooked, add the shallots and brown. Add the rabbit and cook until and browned on all sides. Pour in the wine to deglaze the pan. Add the Jus de Poulet, Tomates Concassées, mushrooms, and bouquet garni. Cover and cook over low heat for about 1 hour and 15 minutes. Add the olives and cook for 15 minutes longer. Thicken slightly with beurre manié if necessary and season with salt and pepper to taste. Remove and discard the bouquet garni. Serve with Purée de Pommes de Terres (see page 123).

❧ *Chef's Truc* ❧

PITTING OIL-CURED BLACK OLIVES: I use oil-cured black olives for this dish because of their powerful intensity. From Sicily and North Africa, these shriveled-looking olives can be easily pitted. Just press each olive with your thumb to flatten, and the pit will squeeze out. Separate each pitted olive into 2 halves before using. They will keep for 2 to 3 months if refrigerated.

PALOURDES FARCIES

STUFFED MAINE BUTTON CLAMS

*M*aine *raises some of this country's finest clams. Button-sized means just that: clams the size of a button. What makes this dish so good is the small size and delicate flavor of the clams I use. This simple dish makes a wonderful hors d'oeuvre for an informal gathering.*

.... SERVICE FOR 4 ....

Steaming the Clams

Using a clam knife, pry open the clams by inserting the knife into the curved recess near the pointy end of the clam. (This is where the clam shells are kept shut by the adductor muscle.) Twist the knife until you can push it in all the way, then cut apart the two shells. Scrape any meat off the top shells, then pull off and discard.

Combine the bread crumbs, oil, parsley, and garlic. Divide the mixture among the shells and pat it onto each of the clams. Top each clam with a piece of bacon. (You can prepare the clams 1 day ahead up to this point.)

When ready to serve, preheat the broiler until hot. Place the clams on a shallow baking pan and broil until bubbling. Serve hot.

Chef's Truc

CLEANING CLAMS: Buy the smallest clams you can find. Choose them for uniformity of size also. Scrub the clams with a brush and plenty of cold water. Soak in a sinkful of cold water for about 20 minutes so they will purge themselves of sand. Discard any with broken shells. Look for any clams that aren't tightly closed. If they are just slightly open, try pressing their edges together. If the clam closes up, it is alive and healthy. Discard any that gape open. Scrub the clams up to 1 day before cooking them. Keep them cold and moist.

THE CLAMS

32 Maine button clams, scrubbed

2 cups fresh soft bread crumbs

6 tablespoons olive oil

6 tablespoons finely chopped Italian parsley

2 cloves garlic, peeled and chopped

½ pound thick-cut bacon,

cut into 32 squares

SALADE DE ST. JACQUES AVEC CREVETTES GRILLÉES PARFUMÉES AUX BETTERAVES ROUGES

SALAD OF GRILLED SEA SCALLOPS AND SHRIMP

WITH BEET VINAIGRETTE

A brilliant magenta beet vinaigrette makes this light, simple salad an eye-catcher. Make it ahead up to the point of grilling the scallops and reheating the vegetables. I always roast beets to maintain all their sugary flavor. This intensity and wonderful color is lost if the beets are boiled. The Beet Vinaigrette is wonderful with other grilled fish and seafood. I also serve this grilled seafood accompanied by my Salade d'Haricots Verts (see page 126), as shown in the photo on the next page.

························· SERVICE FOR 6 ·························

THE SALAD AND MARINADE

¼ *pound green beans, trimmed and julienned*

¼ *pound snow peas, trimmed and julienned*

1 *carrot, peeled and julienned*

1 *tablespoon dry sherry*

1 *tablespoon port*

2 *fresh basil leaves, thinly sliced*

Juice of ½ a lemon

¾ *pound jumbo sea scallops,*
   tough muscles removed

¾ *pound jumbo shrimp, peeled*
   (leave tail shell on) and deveined

1 *tablespoon sesame seeds*

1 *teaspoon dark roasted sesame oil*

2 *tablespoons olive oil*

1 *tablespoon sherry vinegar*

THE BEET VINAIGRETTE

1 *large beet, scrubbed*

½ *cup olive oil*

2 *tablespoons sherry vinegar*

Salt and white pepper

Preparing the Salad

Bring a small pot of salted water to a boil. Blanch the vegetables for 1 minute or until brightly colored. Drain and refresh under cold running water, then drain on paper towels and set aside.

Whisk together the sherry, port, basil, and lemon juice. Marinate the scallops and shrimp for 1 hour.

Preheat the oven to 325°F. Place the sesame seeds in a small pan and lightly toast, shaking occasionally. Toast until lightly colored, about 6 to 8 minutes. Remove to a cool pan and set aside.

Making the Beet Vinaigrette

Increase the oven temperature to 400°F. Wrap the beet in foil and roast for 1 hour, or until soft when stuck with a skewer. Remove from oven and let cool to room temperature. Peel the beet and cut into chunks. In a blender, place the olive oil, vinegar, salt, and pepper. Add the beet chunks and blend until smooth. Strain through a fine sieve and set aside.

Assembling the Salad

Preheat the grill until white hot. Remove the scallops and shrimp from the marinade. Drain and toss with 1 tablespoon of the olive oil. Grill over high heat, marking each scallop with criss-cross grill lines.

Warm the remaining tablespoon olive oil, sesame oil, sherry vinegar, and the toasted sesame seeds in a small pan until hot. Add the green beans, snow peas, and carrots and cook for 30 seconds. Place the vegetables in a mound in the center of each of 6 salad plates. Place the grilled scallops and shrimp around the salad. Drizzle the plates with the Beet Vinaigrette and serve.

POUSSIN GRILLÉ À LA MOUTARDE, SAUCE CHORON

GRILLED CORNISH HEN WITH DIJON MUSTARD AND SAUCE CHORON

I've always loved this dish. It's so simple and so good. The crumb crust keeps the chicken moist and juicy inside. Here, just a few inexpensive ingredients make a dish you will be proud to serve. The Sauce Choron is a simple variation on Sauce Béarnaise. The addition of a little tomato paste adds sweetness and a bite of acidity, and tints the sauce pink.

.... SERVICE FOR 4 ....

THE POUSSIN GRILLÉ

Two 1-pound Cornish game hens

2 tablespoons Dijon mustard

1 cup fresh bread crumbs

1 tablespoon unsalted butter, softened

Salt and white pepper

THE CHORON SAUCE

1 cup Sauce Béarnaise (see page 176)

1 tablespoon tomato paste

Preparing the Poussin and Sauce

Preheat the oven to 400°F.

Turn the hens over so their backs face you. Using poultry shears, cut along one side of each backbone. Then cut down the second side of the backbones and remove. Using your fingers, pull out and discard the V-shaped wishbone or collar bone at the top of breast. Now remove the rib cage. (Set aside bones for a Jus de Poulet if desired.) Split each hen in half between the breasts and season with salt and pepper. Spread the mustard over the chicken, then sprinkle with bread crumbs, patting lightly to set them in place.

Place the hens skin-side up in a baking dish just large enough to hold them. Dot with the butter. Roast until browned and crispy, about 30 to 40 minutes. Jiggle the leg joint where it meets the body. It should move freely. If it feels at all springy, place back in the oven for a few minutes.

Meanwhile, whisk the tomato paste into the Sauce Béarnaise. Serve the hens hot, accompanied by a sauceboat of the Sauce Choron.

❧ *Chef's Truc* ☙

TESTING CHICKEN FOR DONENESS: Another way to tell if the chicken is done is to stick a metal skewer into the joint of the chicken leg. Hold it there for half a minute than pull the skewer out and touch it to the inside of your wrist. The metal should feel warm to hot. Press the incision. The juices that run out should be clear and golden rather than pink. It's important to tell when the chicken is just done, because you don't want to overcook it.

QUICHE AUX AUBERGINES

EGGPLANT QUICHE

I like to accompany this quiche with a simple tomato salad. I peel and thinly slice vine-ripened New Jersey tomatoes then dress them with good olive oil, salt and freshly ground black pepper, and a sprinkle of Balsamic or sherry vinegar. Scatter shreds of basil over the salad and serve.

MAKES ONE 9-INCH QUICHE

Baking the Pastry Shell

Preheat the oven to 350°F. Lightly dust the counter, the rolling pin, and the dough with flour, then roll out evenly. Place the dough in a 9-inch quiche pan with a removable bottom. Trim the edges so they are even with the top. Line the shell with a piece of heavy-duty foil and fill with beans or pie weights. Bake until cooked but not colored, about 15 minutes. Remove the foil and weights and cool.

Preparing the Filling

Pierce the eggplants with a fork and bake at 350° F. until soft, about 45 minutes. Remove the skin and coarsely chop the eggplants and mix with the eggs. Place the cream cheese and heavy cream in the bowl of a mixer. Beat with the paddle attachment until smooth, then add the eggplant mixture, and season with salt, pepper, and nutmeg to taste. Pour into the baked quiche shell, then cover with grated Gruyère cheese. Bake until set in the middle, about 30 minutes.

THE PASTRY SHELL

1 pound *Pâte Brisée* (see page 214)

THE QUICHE FILLING

2 pounds eggplant (firm and shiny)

2 eggs

8 ounces cream cheese

2 tablespoons heavy cream

8 ounces Gruyère cheese, grated

Salt, white pepper, and ground nutmeg

RATATOUILLE À MA FAÇON

MY OWN VERSION OF PROVENÇAL VEGETABLE STEW

To me, traditional ratatouille is often heavy and oily. I like the flavors of the vegetables to come through. Here I cook the vegetables all together, puree them, and then dress them with extra-virgin olive oil. Raw olive oil is much lighter because its volatile flavor essences haven't been destroyed by heat. Try it my way.

.... SERVICE FOR 8 ....

THE RATATOUILLE

2 large red bell peppers, seeded and
    coarsely chopped

2 large onions, peeled and coarsely chopped

2 large eggplants, peeled and
    cut into 1-inch cubes

5 medium zucchini, cut into 1-inch cubes

5 to 6 cloves garlic, peeled and
    coarsely chopped

½ cup extra-virgin olive oil

Bouquet garni (2 sprigs fresh thyme,
    2 bay leaves, 10 black peppercorns,
    2 whole cloves)

Two 28-ounce cans whole peeled
    plum tomatoes, drained, seeded,
    and coarsely chopped

Salt and white pepper

2 tablespoons chopped fresh Italian parsley

Making the Ratatouille

In a large, heavy casserole, combine the bell peppers, onions, eggplant, zucchini, bouquet garni, and garlic along with 2 tablespoons of the olive oil. Cook, stirring occasionally, until the vegetables soften and release their juices. Add the tomatoes and continue to cook until the juices reduce to a syrup, about 10 to 15 minutes.

Remove from the heat then pull out and discard the bouquet garni. Puree the vegetables using a hand-held blender. Stir in the remaining olive oil and the chopped parsley. Season generously with salt and pepper. Serve warm or cold.

ROSE'S CANNELLONI

ROSE GUARRERA'S CHICKEN AND SPINACH-FILLED CANNELLONI

I've never tasted better cannelloni than these made by my very good friend, Rose Guarrera. Rose was an extraordinary Italian cook, probably the best I've ever known. She was like a second mother to me. She was always my friend, in sad moments and in happy moments. Her cannelloni were like velvet. They melted in your mouth. We could never make them quite as good as hers though this recipe comes close.

······································· SERVICE FOR 6 TO 8 ·······································

Preparing the Béchamel Sauce

In a medium saucepan, melt the butter, then add the flour, stirring until smooth. Pour in the milk and cream all at once. Whisk vigorously, then return to the heat and cook, whisking constantly, until thick. Season with salt, pepper, and nutmeg and set aside.

Preparing the Tomato Sauce

Heat the oil in a heavy-bottomed saucepan. Add the onions and cook until translucent. Add the garlic and cook 1 minute longer. Stir in the chopped tomatoes. Bring to a boil and simmer for 30 minutes, stirring occasionally. Cool.

Preparing the Filling

In a shallow pan, bring the Fond Blanc de Volaille to a boil. Add the chicken breasts, then reduce the heat down to a bare simmer. Poach the chicken breasts about 5 minutes, or until firm to the touch but still juicy. Cool slightly in the broth, then drain. Coarsely chop the cooked chicken, then transfer it to a food processor and finely chop.

Squeeze all of the water out of the defrosted spinach and chop very finely. Mix with the chicken. Add enough of the Béchamel Sauce to hold the filling together. (The consistency should be almost like a mousse.) Add the Parmigiano, then stir in the parsley and basil. Season with salt and pepper to taste.

Preparing the Pasta

Roll out the pasta dough in sheets approximately 12 inches long. Cut each sheet into 3-inch squares. Bring a medium pot of salted water to a boil. Cook the pasta squares for 2 minutes each. Remove from the water and refresh under cold running water. Drain on a towel.

Assembling the Cannelloni

Preheat the oven to 375°F. Place 1 tablespoon of filling on each pasta square and roll up. Pour a film of Tomato Sauce into a baking dish. Lay the cannelloni side-by-side in a single layer on top. Spread the Béchamel over the cannelloni, then spoon a thin layer of the Tomato Sauce over the Béchamel. Sprinkle with a little Parmigiano cheese. Bake about 40 minutes, or until the sauce is bubbling hot. Let cool 10 minutes before serving.

THE BÉCHAMEL SAUCE

9 tablespoons flour

¼ pound (1 stick) unsalted butter

1½ cups milk

1½ cups heavy cream

Salt, white pepper, and ground nutmeg

THE TOMATO SAUCE

¼ cup olive oil

1 medium onion, peeled and diced

2 to 3 cloves garlic, peeled and finely chopped

One 28-ounce can whole imported San Marzano tomatoes, strained, seeded, and chopped

Salt and black pepper

THE FILLING AND PASTA

2 cups Fond Blanc de Volaille (see page 214)

6 chicken breasts, trimmed

One 10-ounce box frozen spinach, defrosted

½ cup (about) Béchamel Sauce

¾ cup grated Parmigiano-Reggiano cheese plus ¼ cup for sprinkling on top

2 tablespoons finely chopped fresh Italian parsley

¼ cup thinly sliced fresh basil leaves

Salt and white pepper

1 pound Pâte aux Oeufs (see page 215)

SALADE LYONNAISE

LYON STYLE SALAD WITH POTATO, EUROPEAN CURLY ENDIVE AND BACON

This is my version of the traditional main-dish salad from my home: Lyon. It happens that I dislike bread in a salad, so instead of croûtons I use potatoes, which I love. If you can't find the European frisée, buy several heads of regular curly endive and use only the tender inner leaves for this salad. (The outer leaves are delicious braised in butter and olive oil.)

SERVICE FOR 4

THE SALAD

2 tablespoons unsalted butter

*2 Idaho potatoes, peeled and diced
    into ½-inch cubes*

Salt

*½ pound thick-cut bacon,
    cut into ¼-inch dice*

2 heads frisée (European pale curly endive)

1 tablespoon white vinegar

4 eggs

THE VINAIGRETTE

½ cup olive oil

¾ cup walnut oil

¼ cup sherry vinegar

1 teaspoon Dijon mustard

Salt and white pepper

Preparing the Salad

Melt the butter in a sauté pan over medium heat until sizzling. Add the potatoes and cook until golden brown in color and cooked through. Drain on paper towels and sprinkle with salt while still hot and set aside. Cook the bacon until browned and crispy. Drain, discarding the fat and set aside.

Cut away any outer dark green leaves of the frisée. Slice off 1 inch from the bottom of each head and discard. The remaining leaves should be pale green or white in color. Fill a sink with cold water. Separate the leaves and place in cold water to soak. Swish them around vigorously to release any sand. Spin dry or dry on towels.

Assembling the Salad

Bring a small pan of water with the white vinegar to a rolling boil. Carefully break open each egg and drop, one at a time, into the rolling boil at the center of the pan. Reduce the heat and poach the eggs until the whites have set, but the yolks are still liquid, about 3 minutes.

Meanwhile, whisk together the vinaigrette ingredients. Toss the frisée with enough vinaigrette to lightly coat. Reserve the remaining vinaigrette for another use. Reheat the potatoes and bacon, if necessary, and spoon over the salad. Using a skimmer, remove 1 poached egg at a time from the water, let drain for a few seconds, then place in the center of the salad. Serve immediately.

Chef's Truc

POACHING PERFECT EGGS: You'll really notice the difference if you use farm-raised organic eggs. The freshest eggs poach the best because they are firm enough to keep their shape. To cook ahead, poach in the acidulated water as above, but take the eggs out 1 minute sooner. Have ready a shallow pan of ice water. As you remove each egg, carefully lay it into the ice water to stop the cooking. (You can store the eggs like this overnight.) The next day, reheat the eggs, 1 to 2 minutes only, in a pan of simmering water. If you make the eggs ahead, use extra-large eggs because they won't overcook as easily.

Salade d'Endives aux Noisettes et Gruyère

Belgian Endive Salad with Hazelnut Oil, Walnuts, and Gruyère Cheese

Here I accent the refreshing, slightly bitter endive with a marriage of fresh shelled walnuts and nutty-sweet but assertive Gruyère cheese. Rather than dressing the salad with walnut oil, I use forthright hazelnut oil to round out the soft nutty taste of the walnuts. Because nuts have a slightly bitter quality, they complement the endive beautifully.

.... SERVICE FOR 4 ....

THE SALAD

7 Belgian endives

1 teaspoon Dijon mustard

2 tablespoons red wine vinegar

Salt and white pepper

5 to 6 tablespoons hazelnut oil

½ cup walnuts, coarsely chopped

¼ pound Gruyère cheese, diced

¼ cup finely snipped fresh chives

Preparing the Salad

Discard any wilted outer leaves from the endives. Cut out and discard the cone-shaped core from the bottom of each endive. Remove about 15 of the outer leaves and set aside. Slice the inner leaves crosswise into ¼-inch-wide strips.

In a mixing bowl, whisk together the mustard, vinegar, and season to taste with salt and pepper. Slowly pour in the hazelnut oil, whisking until the dressing is emulsified (creamy looking). Reserve 1 to 2 tablespoons of the dressing, and gently toss the remainder with the sliced endives, walnuts, and cheese until well coated.

Serving the Salad

Place a mound of salad on each of 4 chilled salad plates. Dip the tips of the reserved whole leaves in the remaining vinaigrette, then dip each leaf tip in chives. Arrange the leaves around the salad so that they look like flower petals.

✑ Chef's Truc ✑

STORING WALNUT AND HAZELNUT OILS: Walnut and hazelnut oils are marvelous additions to a pantry. I like to combine walnut and olive oil as in my Vinaigrette Maison. I also season my potato puree with hazelnut oil. The only problem is, like the nuts they're made from, these oils easily become rancid. Buy only from a store that sells enough to keep it fresh. Keep refrigerated after opening and be sure to taste the oil before using it. Discard if there is any moldy or unpleasant taste.

SOUFFLÉ AU GRUYÈRE

GRUYÈRE CHEESE SOUFFLÉ

This is a soufflé for purists. I make it with imported Gruyère, a mountain cheese made with a washed rind, that comes from Alpine France and Switzerland. Other cheeses in this category are Beaufort, Comté, and Emmenthal. A chefs' favorite because its nutty flavor marries well with other savory foods, Gruyère also melts beautifully into long, silky strands.

.... SERVICE FOR 6 ....

Preparing the Soufflé

Preheat the oven to 375°F. Brush 6 individual soufflé dishes with 1 tablespoon soft butter and dust with flour.

In a medium heavy-bottomed saucepan, melt the butter, then stir in the 6 tablespoons flour until smooth. While whisking, pour in the scalded milk. Bring to a boil and cook for 4 minutes. Remove from the heat and stir in the cheese. Whisking constantly, add the yolks, one at a time. Place back on medium heat and cook slightly to thicken. (Cook only until you see the first bubble; do not let it boil.) Remove from the heat immediately and beat slightly to cool and add the salt, pepper, nutmeg, and cayenne to taste.

In a dry, clean bowl, beat the egg whites with a pinch of salt until medium-firm peaks form. Fold the whites half at a time into the cheese sauce. (Mix up and down rather than stirring to maintain the air bubbles in the whites.) Divide the batter between the 6 soufflé dishes. Place the soufflés on a baking sheet. Bake for 15 minutes or until the they have puffed but are still a bit liquidy inside. Serve immediately.

☙ Chef's Truc ❧

BEATING EGG WHITES: Don't overbeat your egg whites. They should hold their shape with soft peaks. If overbeaten, the whites won't mix smoothly with your soufflé base and the texture will be grainy.

THE SOUFFLÉ

7 tablespoons unsalted butter

6 tablespoon all-purpose flour

2 cups milk, scalded

6 ounces Gruyère cheese, shredded

8 eggs, separated

Salt, white pepper, and ground nutmeg

Pinch of cayenne

Tartelette aux Pommes de Terre et Bleu de Roquefort avec sa Petite Salade

Potato and Roquefort Cheese Tart and a Small Salad

Here a simple dish has a little twist to give it another dimension. I combine Roquefort, France's ultra-creamy, cave-ripened sheep's milk blue cheese, with pungent, melting Gruyère from the Alps. The Roquefort melts down into the potatoes while the Gruyère stays on top and forms a glaze, or gratinéed crust.

············ SERVICE FOR 6 ············

THE TARTELETTE SHELLS

1 pound Pâte Brisée (see page 214)

THE FILLING

4 Idaho potatoes, peeled and diced

¼ pound Roquefort cheese, crumbled

¼ pound Gruyère cheese, grated

Salt and white pepper

½ pound mesclun greens,
*   gently washed and dried*

6 tablespoons Vinaigrette Maison
*   (see page 216)*

Baking the Tartelette Shells

Preheat the oven to 375°F. Roll out the dough on a floured surface, then cut out six 3-inch-round individual tartlette shells of pastry. Chill to set the pastry. Line each pastry tart with aluminum foil, then fill with beans or pie weights. Bake until light brown, about 15 minutes. Let cool. Then remove beans and foil and cool the shells completely.

Preparing the Filling

Bring a medium pot of salted water to a boil. Add the potatoes and bring back to a boil. Reduce the heat and cook until firm but cooked through. Drain and set aside. Divide the Roquefort cheese among the shells, and sprinkle in the bottoms. Cover with the cooked potatoes. Top with the Gruyère cheese. Set aside. (The tarts can be made up to 2 days ahead until this point.)

Finishing the Dish

Preheat the oven to 350°F. Bake the tartelettes until golden brown and bubbling, about 7 minutes. Toss the mesclun with the Vinaigrette Maison. Serve each tartelette accompanied by a mound of the salad.

GÂTEAU AUX NOIX DE PACANES

SOUR CREAM PECAN COFFEE CAKE

I learned to love pecans when I moved to the United States. This nut is native to North America and is in the hickory family. It has the highest oil content of any nut (70%). The fresh crop of pecans comes in autumn, so that's a good time to buy these highly perishable nuts. Store them in the freezer, especially in hot summer months

MAKES TWO 8-INCH CAKES

Making the Pecan Filling

Combine the sugar, flour, cinnamon, and salt. Cut in the butter by rubbing the bits of butter and the flour mixture with your fingers. When the mixture is crumbly and no chunks of butter remain, sprinkle in the nuts and toss. Set aside.

Preparing the Cake Batter

Preheat the oven to 350°F. Lightly spray two 8-inch cake pans with nonstick spray. Whisk together the flour, baking powder, baking soda, and salt in a large bowl. In a mixer, cream the butter, sugar, and vanilla, beating until light and fluffy. Add the eggs, one at a time. Add the dry ingredients alternating with the sour cream, beginning and ending with the dry ingredients.

Spread one-quarter of the batter onto the bottom of each of the prepared pans. Cover each layer of batter with one-quarter of the pecan filling. Repeat with one-quarter more of the batter and one-quarter more of the filling. Bake 45 minutes, or until a toothpick inserted in the middle comes out clean. Cool the cakes in the pan for 10 minutes. Invert, then invert again onto a serving platter. Dust with confectioners' sugar and serve. (This cake freezes for up to 1 month extremely well. Just be sure to wrap air tight.)

THE PECAN FILLING

½ cup sugar

¼ cup all-purpose flour

2 teaspoons ground cinnamon

¼ teaspoon salt

4 tablespoons unsalted butter, cut into bits

¾ cup chopped pecans

THE CAKE BATTER

2¾ cups all-purpose flour

1 tablespoon baking powder

½ teaspoon baking soda

½ teaspoon salt

½ pound (2 sticks) unsalted butter, softened

1½ cups sugar

1½ teaspoons vanilla

3 eggs

1 cup sour cream

Confectioners' sugar (for dusting)

Tarte Tatin
Caramelized Upside-Down Apple Tart

*I*mmortalized by the Tatin sisters, tart tatin was introduced to Parisians at Maxim's at the turn of the century. This tart combines just a few basics ingredients. But, what results! When it's properly made and fresh, I can't think of anything better. To caramelize the apples, it helps to have a heavy cast-iron skillet. If you like tart apples, use Granny Smiths. If not, Golden Delicious or MacIntosh work well. A mixture of apples is a good compromise.

SERVICE FOR 8

THE PÂTE BRISÉE

1 pound Pâte Brisée (see page 214)

THE APPLE FILLING

6 tablespoons unsalted butter

¾ cup sugar

6 apples, peeled, cored, and quartered

Preparing the Pâte Brisée

Lightly dust the counter, a rolling pin, and the dough with flour. Then roll out the dough evenly into a circle large enough to overlap the edges of a 9-inch cast-iron skillet. Refrigerate while you prepare the apple filling.

Preparing the Apple Filling

Preheat the oven to 375°F. Place the butter and sugar in a 9-inch cast-iron skillet or cake pan. Heat directly over low heat until the butter has melted and the sugar is moistened. Arrange the apples, side by side, squeezing them in, until no more apples will fit. Cook over medium heat for 10 minutes, then remove the pan from the heat. The apples will have shrunk, so add another 3 or 4 quarters so they're packed together again.

Return to the heat and cook over medium-high, turning the pan occasionally to avoid hot spots, until a light-colored caramel has formed underneath. Place the circle of the Pâte Brisée over the top. Tuck the pastry down around the edges so it will cup the apples when inverted. Transfer the pan to the oven and bake for 20 minutes or until the pastry is golden. Remove the pan from the oven and allow the tart to cool until the liquid from the apples congeals. Rewarm the pan slightly over direct heat, then invert onto a serving dish. Cut into wedges and serve immediately.

GÂTEAU AUX POMMES

APPLE CAKE

We use Granny Smiths for this cake. Another choice is Golden Delicious, which are good in the beginning of their season when they're still green. If yellow, the apples will be mealy and not firm enough for this cake. In France, we prefer Pommes Reinettes, a variety not grown in this country. Golden Delicious is the closest. If you have access to old-fashioned apple varieties, try Macoun, which are outstanding in this cake.

MAKES ONE 6-CUP BUNDT CAKE

THE CAKE

1 ½ cups all-purpose flour

1 cup plus 3 tablespoons sugar

½ teaspoon salt

1 ½ teaspoons baking powder

3 apples, peeled, cored and chopped

1 teaspoon ground cinnamon

2 tablespoons orange juice

Grated zest of 1 orange

1 ¼ teaspoons vanilla

2 eggs

½ cup vegetable oil

Making the Cake

Preheat the oven to 350°F. Generously butter and flour a 6-cup Bundt pan. Combine the flour, 1 cup of the sugar, salt, and baking powder, and set aside. Combine the apples, the remaining sugar, and cinnamon and set aside.

Beat together the orange juice, orange zest, vanilla, and eggs. Pour in the oil and beat until well incorporated. Stir into the dry ingredients and mix. Pour half the batter into the prepared pan, cover with half the apples, then repeat with the remaining batter and apples, ending with a layer of apples. Bake for 1 hour or until the cake pulls away from the sides of the pan. Cool 10 minutes, then invert. Invert again onto a serving plate, with the apple layer on top.

Gâteau Bourbon aux Épices

Bourbon Spice Cake

Bourbon is an American liquor, distilled from corn, that has a two-hundred year tradition. I like using it in this cake because of its powerful flavor and aroma. Like most liquor-infused cakes, this one is best served with a pot of fresh brewed café filtre. This cake freezes perfectly. If you like, double the recipe and freeze one.

.... MAKES ONE 10-INCH CAKE ....

Baking the Cake

Preheat the oven to 350°F. Generously butter and flour a 10-inch cake pan. Combine the flour, baking power, baking soda, spices, and salt, and set aside. Combine the buttermilk and bourbon. In a mixer, cream the butter and sugar together with a paddle attachment until light and fluffy. Add the eggs, one at a time, beating well between additions. Add about one-quarter of the dry ingredients alternating with about one-third of the buttermilk-bourbon mixture. Keep alternating, beginning and ending with the dry ingredients.

Pour the cake batter into the prepared pan. Bake for 45 minutes or until a toothpick inserted in the middle comes out clean. Cool 10 minutes in the pan, then invert onto a cooling rack. Cool, then dust with confectioners' sugar and serve.

Chef's Truc

GRINDING FRESH SPICES: To experience the full savor and perfume of the spices, grind your own from whole seeds. Dedicate a small coffee grinder for this purpose. Grind 1 to 2 tablespoons of whole spices at a time, storing in a tightly sealed glass jar. When measuring, don't be tempted to add a little extra. These spices are full of powerful volatile oils. Too much can make your cake taste unpleasantly medicinal.

THE CAKE

2 cups cake flour

1 tablespoon baking powder

1 teaspoon baking soda

1 teaspoon ground ginger

1 teaspoon ground cinnamon

½ teaspoon ground cardamom

½ teaspoon ground allspice

½ teaspoon ground cloves

¼ teaspoon salt

¾ cup buttermilk

½ cup good-quality bourbon

½ pound (2 sticks) unsalted butter, softened

1¼ cups sugar

2 eggs

Confectioners' sugar (for dusting)

Les Fonds
de Cuisine

BASIC RECIPES

DEMI-GLACE
CONCENTRATED VEAL REDUCTION

MAKES 1 QUART (4 CUPS)

10 pounds veal marrow bones,
cut into 2-inch-long pieces

2 carrots, peeled

2 ribs celery

2 ripe tomatoes (or canned)

2 tablespoons tomato paste

10 black peppercorns

1 whole onion, unpeeled

2 sprigs fresh thyme

1 bay leaf

Preheat the oven to 450°F. Roast the veal bones in a roasting pan until deep brown in color. (Take care not to burn, which will cause bitterness.) Place the bones in a large stockpot with the remaining ingredients. Fill the pot with cold water and bring to a boil. Skim as necessary and reduce the heat to a bare simmer. Cook slowly for 12 hours. Strain the liquid and chill. This will keep for 2 weeks if refrigerated. Remove the solidified fat before using.

Chef's Truc

BUYING DEMI-GLACE: Our Demi-Glace sauce, a complex reduction based on roasted veal bone broth, is a major project for the home cook. You can buy a small container of good quality demi-glace to make things a little easier (see Sources page 219).

FOND D'AGNEAU
RICH LAMB STOCK

MAKES 4 QUARTS

5 pounds lamb bones

1 bay leaf

2 whole ribs celery

1 whole onion, unpeeled

2 whole carrots

1 sprig fresh thyme

10 crushed black peppercorns

Place the lamb stock ingredients in a large stockpot then fill with cold water to cover by 4 inches. Bring to a boil, skimming as necessary. Reduce the heat to a bare simmer and cook slowly for 2 hours. Strain the liquid and chill, removing any solidified fat. This stock will keep for about 1 week.

JUS D'AGNEAU
LAMB BROTH

MAKES ABOUT 4 QUARTS

1 pound lamb bones

1 bay leaf

2 tablespoons vegetable oil

3 cups mirepoix (see page 217)

6 to 8 cloves garlic

1 whole ripe tomato, quartered

½ bunch fresh thyme

1 sprig fresh rosemary

4 mushrooms, cleaned

10 crushed black peppercorns

1 cup dry white wine

4 quarts Fond d'Agneau
(see recipe, this page)

Preheat the oven to 400°F. Roast the lamb bones in a roasting pan until well browned. (They can burn easily, so watch them carefully.) In a large stockpot, brown the vegetables and herbs in the oil. Add the bones, peppercorns, white wine, and Fond d'Agneau. Bring to a boil, skimming as necessary. Reduce the heat to a bare simmer and cook slowly for 2 hours. Strain and chill, removing any solidified fat. This will keep well for up to 2 weeks.

JUS DE VEAU
VEAL BROTH

MAKES 1 QUART (4 CUPS)

10 pounds veal loin bones,
2-inches long

2 carrots, peeled

2 ribs celery

2 ripe tomatoes

1 head garlic, unpeeled

10 crushed black peppercorns

1 whole onion, unpeeled

2 sprigs fresh thyme

1 bay leaf

2 cups Demi-Glace
(see recipe, this page)

Preheat the oven to 450°F. Roast the veal bones in a roasting pan until deep brown in color. (Take care not to burn them, which will cause bitterness.) Place the bones in a large stockpot with the remaining ingredients. Cover the ingredients with 6 inches of cold water and bring to a boil. Skim off any foam as necessary and reduce the heat to a bare simmer. Cook for 6 hours. Strain and chill, removing the solidified fat. This will keep 1 to 2 weeks in the refrigerator or 1 month in the freezer.

FOND DE HOMARD

RICH LOBSTER STOCK

MAKES 2 QUARTS

2 tablespoons unsalted butter

½ cup coarsely chopped celery

½ cup coarsely chopped onion

¼ cup coarsely chopped carrots

1 leek (white part only),
     cleaned and chopped

1 lobster (can be a cull or
     imperfect lobster), killed
     and cleaned (see page 24)

5 sprigs fresh tarragon

½ cup dry white vermouth

½ cup Harvey's Bristol Cream
     sherry

1 teaspoon tomato paste

2 quarts (8 cups) Fond Blanc de
     Volaille (see page 214)

In a large heavy stockpot, melt the butter until sizzling, then add the celery, onions, carrots, and leek along with the tarragon sprigs. Cook the vegetables until transparent. Add the lobster to the pot and cook until the shell turns bright red. Add the vermouth and sherry, bring to a boil, then reduce the liquid by half. Stir in the tomato paste and the Fond Blanc de Volaille and bring to a boil again. Simmer on very low heat for 1½ hours, skimming occasionally. Strain the stock through a sieve, pressing well to extract all the juices. Discard the solids and set aside the stock. This stock can be made up to 2 days ahead or 1 to 2 weeks ahead if frozen.

FUMET DE POISSON

FISH ESSENCE

MAKES 1 QUART (4 CUPS)

5 pounds clean and sweet-
     smelling, non-oily fish bones

2 ribs celery

1 whole onion, unpeeled

1 sprig fresh thyme

1 bay leaf

10 crushed black peppercorns

2 cups dry white wine

1 gallon (4 quarts) cold water

Rinse the fish bones in cold water, cutting off and discarding the heads if not already done. Place in a large stockpot with the remaining ingredients. Add water and bring to a boil. Skim off any foam as necessary and reduce the heat to a bare simmer. Cook for 35 to 40 minutes. Strain and chill, removing any solidified fat. This stock will not keep beyond 3 days. Place in a tightly sealed container and freeze for up to 1 month.

Chef's Truc

USING DIFFERENT FISH IN STOCKS: Flat fish, such as sole or halibut, give the most gelatinous stocks. Red snapper makes a light, clear stock. Just be sure the bones smell sweet. Always remove the fish heads, using only the skeletons for your stock.

JUS DE MOULES

MUSSEL BROTH

MAKES 1 QUART

5 pounds cultivated mussels,
     scrubbed and debearded

10 whole shallots, peeled

2 cups dry white wine

1 sprig fresh thyme

1 bay leaf

Heat a large empty saucepan on the stovetop until hot. Add the mussels and the shallots. Cover the pot until the mussels open. Add the wine, thyme, and bay leaf and cover with cold water. Bring to a boil, remove from heat, and strain. This will keep only 2 days in the refrigerator or up to 1 month in the freezer.

JUS DE LÉGUMES

VEGETABLE BROTH

MAKES 2 QUARTS

3 carrots, peeled and coarsely
     chopped

1 onion, unpeeled and coarsely
     chopped

1 red bell pepper, coarsely
     chopped

1 bunch fresh Italian parsley

4 large white mushrooms, cleaned
     and chopped

2 ribs celery, coarsely chopped

1 leek, cleaned and chopped

2 ripe tomatoes, chopped

10 crushed black peppercorns

1 sprig fresh thyme

½ head garlic

3 shallots

Place all ingredients in a large stockpot. Cover with cold water and bring to a boil. Reduce the heat to a bare simmer and cook for 1 hour. Puree the liquid in blender. Strain and chill. This will keep for up to 4 days in the refrigerator or up to 1 month in the freezer.

FOND BLANC DE VOLAILLE
WHITE CHICKEN STOCK
MAKES 4 QUARTS

15 pounds chicken bones (backs, necks, wings, drumsticks)

2 onions, peeled and coarsely chopped

2 carrots, peeled and coarsely chopped

4 ribs celery, coarsely chopped

1 Bouquet garni (2 sprigs parsley, 1 bay leaf, 2 sprigs thyme)

1 tablespoon black peppercorns

Place all the ingredients in a large stockpot. Cover with cold water. Bring to a boil, reduce heat and simmer over low heat for 4 hours, skimming off any foamy impurities. Strain through a sieve, then chill the pot in a sink filled with ice and water. Refrigerate overnight, then remove and discard the solidified fat on top. This will keep up to 4 days in the refrigerator or up to 1 month in the freezer.

JUS DE POULET
BROWN CHICKEN BROTH
MAKES 2 QUARTS

2 pounds cooked chicken carcasses (or parts)

2 whole onions, unpeeled

½ head celery

2 sprigs fresh thyme

1½ gallons cold water

3 bay leaves

10 crushed black peppercorns

2 whole ripe tomatoes

2 tablespoons vegetable oil

¾ cup dry white wine

Preheat the oven to 350°F. Combine everything but the wine in a roasting pan. Roast, stirring occasionally until everything is well browned. Remove from the oven, pour off the fat and pour in the wine. Scrape everything into a large stockpot and add water. Bring to a boil, skimming as necessary. Reduce the heat to low and cook slowly for 4 to 5 hours or until the liquid is reduce to 2 quarts. Strain the broth into another pot and chill in an ice bath. This will keep up to 4 days in the refrigerator or up to 1 month in the freezer.

PÂTE BRISÉE
SHORTCRUST PASTRY DOUGH
MAKES ABOUT 1 POUND

½ pound (2 sticks) unsalted butter, cut into bits and chilled

¾ cup all-purpose flour

¾ cup cake flour

¼ teaspoon salt

½ cup ice-cold water

Place the butter, flour, and salt in a mixing bowl and super-chill in the freezer for 30 minutes. Using the flat beater of an electric mixer, cut the butter into the flour until the pieces are the size of peas. Remove the bowl from the machine and sprinkle the ice water over the flour mixture tossing together to distribute the water evenly. Pat the mixture together until a ball is formed. (If necessary, add a few more teaspoons of water to gather any dry ingredients remaining in the bowl.) Wrap in plastic, press into a flat block, then refrigerate for 1 hour.

PÂTE SABLÉE
RICH, SWEET SHORTCRUST PASTRY
MAKES ABOUT 1 POUND

½ pound (2 sticks) unsalted butter, softened

½ cup sugar

1 egg

1½ cups cake flour

1½ cups all-purpose flour

In a mixer, cream the butter and sugar until well combined. Beat in the egg. Stir in the flour by hand, until no flour streaks remain. Wrap the pastry dough in plastic wrap, forming it into a flat block, then refrigerate 1 to 2 hours or until firm. To roll out the pastry, lightly dust the counter, dough, and the rolling pin with flour. Roll out the dough, using as little additional flour as possible. (More flour makes the dough tough.)

PÂTE AUX OEUFS

EGG PASTA

MAKES ABOUT 1 POUND
(4 TO 6 PORTIONS)

5 eggs

3 cups durum wheat flour

Place eggs into an electric mixer. Using the paddle attachment, beat the eggs lightly. Add 2½ cups of the flour, beating until the dough forms a smooth, shiny, firm ball and the sides of the mixer are clean. If the dough is still sticky, add the remaining ½ cup flour. Wrap in plastic and refrigerate.

PÂTE AU SAFRAN

SAFFRON PASTA

MAKES ABOUT 1 POUND
(4 TO 6 PORTIONS)

Large pinch of saffron threads

2 tablespoons hot water

3 cups durum wheat flour

4 eggs

Steep the saffron in the water for 20 minutes. Combine the saffron "tea" with the flour in a mixer and beat, using the paddle attachment, on low speed until thoroughly combined. Add 2 eggs and mix, then add the remaining eggs, beating just until the dough forms a ball. Wrap in plastic and refrigerate.

PÂTE AUX TOMATES

TOMATO PASTA

MAKES ABOUT 1 POUND
(4 TO 6 PORTIONS)

4 cups durum wheat flour

½ cup tomato paste

4 eggs

Combine the flour and tomato paste in a mixer on low speed until thoroughly combined. Add 2 eggs and mix until combined. Add the remaining eggs, beating just until the dough forms a ball. Wrap in plastic and refrigerate

PÂTE AUX ÉPINARDS

SPINACH PASTA

MAKES ABOUT 1 POUND
(4 TO 6 PORTIONS)

3 eggs plus 1 yolk

3 cups durum wheat flour

*½ cup cooked spinach,
    squeezed dry*

Combine the spinach and 1 egg plus a yolk in a food processor and blend until pasty. Combine the spinach paste with flour in the mixer and beat on low speed, using the paddle attachment, until thoroughly combined. Add 2 eggs and mix thoroughly until the dough forms a ball. Wrap in plastic and refrigerate.

Chef's Truc

MAKING DOUGH AHEAD: If making the dough ahead, wrap in plastic and refrigerate, using within 2 days. Otherwise, wrap the dough in plastic wrap and allow it to rest at room temperature for 30 minutes before rolling out with a pasta sheeter.

BEURRE MANIÉ

KNEADED BUTTER (FOR THICKENING SAUCES)

MAKES ABOUT 1 CUP

¼ pound (1 stick) butter, softened

½ cup all-purpose flour

Combine equal amounts of the butter and flour. Mix by hand until the consistency is pasty. Refrigerate it to use as needed. Add small amounts of the Beurre Manié to a simmering sauce. Wait until the sauce comes back to a boil and thickens before adding more, if necessary. This way, you can control the consistency of your sauce.

SAUCE MAYONNAISE

HOMEMADE MAYONNAISE

MAKES ABOUT 1 CUP

1 whole egg

1 teaspoon Dijon mustard

Salt and white pepper

1 tablespoon red wine vinegar

1 cup vegetable oil

Place the egg, mustard, salt, pepper and vinegar in the bowl of a food processor and process 30 seconds. With the machine still running, slowly drizzle in the oil, drop by drop at first. Keep adding the oil until it all has been absorbed. The mayonnaise should be thick and creamy. If necessary, thin with a little tepid water and set aside.

VINAIGRETTE MAISON

HOUSE VINAIGRETTE

MAKES ABOUT 1½ CUPS

6 tablespoons sherry vinegar

1 teaspoon Dijon mustard

½ cup extra-virgin olive oil

½ cup walnut oil

*Salt and freshly ground
    black pepper*

Place the vinegar, and mustard in a blender (or use a hand-held blender). Blend until creamy, then slowly pour in both oils. Keep blending until emulsified. Season with salt and pepper to taste.

BEURRE CLARIFIÉ

CLARIFIED BUTTER

MAKES ABOUT 4 CUPS

2 pounds unsalted butter

Preheat oven to 350°F. Place butter in a heavy, ovenproof pot. Melt for about 30 minutes. Carefully, trying not to disturb the layers, remove from the oven. Ladle off the white foam layer on top. (This is excellent added to cream soups or to potato puree.) Ladle off all the clear, yellow butterfat, placing it in a storage container. When you get close to the bottom of the pot, you will see a layer of milk below the butterfat. Pour this remaining butterfat and milk layer gently into another container.

Allow the contents of both containers to harden in the refrigerator. The first container will contain pure clarified butter, which will keep for 2 months in the refrigerator. The second container will have separated into 2 layers: a butterfat layer and a milky layer. Remove the solid butter layer and set aside. Pour off and discard the milky layer. Rinse off the butter layer under cold water to remove any remaining milky solids.

CRÈME FRAÎCHE
RIPENED CREAM
MAKES 1 QUART

1 quart (4 cups) heavy cream

(non ultra-pasteurized

if possible)

½ cup buttermilk

In a clean stainless steel or glass bowl, whisk together the cream and buttermilk to combine. Cover tightly and leave at room temperature for 12 hours. Alternately, leave in a very low oven. This can be a gas oven with just the pilot lit or an electric oven set as low as possible. The cream should thicken to the consistency of yogurt and have a pleasant sour smell. If it hasn't thickened enough after 12 hours, leave 4 to 6 hours longer, then refrigerate. Crème fraîche will keep very well in the refrigerator for up to a month if tightly covered.

MIREPOIX
COOKING VEGETABLES
MAKES ABOUT 6 CUPS

1 pound onions, cut into

1-inch dice

1 pound carrots, peeled and

cut into 1-inch dice

1 head celery, cut into

1-inch slices

Mix until well combined and use as needed. Store, tightly covered, in the refrigerator for up to 3 days.

TOMATES CONCASSÉES
FRESH TOMATO DICE
MAKES 3 CUPS

6 large ripe tomatoes

Drop the tomatoes into a large pot of boiling water for about 20 seconds or until the tomato skin loosens from the flesh. At this point, skim the tomatoes from the water and refresh them in a bowl of ice water to stop the cooking. Peel, then cut them in half (through the equator) exposing the seed pockets. Scoop out the seedy pulp and either save for a stock or discard. Dice and set aside. Use immediately or refrigerate up to 1 day.

Glossary of French Culinary Terms

Beurre Manié: Meaning "kneaded butter." A paste made of softened butter and flour, usually in equal amounts, used for thickening sauces.

Beurre Noisette: "Hazelnut" butter or butter cooked until it browns and has a hazelnut-like flavor and aroma.

Bouquet Garni: A small, tied bouquet of herbs and aromatics used to flavor soups, broths and stews. Chef Perrier uses Italian parsley, French thyme, bay leaf, and black peppercorns.

Brunoise: A culinary term for tiny, even dice of vegetables, about ⅛-inch cubes.

Cassolette: A small individual ceramic container or metal pot in which certain hot dishes are heated and served. At Le Bec-Fin, the cassettes are silver and used for escargots.

Chef's Truc: A trick of professional chefs; a special knack for doing things.

Concasser: A culinary term meaning to finely chop. In this book it refers to peeled, seeded, and diced raw tomatoes; it also refers to chopped up bones for stock or to chopped herbs.

Coulis: A liquid puree of cooked or raw vegetables or fruits, used either as a sauce or to enhance a sauce. In this book, we refer to Parsley Coulis, Yellow Pepper Coulis, Tomato Coulis, and Mango Coulis.

Court-bouillon: A quickly cooked seasoned, aromatic broth, used mainly for cooking seafood, but also used to cook meats such as sweetbreads. *Court-bouillon* often contains an acid, such as white wine and lemon juice.

Couverture: A type of high-quality chocolate used for creating pastry items such as cakes and candies. *Couverture* chocolate has a large percentage of cocoa fat (about ⅓ of its total weight), which enables it to form a thin, hard, shiny shell.

Cru: The French term for a growth, used for a designated wine region or locality. The term is also used for chocolate to describe the specific region where the cocoa beans are produced.

Dodine: Similar to a ballontine, a type of garnished terrine—a dish of boned, stuffed and braised meats, fish, or poultry, made in a special, U-shaped mold.

Flamber: To pour wine and spirits into a dish and ignite it to make a sauce from the pan juices. *Flambéing* enhances the flavor of wine and spirits while burning off the excess alcohol. To *flambé* a spirit with a low alcohol content, always heat the spirit before lighting; it will ignite much more easily.

Frémir: To "tremble." A culinary term used to describe a properly cooking stock that barely trembles, with just an occasional bubble coming to the surface.

Fricasser: An old French culinary term meaning to stew cut-up meats, fish or poultry in a brown or a white stock to make its sauce. A Fricassée often contains cream.

Haricots Verts: Literally "green beans," the term is used on French menus for young pencil-thin green beans, picked daily so they'll all be the proper size.

Julienne: A term for cutting vegetables into thin, even matchstick shapes. This can be done on a mandoline or using a Japanese Benriner cutter.

Mesclun: A word, originating in Niçoise dialect, that means mixture. It refers to an assortment of wild-type young greens used for salad, often including chicory, mâche, dandelion, arugula, oak leaf lettuce, and chervil as well as other tender herbs.

Napper: To coat lightly. A sauce should "nap" the spoon when its consistency is right.

Panade: A thickening paste originally made from moistened bread crumbs. Here its made from butter, water, and flour cooked together.

Pluches: Fine sprigs of tender herbs, especially chervil.

Tourner: To "turn," as in turning wood on a lathe. To tourner vegetables is to cut them while turning to create a seven-sided barrel shape.

Sources

Assouline & Ting Inc.
314 Brown Street
Philadelphia, PA 19123
Phone: 215-627-3000
Fax: 215-627-3517

Catalog available

Mail order: Valrhona chocolate, hazelnut and walnut oils, Moroccan lemon confit, black currants in syrup, Moroccan spice mix, dried morels, sheet gelatin, Spanish saffron in a 1-ounce tin (this freezes beautifully), imported caviars, gold leaf sheets, truffles—canned and fresh (in season), black currant vinegar, Helix snails.

Auray
109 South 18th Street
Philadelphia, PA 19103
Phone: 215-665-9220
Fax: 215-575-1155

Mail order: fine French cheeses, including St. Maure, Crottin Chavignol, Reblochon, Morbier, Tomme de Savoie, Brin d'Amour, and Fourme d'Ambert. This company provides the cheeses for Le Bec-Fin.

D'Artagnan
399-419 St. Paul Avenue
Jersey City, NJ 07306
Phone: 1-800-DARTAGN
Fax: 201-792-0588

Catalog available

Mail order: Fresh foie gras, pintade Guinea hen, pigeons, quail, free-range organic chickens, duck fat, magret, fresh turkey, quail eggs, rabbit, and other specialty meats

Guarrera's Quality Meats
800 Catherine Street
Philadelphia, PA 19147
Phone: 215-922-0736
Fax: 215-440-7624

Owner Michael McDonough is the former Maitre D' of Le Bec-Fin. Five years ago he bought this company, which provides most of the meats served at Le Bec-Fin. While Guarrera's does not offer a mail-order service, you are welcome to call him with any meat questions and to get the exact specifications of the meat his butchers cut for the restaurant.

Moore Brothers Wine Co.
7180 North Park Drive
Pennsauken, NJ 08110
Phone: 609-317-1177
Fax: 609-317-0055

Regular newsletter available

Mail order: Gregory Moore, Sommelier at Le Bec-Fin for twenty-five years, operates this new, small, specialty wine company. He sells only personally selected wine including many of the wines from Le Bec-Fin's list.

More Than Gourmet
115 West Bartges Street
Akron, OH 44311
Phone: 330-762-6652
Fax: 330-762-4832

Mail order: Demi-Glace Gold, Glace de Poulet, and Jus de Poulet Lié, all-natural reduction sauces sold in small portion-pack containers for home use. Or call for a retailer in your area.

Previn Inc.
2044 Rittenhouse Square
Philadelphia, PA 19103
Phone: 215-985-1996
Fax: 215-985-0323

Catalog available

Mail order: dodine mold, individual flan rings, tart pans, cast-iron salamander, all types of specialty French cookware and bakeware, Savarin molds, Benriner cutter, crème brûlée dishes.

Samuels & Son Seafood Co.
3407 South Lawrence Street
Philadelphia, PA 19148
Phone: 1-800-290-7810
Fax: 215-336-7813

Mail order: Diver scallops, U-10 shrimp, Rouget de Barbet, fresh Dover sole, exotic oysters, fresh jumbo lump crabmeat, black sea bass, John Dory, cockle clams, pike (in season). Call Dick Coyne with any questions.

Index